History and Culture Series

ESSAYS ON INDIAN CULTURE

Edited by
Dr. Raj Kumar

DISCOVERY PUBLISHING HOUSE
NEW DELHI-110002

Published by:
Namit Wasan
DISCOVERY PUBLISHING HOUSE PVT. LTD.
4383/4B, Ansari Road, Darya Ganj
New Delhi-110 002 (India)
Phone : +91-11-23279245; 23253475; 43596065
E-mail : discoverybooksindia@gmail.com
discoverypublishinghouse@gmail.com
namitwasan9@gmail.com
web : www.discoverypublishinggroup.com

First Published: **2003**

Reprinted: **2021**

ISBN: 978-81-7141-692-9

Essays on Indian Culture

Printed at:
Infinity Imaging Systems
Delhi

Preface

Aim is to collect such essays as revealed the deeper impulses of India. This should enable us to understand re-integration of the Indian culture in the light of modern knowledge.

It is hoped that through such works the harmonies underlying true culture will one day reconcile the disorders of modern India.

Raj Kumar

Acknowledgements

In preparing this collection of essays, I have incurred indebtness and kindness of Professors A.L. Bashan, Lalanji Gopal, G.C. Pande, Suniti Kumar Chatterjee, S. Gopal, K.N. Pannikar, S. Kadhrival, N. Subramaniam and N.R. Ray. I am Thankful to them. Works of K.M. Munshi, Arbindo Ghosh and Radhakrishnan have influenced me. I am beholden to them.

Some of our universities, institutions, their librarians and staff members have been good and helpful, I am grateful to them.

Hard work of my publisher Sri Tilak Wasan and his staff has made all their possible. I am thankful to them.

Raj Kumar

Contents

1

INTRODUCTION

Culture is the characteristic way of life inspired by fundamental values in which a people live. It is the sum total of the values expressed through art, religion, literature, social institutions and behaviour the ever acts of individuals and mass action inspired by collective urges. The dress we wear, the factories we set up or the dams we build are only a part of the 'civilization', the material equipment of life which tends to increase in complexity with scientific progress. But essentially culture has little to do with material equipment of life.

What then constitutes culture. Its first characteristic is continuity. It comes from the past, adjusts itself to the present and moves forward to shape the future. The division of culture in relation to time does not therefore give a true picture of what it really is.

A Culture becomes a flowing stream only when there is continuity of collective life in a people. In other words a distinctive culture comes into existence when a people develop a continuous way of life. Such toninuity expresses itself in various ways; in common traditions and norms of conduct, in common institutions, in a common memory of triumphs achieved, in a common aesthetic outlook, in a capacity for characteristic collective action.

If there are no common traditions, no common culture can come into existence. Nor is a common life possible without common norms of conduct approved by the thinking and active minority and generally accepted by the people.

The most important characteristic of a vital culture is a common outlook among the people which when faced with difficulty resistance of adversity, can generate a collective will to action. In other words the vitality of culture can be measured by the capacity of the dominant minority, and following it the mojority of a people to offer collective resistance in a characteristic way. However they cannot do so when the collective will to resist adverse circumstances is weak; then the culture becomes decadent and the people begin to distintegrate.

Few countries in the world have such an ancient and diverse culture as India's. Stretching back in an unbroken sweep over 5000 years, India's culture has been enriched by successive waves of migration which were absorbed into the Indian way of life.

It is this variety which is a special hallmark of India. Its physical, religious and racial variety is an immense as its linguistic diversity. Underneath this diversity lies the continuity of Indian civilization and social structure from the very earliest times until the present day.

There is perhaps no phenomenon as complex as 'culture'. In a manner of speaking, culture is everything in a particular society, and one can as easily speak of the culture of Hindustani music and Bengali Bhadralok Society as one can of the culture of the working-class, Hindi film-viewers, rickshawpullers, and India's wondernizing elites. Indian culture is no easy composite of varying styles and influences. In the matter of cuisine, for instance, the North and the South share little, and these broad categorizations say little about the distinctions between the peppery hot food of Andhra and the coastal, largely coconut-based, cuisine of Kerala. Likewise, in thinking of architecture, one's mind traverses from the great temple cities of the South—Chidambaram, Rameswaram, Kanchipuram, Madurai, and numerous others—to the architectural splendors of the Vijaynagar empire and the erotic sculptures of Khajuraho to the grand Mughal architecture of Delhi, Agra, and Fatehpur Sikri. And what of modest roadside shrines, the step-wells of Gujarat, or the havelis of Jaisalmer with their impeccable lattice work? But culture is not only a matter of music, dance, art and cinema, for marriage customs, death rites, patterns of pilgrimage to holy cities, modes of raising children, treatment of elders, and innumerable other aspects of everyday life are stitched into the meaning of culture.

MAIN INGREDIENTS OF MODERN INDIAN CULTURE

People

India is a land of great diversity, more heterogenous than any other country in the world.

Four major racial groups have met and merged in India resulting in a complex demographic profile. The pale-skinned Europoid entered from the western mountain passes, encountering settled populations of *Dasyu,* the dark skinned ones of Rig Vedic description.

The *Aryans* established a dominant presence in the northwest and the Gangetic plain, but the people of Mongoloid descent remained undisturbed in the Himalayan region and the highlands of the northeast. Their affinity with the southeast Asian world is remarkable and is reflected in the motifs used in the crafts. Though the Mongoloid people influenced the racial pattern of tribes in the eastern provinces of Orissa and Bihar, by and large, they stayed within central India. Southerners in peninsular India might have had a link with Negroid racial elements, as deduced from contemporary populations with dark skins and tightly curled hair. But the only true Negrito are isolated in the Andaman Islands.

The ethnic diversity is reflected in the variety of languages and dialects used in India—17 major languages and 900 dialects or closely related subsidiary languages. The Indo-European group, particularly the sub-branch of the Indic languages, concentrated as dialects of northwest India and the Gangetic plains, share a linguistic pool with modern French, English, Greek and Persian, indicative of migrations of Europoid people. The Dravidian language family alone consists of 23 languages. Tamil is spoken in Tamilnadu, Telugu in Andhra Pradesh, Kannada in Karnataka and Malayalam in Kerala.

Tribal groups of Graon, Munda and Santhal scattered through the highlands of eastern and central India use the languages of the Austro-Asiatic family, but many of the dialects with only oral traditions have lost.

Less than one per cent of modern India's population-comprising the Mazo, Naga, Lushai and Khasi, to name a few tribes—is inheritor to the languages of the Tibeto-Burman family. Secluded by geography and, later, protected by policy, their ethnological and linguistic identity has survived. Christian missionaries have contributed to the standardization of some of these languages.

Festivals

India is a country of subcontinental dimensions. It is an ancient civilisation and an inheritor to a rich and diverse cultural tradition. The Fairs and Festivals celebrated across the length and breadth of the land present a fascinating pageant and showcase the resplendence of its arts and crafts tradition. Some festivals are of religious nature, others are linked with the lives of the people, change of seasons and harvesting. There are fairs which in past played an important role in the commericial life of the people and continue to be celebrated with great gusto.

* Holi
* Diwali
* Dussehra
* Baisakhi and other harvest festivals
* Onam
* Eid
* Maha-Mastikabhishek
* Guru Purnima
* Regional Festivals

Indian Classical Dances

Indian Classical Dance has many forms and also a strong regional flavour. In Indian mythology, *Shiva* the supreme deity is *Nataraja* the cosmic dancer. The universe comes into existence and disintegrates into nothingness, keeping time with his footfallls. This cycle is repeated infinitely. The dance has both elements—*tandava,* the virile masculine dimension, and *lasya,* the lyrical feminine grace. There are also other mythological accounts that narrate the origin of dance. One recounts how Sri Krishna assumed the form of an enchantress to beguile and destroy the demon Bhasmasur.

The revival of classical dance was painstakingly accomplished, assisted by scholars who researched the poses engraved in stone sculptures adorning temple walls.

The various dance forms of India include the popular Bharat Natyam of Tamil Nadu; the Kuchipudi style of dance, somewhat similar to the former, of Andhra Pradesh;

the Kathakali, an elaborate dance drama where the dancers wear elaborate facial masks and make up and dance to the clash of cymbals and the beat of percussion instruments; the Kathak of Uttar Pradesh and Rajasthan which is a dance form heavily influenced by the Moghul court dances which is danced to the accompaniment of Persian musical instruments; the graceful Manipuri dance of Manipur, where the female dancers slowly sway to the beat of a single male drummer; the Odissi of Orissa, which is both graceful and intricate.

Of all these dance forms, Bharat Natyam is believed to be the oldest and the purest Indian classical dance. It gets its name from *Natya Shastra* and its author, the sage Bharata and is the oldest treatise on Indian dance, drama and music (2nd century AD.)

The uniqueness of Indian classical dances is that they are all devotional in content. In fact Bharat Natyam was till the early 20th century, only performed by *'devadasis'* or maids of God, in temples.

Music

Indian classical music is divided broadly into *Hindustani* (North Indian) and *Carnatic* (South Indian). The styles are very different from each other, both in content and rendering. The ragas are similar, though they go by different names content and rendering. The ragas are similar, though they go by different names and treated differently in each style.

The Hindustani music offers a variety of forms like· *khayal, dhrupad, thumri, tappa and ghazal.* Among these, the *khayal* is the most widely performed classical music form. A *thumri* is usually sung as an accompaniment to *kathak. Dhrupad* is the strictly classical form of music. The tappa is a lighter form of music which requires a good degree of proficiency.

North Indian music is recognised by the specific school it belongs to. This is denoted by the word *gharana,* which literally means 'family'. Some of the well known gharanas are Agra, Jaipur, Delhi and Gwalior.

Carnatic music is more rigid and structured. A concert follows a set style and order of rendering the compositions. They are free to explore the raga in which the composition is being rendered and improvise within the structure. *Varnam, kriti* and *tillana* are some forms of *Carnatic* music.

Since this form of music is deeply spiritual and has a devotional bias, the compositions reflect these aspect. Literary content is an important component of Carnatic music Musicians generally render the compositions of the musical trinity of Tyagaraja, Muthuswami Dikshitar and Shyama Shastri.

Indian Musical Instruments

There are many ancient and contemporary musical instruments in India. Among the well known instruments of North India are *sitar, sarod, sarangi, santoor, flute, shehnai* and *rudraveena*. Percussion instruments include the *tabla and pakhawaj.* Of these, the tabla is used most often in music concerts as an accompaniment.

South Indian musical instruments include the violin, veena, gottuvadyam, flute and nadaswaram. Violin is used as an accompaniment with vocal music but also as a solo instrument. There is more variety in persuccion instruments of the south. *Mridanagam, ghatam, ganjira* and *thavil* are used as accompaniments. Of these, *thavil* is used only with *nadaswaram,* while *mridangam* is a must for any concert, be it vocal or instrumental, the other two viz., *ganjira* and *ghatam* are optional.

Cinema in India

On Dec. 28, 1895, Lumiere Brother Auguste and Louis, exhibited their cinematography in the first public show in Paris. Six months or so later, their assistant, Marius Sestier brought it to India. He presented the first show at Watson Hotel in Bombay on July 7, 1886. Today, India is among the top film producing countries in the world, producing films in many Indian languages.

The first story film, *Pundalik,* was shot in 1912. However, it didn't run successfully. The first film that was a commercial success was *Raja Harishchandra* by Dadasaheb Phalke in 1913, which ran nearly a month at a time when films hardly ran for a week. Initially movies were only made on methodological and religious subjects but slowly, other themes were also taken up.

Today, the Indian film industry turns out over 800 films a year in various languages, principal among them being, Hindi, Telugu and Tamil followed by Kannada and Bangali. The films include huge multi-star extravaganzas whose budgets run into several millions, art films that cater to the discerning film-goers, and commercial films that follows the set formula of the triumph of good over evil with songs and dances.

Though television and video have made their presence felt for many years now, films still hold the audience spellbound in hundreds of theaters across the length and breadth of the country. Perhaps nowhere else in the world have actors and actresses are treated as demi-gods and goddesses, commanding mass adulation bordering on hysteria. The film industry today is a multimillion dollar business providing both direct and indirect employment to thousand of workers.

Adivasi Contributions to Indian Culture and Civilization

Adivasi traditions and practices pervade all aspects of Indian culture and civilization, yet this awareness is often lacking in popular consciousness, and the extent and import of Adivasi contributions to Indian philosophy, language and custom have often gone unrecognized, or been underrated by historians and social scientists.

Although popular myths about Buddism have obscured the original source and inspiration for it's humanist doctrine, it is to India's ancient tribal (or Adivasi) societies that Gautam Buddha looked for a model for the kind of society he wished to advocate. Repulsed by how greed for private property was instrumental in causing poverty, social exploitation and unending warfare—he saw hope for human society in the tribal republics that had not yet come under the sway of authoritarian rule and caste discrimination. The early Buddhist *Sanghas* were modelled on the tribal pattern of social interaction that stressed gender equality, and respect for all members. Members of the *Sanghas* sought to emulate their egalitarian outlook and democratic functioning.

At that time, the tribal republics retained many aspects of social equality that can still be found in some

Adivasi societies that have somehow escaped the ill-effects of commercial plunder and exploitaion. Adivasi society was built on a foundation of equality with respect for all life forms including plants and trees. There was a deep recognition of mutual dependence in nature and human society. People were given respect and status according to their contribution to social needs but only while they were performing that particular function. A priest could be treated with great respect during a religious ceremony or a doctor revered during a medical consultation, but once such duties had been performed, the priest or doctor became equal to everyone else. The possession of highly valued skills or knowledge did not lead to a permanent rise in status. This meant that no individual or small group could engage in overlordship of any kind, or enjoy hereditary rights.

Such a value-system was sustainable as long as the Adivasi community was non-acquisitive and all the products of society were shared. Although division of labor did take place, the work of society was performed on a cooperative and co-equal basis without prejudice or disrespect for any form of work.

It was the simplicity, the love of nature, the absence of coveting the goods and wealth of others, and the social harmony of tribal society that attracted Gautam Buddha, and had a profound impact on the ethical core of his teachings.

(To this day, sharing is a vital and integral part of the philosophy of the Mullakurumba Adivasis of South India. When the Mullakurumbas go hunting a share is given to every family in the village, even those who may be absent, sick or cannot participate for any other reason. An extra portion is added for any guest in the village and even a non-tribal passersby will be offered a share. Not sharing is something they find difficult to comprehend.)

Nevertheless, tribal societies were under constant pressure as the money economy grew and made traditional forms of barter less difficult to sustain. In matters of trade, the Adivasis followed a highly evolved system of honour. All agreements that they entered into were honoured, often the entire tribe chipping into honour an agreement made by an individual member of the tribe. Individual dishonesty or deceit were punished severely by the tribe. An individual who acted in a manner that violated the honour of the tribe faced potential banishment and family members lost the right to participate in community events during the period of punishment. But often, tribal integrity was undermined because the non-tribals who traded with the Adivasis reneged on their promises and took advantage of the sincerity and honesty of most members of the tribe.

Tribel societies came under stress due to several factors. The extension of commerce, military incursions on tribal land, and the resettling of Brahmins amidst tribal populations had an impact, as did ideological coercion or persuasion to attract key members of the tribe into "mainstream" Hindu society. This led to many tribal communities becoming integrated into Hindu society as *jatis* (or castes) while others who resisted were pushed into the hilly or forested areas, or remote tracks that had not yet been settled. In the worst case defeated Adivasi tribes were pushed to the margins of settled society and became discriminated as outcastes and "untouchables".

But spontaneous differentiation within tribal societies also took place over time, which propelled these now unequal tribal communities into integrating into Hindu society without external violence or coercion. In Central India, ruling dynasties emerged from within the ranks of tribal society.

In any case, the end result was that throughout India, tribal deities and customs, creation myths and a variety of religious rites and ceremonies came to absorbed into the broad stream of "Hindu" society. In the Adivasi traditions, ancestor worship, worship of fertility gods and goddesses (as well as male and female fertility symbols), totemic worship-all played a role. And they all found their way into the practice of what is now considered Hinduism. The widespread Indian practice of keeping '*vratas*', i.e. fasting for wish-fulfillment or moral cleansing also has Adivasi origins.

Mahashweta Devi has shown that both Shiva and Kali have tribal origins as do Krishna and Ganesh. In the 8th century, the tribal forest goddess or harvest goddess was absorbed and adapted as Siva's wife. Ganesh owes it's origins to a powerful tribe of elephant trainers whose incorporation into Hindu society was achieved through the deification of their elephant totem. In his study fo Brahmin lineages in Maharashtra, Kosambi points to how many Brahmin gotras (such as *Kashyapa)* arose from tribal totems such as *Kachhapa* (tortoise). In Rajasthan, Rajput rulers recognised the Adivasi *Bhil* chiefs as allies and *Bhils* acquired a central role in some Rajput coronation ceremonies.

India's regional languages such as Oriya, Marathi or Bengali developed as a result of the fusion of tribal languages with Sanskrit or Pali and virtually all the Indian languages have incorporated words from the vocabulary of Adivasi languages.

Adivasis who developed an intimate knowledge of various plants and their medicinal uses played an invaluable role in the development of Ayurvedic medicines. In a recent study, the All India Coordinated Research Project credits Adivasi communities with the knowledge of 9000 plant species-7500 used for human healing and veterinary health care. Dental care products like *datun*, roots and condiments like *turmeric* used in cooking and ointments are also Adivasi discoveries, as are many fruit trees and vines. Ayurvedic cures for arthritis and night blindness owe their origin to Adivasi knowledge.

Adivasis also played an important role in the development of agricultural practices—such as rotational cropping, fertility maintenance through alternating the cultivation of grains with leaving land fallow or using it for pasture. Adivasis of Orissa were instrumental in developing a variety of strains of rice.

Adivasi musical instruments such as the *bansuri* (flute) and *dhol* (drum), folk-tales, dances and seasonal celebrations also found their way into Indian traditions as did their art and metallurgical skills.

In India's central belt, Adivasi communities rose to considerable prominence and developed their own ruling clans. The earliest Gond kingdom appears to date from the 10th C. and the Gond Rajas were able to maintain a relatively independent existence until the 18th C., although they were compelled to offer nominal allegiance to the Mughal empire. The Garha-Mandla kingdom in the north extended control over most of the upper Narmada valley and the adjacent forest areas. The Deogarh-Nagpur kingdom dominated much of the upper Wainganga valley, while Chanda-Sirpur in the south consisted of territory around Wardha and the confluences of the Wainganga with the Penganga.

Jabalpur was one of the major centers of the Garha-Mandla kingdom and like other major dynastic capitals had a large fort and palace. Temples and palaces with extremely fine carvings and erotic sculptures came up throughout the Gond kingdoms. The Gond ruling clans enjoyed close ties with the Chandella ruling clans and both dynasties attempted to maintain their independence from Mughal rule through tactical alliances. Rani Durgavati of Jabalpur (of Chandella-Gond heritage) acquired a reputation of legendary proportions when she died in battle defending against Mughal incursions. The city of Nagpur was founded by a Gond Raja in the early 18th century.

ADIVASIS AND THE FREEDOM MOVEMENT

As soon as the British took over Eastern India tribal revolts broke out to challenge alien rule. In the early years of colonization, no other community in India offered such heroic resistance to British rule or faced such tragic consequences as did the numerous Adivasi communities of now Jharkhand, Chhatisgarh, Orissa and Bengal. In 1772, the Paharia revolt broke out which was followed by a five year uprising led by Tilka Manjhi who was hanged in Bhagalpur in 1785. The Tamar and Munda revolts followed. In the next two decades, revolts took place in Singhbhum, Gumla, Birbhum, Bankura, Manbhoom and Palamau, followed by the great Kol Risings of 1832 and the Khewar and Bhumij revolts (1832-34). In 1855, the Santhals waged war against the permanent settlement of Lord Cornwallis, and a year later, numerous adivasi leaders played key roles in the 1857 war of independence.

But the defeat of 1858 only intensified British exploitation of national wealth and resources. A forest regulation passed in 1865 empowered the British government to declare any land covered with trees or brushwood as government forest and to make rules to manage it under terms of it's own choosing. The act made no provision regarding the rights of the Adivasi users. A more comprehensive Indian Forest Act was passed in 1878, which imposed severe restrictions upon Adivasi rights over forest land and produce in the protected and reserved forests. The act radically changed the nature of the traditional common property of the Adivasi communities and made it state property.

As punishment for Adivasi resistance to British rule, "The criminal Tribes Act" was passed by the British Government in 1871 arbitrarily stigmatizing groups such as the Adivasis (who were perceived as most hostile to British interests) as congenital criminals.

Adivasi uprisings in the Jharkhand belt were quelled by the British through massive deployment of troops across the region. The Kherwar uprising and the Birsa Munda movement were the most important of the late-18th century struggles against British rule and their local agents. The long struggle led by Birsa Munda was directed at British policies that allowed the *zamindars* (landowners) and money-lenders to harshly exploit the Adivasis. In 1914 Jatra Oraon started what is called the Tana Movement (which drew the participation of over 25,500 Adivasis). The Tana Movement joined the nation-wide Satyagrah Movement in 1920 and stopped the payment of land-taxes to the colonial Government.

During British rule, several revolts also took place in Orissa which naturally drew participation from the Adivasis. The significant ones included the Paik Rebellion of 1817, the Ghumsar uprisings of 1836-1856, and the Sambhalpur revolt of 1857-1864.

In the hill tribal tracts of Andhra Pradesh a revolt broke out in August 1922. Led by Alluri Ramachandra Raju (better known as Sitarama Raju), The Adivasis of the Andhra hills succeeded in drawing the British into a full-scale guerrilla war. Unable to cope, the British brought in the Malabar Special Force to crush it and only prevailed when Alluri Raju died.

As the freedom movement widened, it drew Adivasis into all aspects of the struggle. Many landless and deeply oppressed Adivasis joined in with upper-caste freedom fighters expecting that the defeat of the British would usher in a new democratic era.

Unfortunately, even fifty years after independence, Dalits and Adivasis have benefited least from the advent of freedom. Although independence has brought widespread gains for the vast majority of the Indian population, Dalits and Adivasis have often been left out, and new problems have arisen for the nation's Adivasi populations. With the tripling of the population since 1947, pressures on land resources have played havoc on the lives of the Adivasis. A disproportionate number of Adivasis have been displaced from their traditional lands while many have seen access to traditional resources undercut by forest mafias and corrupt officials who have signed irregular commercial leases that conflict with rights granted to the Adivasis by the Indian constitution.

It remains to be seen if the grant of statehood for Jharkhand and Chhatisgarh ameliorates the conditions for India's Adivasis. However, it is imperative that all Adivasi districts receive special attention from the Central government in terms of investment in schools, research institutes, participatory forest management and preservation schemes, non-polluting industries, and opportunities for the Adivasi communities to document and preserve their rich heritage. Adivasis must have special access to educational, cultural and economic opportunities so as to reverse the effects of colonization and earlier injustices experienced by the Adivasi communities.

At the same time, the country can learn much from the beauty of Adivasi social practices, their culture of sharing and respect for all—their deep humility and love of nature and most of all—their deep devotion to social equality and civic harmony.

NOTES & REFERENCES :

1. What is living and what is Dead in Indian Philosophy-Debiprasad Chattopadhyaya.

1b. Stcherbasky: Buddhist Logic (New York, 1962), Papers of Stcherbasky - (Calcutta - 1969, 71)
2. The Indian Historical Review, Vol. 16:1, 2. Baidyanath Saraswati's Review of P.K.Maity, *Folk-Rituals of Eastern India.*
3. Bulletins of the ICHR (Indian Council of Historical Research).
4. Studies in the Histery of Science in India (Edited by Debiprasad Chattopadhyaya).
5. Adivasi: A Symbiotic Bond—Mari and Stan Thekaekara (Hindu Folio, July 16, 2000).

Note: The term Adivasi has been used broadly to represent those classified as Scheduled Tribe under the Indian constitution. Roughly speaking, the term translates as aboriginal or native people (or native dwellers).

Some Dalit activists now prefer to also be characterized as Adivasis. Others seek to bring all of India's oppressed groupings under the'Bahujan Samaj' umbrella. While the term Harijan is largely out of favour, there are some who simply identify with the government designated terms ST (scheduled tribe) and SC (scheduled caste).

Although, districts with large Adivasi populations are to be found almost throughout India, the majority of India's Adivasis hail from Jharkhand, Chhatisgarh and Orissa. Tripura, Arunachal, Manipur, Meghalaya, Mizoram and Nagaland also have large Adivasi populations. There are also districts in Assam, Madhya Pradesh, Rajasthan, Gujarat, Maharashtra, Andhra and Tamil Nadu with sizeable Adivasi poulations.

2

CULTURE DEFINED

Culture is, no doubt, a comprehensive term. Dr. Julian Huxley, then Executive Secretary of the Preparatory Commission for UNESCO, who put forward the idea of the UNESCO Publication, *History of Mankind*, in 1946, wrote:

The chief task before the Humanities today would seem to be to help in constructing a history of the development of the human mind, notably in its highest cultural achievements. For this task, the help of art critics and artists will be needed as well as of art historians; of anthropologists and students of comparative religion as well as of divines and theologians; of archaeologists as well as of classical scholars; of poets and creative men of letters as well as of professors of literature; as well as the whole-hearted support of the historians.

It is well known that the anthropologists, who claim to have culture as their special field of study, are themselves not agreed on the connotation of the word. Anthropologists like Weber and MacIver are inclined to make a distinction between culture and civilization, restricting civilization to science and technology and culture to philosophy, religion, and the arts. But Kroeber uses the word "culture" as the customary term applicable alike to high or low products of societies. "Civilization" is used as a term for the larger and richer cultures, carrying an overtone of high development of a specific society.

I am inclined to accept Kroeber's definition of "civilizaiton" as "the historically differentiated and variable mass of customary ways of functioning of human societies", because of its comprehensiveness. He analyzes the components of culture at three levels: basic culture, social culture, and value culture. He pleads that this classification is only a conceptual axis which facilitates understanding and is bound to be capricious, if pushed too far. He himself posits language as a fourth component, morality and law as a fifth, and fashion as a sixth component. This is a good enough framework for an analytical presentation.

What I am concerned with here is "value culture" or "fine culture". The common man has this in mind when he speaks of "culture". It means the value-system of the individual, his scale of values and also the national pattern of culture to which he himself belongs. In this sense, culture is the pursuit of perfection in life. Powys describes culture as creative self sculpture. Perfection may always remain an unrealized ideal because there may be various levels in perfection too. The Duke of Windsor, when he was Prince of Wales, seems to have remarked: "Culture? It's a fine idea. I wish man will be able to realize it some day."

It is not growing like a tree that makes a man cultured. Age by itself is no criterion of culture. Culture does not necessarily consist in an intense attachment to any idea or doctrine. An attachment of this kind may generate fanaticism but not culture. In these days of increasing specialization, one cannot say that a specialist or an expert in a narrow field of knowledge is necessarily a cultured man. Expertise in a subject does not always go with culture. The uncultured man, as Powys said, displays his ideas lightly like a man who jingles the few coins he has in his pocket.

Culture implies the pursuit of perfection in all walks of life. It was Matthew Arnold who spoke of the pursuit of perfection fulfilling itself in two ways: the Hellenism of the Greeks and the Hebraism of the Jews. Hellenism, according to Arnold, denotes the spontaneity of consciousness and Hebraism the strictness of conscience. One stresses delight, heart-ease or *ananda* and the other the ethical aspect: purity of conduct, *tapasya* or askesis. If culture is the pursuit of perfection, it stands for perfection in purity of thought, feeling as well as deed. A cultured man is the integrated man. He is not divided within himself and against himself. He has overcome this self-division. An unevolved individual suffers continuously from self-division. His words belie his deeds and his thoughts his feelings. On the other hand, a cultured man's thoughts, feelings, and deeds are in harmony with each other. He achieves, in his own personality. a happy synthesis of knowledge, works and nobility of feeling. Like Wordsworth's happy warrior, a cultured man unites in his own personality the twin phases of action and contemplation. Like the bee that Swift, and later Matthew Arnold spoke of, he compasses the two ends of sweetness and light in his own being.

Culture, therefore, consists in a harmonious and balanced cultivaiton of all the faculties in man: intellect and emotion, intuition and sense perception, flesh as well as spirit Nero, the Roman emperor, had a perverted mind. His hunger for unusual sights, quite apart from their moral or even human implications, made him a neurotic and sadist. Cleopatra was too much plunged in the life of the senses to be regarded as a cultured lady. She became all "air and fire" only when Antony died and she realized the futility of physical passion.

This is at least true of Shakespeare's Cleopatra. An undue attachment to a life of spirit can also lead to lack of culture. Tagore's *Sanyasi* spent twenty to thirty years in the Himalayas, practising penance, and felt that he had attained the Divine. But he discovered, to his utter horror, that, on his return a simple beggar girl aroused in him an overwhelming emotion, giving the lie to his impressions that all such emotions had been extinguished within him. The ascetic's denial betrays as much lack of culture as the sensualist's entanglement with the senses. A wrongly felt intuition can lead to hasty and impulsive and, therefore, uncultured action as illustrated by the hero of W.B. Yeats' *The Unicorn From The Stars.*

However great an artist may be, uncontrolled emotion is sure to demonstrate his lack of culture. Strindberg, the great dramatist, for example, used to go mad whenever his cooks forsook him. An excessive reliance on the intellect may also lead to an unhealthy attitude in life. One may become a cynic and live life in a manner utterly devoid of taste or joy. There is a Sanskrit verse which points out that human beings are like pieces of wood adrift at sea. They float together for a while and then get separated. This may be true. At the same time, even a moment of companionship can be enduring and as full of joy as eternity. Browning gives a fine picture of this state of experience in his poem *The last Ride Together*. The cynic loses the beauty and harmony which reside in an emotional and intuitive approach to life.

Neglect or carelessness even in the observance of minor rules of health or conduct may reveal a proportionate lack of culture in highly gifted men. Gandhiji has narrated in his autobiography, how Gopal Krishna Gokhale, who was regarded by him as his political *guru*, never took any physical exercise. It was this neglect of health that brought about his premature end. But to make a fetish of one's health also means taking to a bye-lane which may or may not have the stamp of culture on it. There is a stroy woven round Gorakhnath who was an adept in *hatayoga* and excelled in many endurance tests and feats. When he met another saint, Allama Prabhu, Gorakhnath offered Prabhu a sword, challenging Prabhu to kill Gorakhnath, if he could. Allama struck with all his vehemence and the sword glanced back, hardly touching Gorakhnath's skin, as if it had been flourished against a flint. But Allama offered the same sword to Gorakhnath inviting him to strike at Allama Prabhu with it. When Gorakhnath tried to cut Prabhu's body into two, the sword passed through the body as if through air and the two separated halves were united again, like air itself. Culture, which is perfect in all its parts, is like air rather than earth. One can specialize and master a particular craft or discipline; but the cultured man is as unattached and as universal as air.

Even a mystic, who is not actively aware of his own time and place and is lost in his brooding on eternity, does not fit into our definition of culture. He may be of all time. But he has to belong to his own time and place and contribute actively to the progress and well-being of his fellowmen, if he is to be regarded as a cultured person.

This brings us to the consideration of an adequate formula for defining the cultured man. Culture implies an integrated personality and neither time nor eternity can be left out of it. The cultured man reconciles the universal with the particular and the claims of time with the claims of eternity. Taine, the French literary historian, spoke of the race, the moment, and the milieu as factors determining the form and substance of literary history in a given epoch. But he left out an all-important factor: the personality of the individual. The human personality, as sages and prophets have proved on their own pulses, can rise to any level of perception or consciousness, hardly dreamed of by others. But this perception also has to reckon with the three other factors, if the individual is to function in the spirit of true culture. It is likely that each one of these factors may lead to deviation or distortion in one or the other way, it it is turned into a hobby horse and pursued in excess. To take a few instances from literary history, Kipling's writings were frequently disfigured by his sense of racial pride. There came into his poetry a jingoistic note which detracted considerably from its enduring significance. As for environment, one has to judge whether conformity to or revolt against it is justified from the point of view of culture. Pandit Malaviyaji, an orthodox Hindu who modelled his behaviour on what the scriptures, even the apocryphal scriptures, said, set them side and went to England for the Round Table Conference in spite of the fact that orthodoxy banned journeys across the seas. Gandhiji, who cared only for truth and even put it far above the freedom of India, rode on the crest of the wave, caught the Time Spirit by its forelock and launched the movement of non-violent non-cooperation against the British because that moment in the life of the nation needed it.

If one were to speak of men of letters who realized this ideal of culture in their own lives, one could mention Kalidasa and Shakespeare. They belonged to their age but they also were of all time. The poetry of Kalidasa is a vivid portrayal of the problems, the pressures, the glory, and the splendour of the Gupta period. But it also sets forth the eternal verities in an unmistakable manner. Shakespeare's plays fulfil themselves in a similar way. The entire Elizabethan England can be found in his plays. At the same time his heroes and heroines are types and individuals that can be met with in all countries in any age.

The cultured man is not just interested in perfecting himself. He also helps to perfect the world because his passion for perfection does not end only with himself. Culture may be an end in itself. But the very fact that a person is cultured makes its own contribution to the society around him. Viewed nationally, culture is a means to an end, the end being the happiness and all-round prosperity of one's own country and of humanity.

Philosophy and religion, the fine arts, Nature, love and friendship are some of the channels which can irrigate human lives and lead to a worldwide harvest of culture. If the philosopher, the man of religion, the artist and poet are not men of culture, at least in the creative springs of their personality, their writings will not make for the diffusion of culture. One has therefore to be careful in surrendering oneself to any specific philosophy or work of art. It may be that some of the limitations of the artist or the thinker project themselves into his work. The impassioned prose of Nietzsche was full of power and energy. But along with power and movement, there was no adequate measure of light. The light available was obscured by the turbidity of his impulsiveness. The result was that Nietzsche sowed the wind and reaped the whirlwind called Hitler.

A love of Nature, truth and friendship, and the company of the good and great can diffuse the authentic values of culture effectively. These are the graces of life that contribute substantially to the greatness of a civilization.

The coming generation may do well to remember that action alone is not the *summun bonum* of life. Macbeth, the villianhero of Shakespeare's great tragedy, acted impulsively and spent the rest of his life in desperate repentance. On the other hand, Hamlet lived a life of utter indecision and by the time he was inclined to act, it was too late. Thought, feeling, and action have to blossom simultaneously, like three roses on a stem, and express the root-intuition of the complete personality. If precedence has to be given till this becomes possible, it will have to go to intensive thinking and deep feeling. An agility of judgment, changing as new facts come into our ken, a purity of feeling, which is untainted by any preference or prejudice, and a readiness to act to the extent necessary without fear or favour, once the decision is made, are the sure marks of a cultured personality fully formed or in the making.

It is now clear that there can be no foreground without its background relief, no effective specialization unless it is backed up by a wide, fundamental knowledge of other departments of thought and of life and reality. Book-worms can be boring. But subject-worms run the risk of being dehumanized, becoming efficient tools and, for that very reason, lifeless or insensitive to the beauty and movement of life.

Lastly, the contemplation of eternity should not obscure the vision of the social scene animated and active all around us. Nor should our complete absorption in the social scene make us oblivious of the verities that abide long after our lips are dumb and our hands and feet are clay. For, after all,

We are such stuff
As dreams are made on and our little life
Is rounded with a sleep.

—

3

EPOCHS OF INDIAN CULTURE

Indian culture must be viewed not in seetions but in continuous time and the long career of our culture can be divided into four distinct ages.

The first, the Age of Expansion, can be traced from the civilisation of the Indus Valley, five thousand years ago, when the country worshipped the Pashupati in the Yoga posture, through the fresh young life during the age of Rigvedic *mantras* and the vigorous youth of the post-Vedic age of Janamejaya Parikshita; through the unbroken continuity during the age of Imperial Magadha (c.700 B.C.-A.D. 320), the Classical Age of the Guptas (A.D. 320-750), and the age of Imperial Kanauj (A.D.750-1000).

The second age of our culture, that of Resistance, can be traced through the age of disintegration (A.D.1000-1300) at the end of which the Sultanate of Delhi became an imperial power in India. At the end of the twelfth century Central Asian hordes flung themselves on India to burn, to loot, to destroy. Indians, who only knew how to wage wars according the laws of Dharma, were staggered by the totalitarian wars forced upon them. They then mobilised defensive resistance in other spheres of life, and the concentrated vigour of the barbarie onslaught was broken. Alien rule was segregated into the narrowest limits; inviolable defences— psychological, social and religious— were raised against any surrender to it.

The beginning of the third age, that of Modern Renaissance, may be traced to the end of the seventeenth century. By about A.D. 1700, Ramdas and Shivaji in Maharashtra, the Gurus in the Punjab and the Rajputs in

Rajasthan had exchanged resistance for aggressive defiance. An expansive mood was in the air. But before Bharat could reap the harvest of this upsurgence, fate subjected her to political and economic domination by Britain. Undaunted, the upsurgence spread to different channels, to unexpected forms and quarters. The movements associated with Ram Mohan Roy, the Great Revolt of 1857, Dayananda Sarasvati, Ramakrishna Paramahansa, Vivekananda, Tilak and Sri Aurobindo, Malaviyaji, Tagore and Gandhiji and the Congress, represent each in their own way, the highwater marks of a progressively expansive attitude. Through the British Universities, established in India to train Indians for subservient careers, the culture forced its way as the Sanskritie revival, a great political awakening and a cultural renaissance. When disarmed after 1857, India projected her usge for self-realisation into a peaceful but all-sweeping movement which reached its climax in the nationwide *satyagragh* activities.

The fourth age commenced on August 15, 1947, when we became masters of our own destiny. But with our freedom has come a crisis in our cultural advancement. We have to face post-war problems, new world forces, and the power of a highly technocratic civilization with its industrial and urban problems, to all of which the fundamental values and the central idea in our culture have to adjust themselves.

In each age culture broadly expresses itself through four principal activities, social, intellectual, emotional and aesthetic, and spiritual. It has, therefore, to be studied in four corresponding aspects:

(a) Social achievements, with reference to institutions like (i) the family,(ii) the social organisation, and (iii) the State;

(b) Intellectual achievements like (i) political and legal concepts, (ii) speculative thought, and (iii) scientific advancement;

(c) Emotional and aesthetic achievements found in (i) religious movements, (ii) linguistic and literary development, (iii) art forms and traditions, and (iv) embellishment of life;

(d) Spiritual achievement—reintegration of fundamental values, and their adjustment to the dominant ideas and conditions of the age so that the Central Idea achieves fresh vigour and velocity.

II

Before the first age of formation began, Aryans in India had inherited the institution of the patriarchal family. The house community of pre-Vedic Aryans all over Asia and Europe lived round the family fire, and consisted of male descendants of a common ancestor. According to Fustel de Coulanges and Schröder, these Aryans, in sharp contrast with the matriarchal races, did not recognise any relationship with the mother or her relatives. Maternal right was foreign to them; only later the paternal right was raised into the parental.

The basic institution of the Vedic Aryans in India was the patriarchate family. The father was the lord and master of the family, both of its members and its assets. Ancestor worship was the central creed.

The *pitris*, manes, watched over the family; they had to be given *pinda*, offerings, at stated intervals or on stated days. When his dead body was consigned to the flames, The Jatavedas (Agni) was called upon to give him over to the *pitris*. A son was, therefore, an indispensable link in the chain which bound a man to his *pitris*; if there was no son, there had to be a son by adoption, *i.e.*, by spiritual birth; but he had to be taken from the same family. "The son is substitute for the father in performing religious rites", say the Vedas. The father, son and grandson owned the family property by right of brith. The *pitri-yajna* and the *tarpana*, the *pindadana* and the *shraddha* kept the spiritual unity indissoluble. The son was the saviour of the family, for he carried the *kula* forward. The basic idea was that the *pitris*, the living males, and the sons, born and to be born, were an indissoluble unit.

The *gotra* was a group of families claiming descent from a common male ancestor and was the unit of society; a federation of *gotras* formed the *jana* which claimed an eponymous hero as the common but remote ancestor. Intermarriage between members of the same *gotra* was forbidden. Five such tribes formed the *pancha-janah* who constituted the conquering race in the Saptasindhu of Rigvedic times. Their common ancestor was Manu.

Manu's law had even then the reputaion of having been handed down from the *pitris;* and to the Aryan it was the law eternal (*esha dharma sanatanah*). He prayed that his race might not stray from the path.

Pride of descent from a common male ancestor carried with it the need to demand unswerving loyalty of the woman married into the family. Purity of descent is in conceivable without it. Marriage, in which man and wife became one, was the most inalienable of spiritual bonds. The purpose of marriage was *garhapatya*, *i.e.* householdership, comradeship in the worship of gods, and procreation of sons to secure heaven for oneself and the *pitris*. The wife was half of oneself, *sharirardha*. A man was complete only when he took a wife and had a son. The fall of a wife was a great lapse. The gods would not forgive it. Thus was established the fundamental value of the identity of man and wife joined by the marriage tie.

These values laid the foundation of Aryan culture. Even Parashurama had to kill his mother because she looked at a Gandharva.

III

The Aryans of the post-Vedie period were settled in the valley of the Yamuna and the Ganga. Large kingdoms ruled by the Aryan clans had come into existence. In this age the patriarchal family unit—*kula*—had become firmly established as the foundation of the society. The father was the supreme *guru* and the master of life. Ajigarta could even sell his son for a hundred cows. The Pandavas had to pass through years of trial on account of their supposed doubtful origin.

With the dawn of history in the seventh century before Christ, Magadha, under the Shishunagas, emerged as the predominant factor in the life of the country.

Our culture entered upon an era of triumphant expansion first under the Shishunagas, Nandas and Mauryas; next under Pushyamitra and the Sungas; and later under the Guptas till A.D. 550. Later on for about four centuries, the culture centered on Kanauj carried on the tradition.

The Age of Expansion ended when in A.D. 940 the Rashtrakuta conquerors of the South broke the power of Kanauj and the Sultans of Ghazni from 997 A.D. onwards carried out their raids rudely shaking the foundations of life. But the North-West had been overrun by the Hunas and allied foreigners; Dakshinapatha, the Deccan, under the Chalukyas, was vying with Uttarapatha, North India, for all-India supremacy and culture began to lose both its purity and creativeness.

The Sutras invested the family with semi-divine sanction. They laid emphasis on the headship of the father, the corporate character of the joint family, and the indissolubility of the *gotra*. The economic basis of the family was the ancestral property; the economic bond was strengthened between the ancestor from whom the property was inherited on one side, and the owner, his son and grandson who acquired interest in it by birth. This laid the foundation of a stable economic order.

Intermarriage between members of the three castes (the *dvijas)* without offending against the principle of *pratiloma* was the rule. Marriage as a spiritual merger of man and wife became a fundamental value. *Paraskara Grihya Sutra* indicates this alchemy: "With thy breath I join my breath, with thy bones my bones, with thy flesh my flesh, and with thy skin my skin." It was the age of Sukanya, Arundhati and Anasuya, of Savitri and Sita. Arjuna in the Gita expresses horror at the lapse of women from chastity, and at sons of mixed descent. A woman's loss of all rights in her father's property and acquisition of rights in the husband's, as laid down by the Smritis, provided the economic basis. In later centuries it accounted for the wonderful tenacity of our social institutions. During the later ages, this value was invested with tragic greatness in the Age of Resistance, thousands of women cheerfully lived up to the idea of going through the sublime self-immolation of the *Jauhar.*

The Gupta empire was dissolved by the inroads made by foreigners in the North and the West. The four allied martial tribes—an interconnubial group—of Pratiharas, Chahamanas, Chalukyas and Paramaras became a military power, fought the East under the Palas of Bengal and the South under the Rashtrakutas and founded the Imperial Gurjaradesha which comprised West Punjab, East Madhyadesha, Rajputana, Malwa and Gujarat, with Kanauj as the capital of India.

From about A.D. 600, the North and South each had its own line of Emperors, the Gurjara-Pratiharas of Kanauj and the Chalukyas and Rashtrakutas of Vatapi and Manyakheta. The cultural classes of the North had been by heredity or education, deeply imbued with the values of Aryan culture. In the South, exeept in the case of Brahmanas, the culture was no more than an ideal pattern in which the existing social conditions were to be cast under the influence of Brahmanas and devout kings. Women in the South were in a sense free from the code which the Smritis enjoined; even in high society they were different from the women of the North, free in their intercourse with men.

With free intermarriage between the North and the South consequent upon frequent wars, intermarriage between the higher classes disappeared in the North. The martial races came to be much married. Disparity of cultural outlook among the families who thus freely intermarried led to a lowering of cultural values. The wife became a mere dependent. Islam also appeared in Sindh and, as is seen in the *Devala Smriti,* the wife forcibly converted to Islam created a new problem unknown before. *Anuloma* marriage became rare. The education of women came to be neglected or was rendered impossible; castes slowly came to be segregated into compartments. The partriarchal family unit and the marriage tie were accepted as sacred values in theory; in practice, among certain sections of the society, they were disregarded.

With the disastrous inroads of Central Asian hordes, the Age of Resistance was reached. I have called this 'the Age of Resistance', because whatever cultural development we find during the period was more a product of determined resistance to the destructive forces which came into India from outside rather than of a direct contact with alien influences.

The Age of Resistance passed through several stages. The first and the darkest period was from Qutb-ud-Din to

Akbar, and the second period of weakening resistance from Akbar to A.D. 1675. The administration of that law laid down by the Dharma-shastras, so far considered to be the duty of good kings, was neglected wherever the foreigners held sway.

The great centres of learning throughout the North were destroyed. The operation of free intellectual and moral forces was arrested. Society developed defensive conservatism. In about eighty years which passed between Medhatithi's commentary on Manu and Vijnaneshvara's commentary on Yajnavalkya, we find society completely changed in its attitude from an expansive almost aggressive, outlook towards world conquest to a frantic attempt at conserving all that happened to be current at the time. The joint family became more rigid; family life was allowed litle scope for freedom. Women, the most coveted of possessions, were protected, treasured in families by infant marriage, and in many cases by *purdah*. The wife was merged in the husband, but was no longer his partner. She tended to deteriorate into a parasite; not that anyone made her so; but fleeing from the terrors of the onrushing tide of destruction, she was helplessly reduced to that position. For instance, nowhere in India today is the *purdah* so rigid as in Rajasthan, which for several centuries bore the brunt of the onrush and, resisting grimly, saved the social structure and cultural traditions.

IV

The second great institution, the social organisation of Chaturvarnya, can also be traced through the different ages. In the early Age of Expansion, particularly in the early *Mantra* period, Brahmana was the professional priest; Rajanya the ruler-king; Vaishya, the villager who constituted the bulk of the Aryan community; Dasyus and Shudras were the non-Aryan, dark-skinned, noseless people with strange gods. But the germ of the Chaturvarnya was there. Those men who as a class dedicated themselves to learning and meditation were recognised as the head of the community. By their far-sighted social wizardry they converted the political supremacy of the Aryans over non-Aryans into a cultural hierarchy of the *dvija*(twice born) and the non-*dvija*. Transition from one class to another came to depend upon conformity to cultural standards rather than birth. The *Purusha Sukta* of the *Rigveda* period has left on record the first clear indication of the four-fold order of society. The four-fold order was devised to broaden and arrange the social system so as to absorb the non-Aryans without sacrificing cultural purity.

In the post-Vedic period, the four-fold order of society became a universal order, the men of learning and nonpossession stood at the head; the Kshatriyas came next, though a clear tendency to look upon them as exalted is discernible. The incident of Brahmana Parashurama being made to suffer a defeat at the hands of Kshatriya Rama is an indication of a rival movement. But as the kingdoms grew, the kings could not do without divine sanction, and it was forthcoming only through protracted and costly sacrifices which a host of Brahmanas alone could perform.

When history opens with Magadha's imperial sway we see the struggle continuing in spite of the traditional arrangement. "The king had to find the *shrotriya*, for he was the half soul of the king; both were the upholders of dharma"say the *Shatapatha* and the *Aitareya Brahmanas*. But the Brahmanas, who had by then become the repositories of learning and statecraft, of poetry and science, were indispensable leaders of the community. They could prescribe law-texts; they could perform sacrifices; they could indulge in philosophic speculations; they could also produce political texts, the greatest of which Kautilya's *Arthashastra*—has few parallels, if any, in the political literature of the world. The theoretical pattern of society as the four-fold order had its antagonists too. Nanda was one of them. *Matsyapurana* refers to irascible and contemptible rulers who tried to destroy the social system.

The foundations of culture were so well laid in Chaturvarnya that, with the period which opened with the rule of Pushyamitra, himself a Brahmana, Chaturvarnya became accepted as an immutable social order. No doubt each province and each movement interpreted it as it liked. Sri Krishna in the *Gita* ranges the four-fold order according to qualities and actions (*guna-karma-vibhagashah.)*

Yudhishthira, in his dialogue with Nahusha, himself expresses a doubt as to the validity of hereditary castes. In the *Mahabharata* Indra enjoins Mandhata to bring all the foreigners into the fold of *dharma*. And Kalidasa's works reflect the beauty and vigour of Chaturvarnya at its best.

In the Age of Expansion, it provided a social pattern of universal application whereby new races were fitted into a living organisation, without destroying its stability and cultural standards. It utilised the principle of hereditary transmission of specialised functions to produce one corporation of men devoted to learning, another of men devoted to the martial arts, and a third of those pursuing trade and commerce. It stabilised society. It enabled the Brahmanas to work for intellectual and literary advancement. It enjoined on the Kshatriyas the duty to protect the social structure, to preserve the law, and by humanising and regulating war, to render the continuity of culture possible. The Vaishyas were to carry on the economic life of the people, undisturbed by political earthquakes. While this order emphasised heredity,it also had elasticity. It enabled outsiders to be absorbed easily or a lower group to rise to a higher level by adopting a more cultured way of life. It provided India with a living social gospel wherewith to make internal life coherent and external conquest full of meaning. Medhatithi says Aryavarta is not between the mountains and the sea; wherever an Aryan ruler spreads his arms, establishes Chaturvarnya and reduces the *mlechchhas* to the position of Shudras, there is Aryavarta.

In the Age of Resistance, Chaturvarnya played its part magnificently. The Brahmanas, driven from their ancient Universities, fled to distant villages, preserved learning and traditions, upheld the Smriti laws, and catered for the educational and religious needs of the people. The Kshatriyas, men and women, died in their thousands, to preserve freedom and faith. The Vaishyas bought from the barbarians safety for themselves and the rest, for their shrines and for their localities, and carried on their vocation with deft thoroughness.

When a cataclysmic upheaval followed the invasion, the Chaturvarnya became the fortress of life. Millions of refugees fled before the onrushing fury; subdivided themselves into rigid sub-castes; preserved their way of life; resisted aliens and their ways by the sharpest of collective instruments—social ostracism and sheer non-recognition of everything alien. If Chaturvarnya had not reacted so defensively, India would have been a charnel-house of Bharatiya culture. If the Kshatriyas resisted in every fort and village and their womenfolk courted fire in order to leave a mighty tradition of unsullied chastity the Brahmanas threw up *acharyas*, *bhaktas* and poets who brought about religious upheaval and literary renaissance and kept alive the inspiration of Sanskrit. The flag of the mercantile fleet of Gujarat owned by the Vaishyas continued to fly in eighty-four foreign ports throughout this age. We, who are blinded by an admiration of the social apparatus of the West, fail to realise that Chaturvarnya was a marvellous social synthesis on a countrywide scale, when the rest of the world was weltering in a tribal state.

"No doubt," says Sydney Low in his *Vision of India*, "that it (Chaturvarnya) is the main cause of the fundamental stability and contentment by which Indian society has been braced up for centuries against the shocks of politics and the cataclysms of nature."

Indian culture has been a dynamic force throughout history, and no better proof of it could be found than in the vitality, tenacity and adaptability of its social structure.

4

THE CONTINUITY OF INDIAN CULTURE

The coming of the Aryans into India raised new problems—racial and political. The conquered race, the Dravidians, had a long background of civilization behind them, but there is little doubt that the Aryans considered themselves vastly superior to them and a wide gulf separated the two. Then there were also some backward aboriginal tribes, nomads or forest-dwellers. Out of this conflict and interaction of races gradually rose the caste system, which, in the course of succeeding centuries, was going to affect Indian life so profoundly. Probably this was neither Aryan nor Dravidian. It was an attempt at the social organization of different races, a rationalization of the facts as they existed at the time. It brought degradation in its train afterwards, and it is still a burden and a curse. But we can hardly judge it from subsequent standards or later development. It was in keeping with the spirit of the times and some such grading took place in most of the ancient civilizations, though apparently China was free from it. There was a four fold division in that other branch of the Aryans, the Iranians, during the Sassanian period, but it did not petrify into caste. Many of these old civilizations, including that of Greece, were entirely dependent on mass slavery. There was no such mass or largescale labour slavery in India, although there were relatively small numbers of domestic slaves. Plato in his Republic refers to a division similar to that of the four principal castes. Medieval Catholicism knew this division also.

Caste began with a hard and fast division between Aryans and non-Aryans, the latter again being divided into the Dravidian races and the aboriginal tribes. The Aryans, to begin with, formed one class and there was hardly any specialization. The word *Arya* comes from a root word meaning to till, and the Aryans as a whole were agriculturists and agriculture was considered a noble occupation. The tiller of the soil functioned also as priest, soldier or trader, and there was no privileged order of priests. The caste divisions, originally intended to separate the Aryans from the non-Aryans, reacted on the Aryans themselves, and as division of functions and specialization increased, the new classes took the form of castes.

Thus at a time when it was customary for the conquerors to exterminate or enslave the conquered races, caste enabled a more peaceful solution which fitted in with the growing specilization of functions. Life was graded and out of the mass of agriculturists, evolved the Vaishyas, or rulers and warriors; and the Brahmanas, priests and thinkers who were supposed to guide policy and preserve and maintain the ideals of the nation. Below these three there were the Shudras or labourers and unskilled workers, other than the agriculturists. Among the indigenous tribes many were gradually assimilated and given a place at the bottom of the social scale, that is among the Shudras. This process of assimilation was a continuous one. These castes must have been in a fluid condition; rigidity came in much later. Probably the ruling class had always great latitude, and any person, who by conquest or otherwise assumed power, could, if he so willed, join the hierarchy as a Kshatriya, and get the priests to manufacture an appropriate genealogy connecting him with some ancient Aryan also.

The word *Arya* ceased to have any racial significance and came to mean 'noble,' just as *un-Arya* means ignoble and was usually applied to nomadic tribes, forest-dwellers, etc.

The Indian mind was extraordinarily analytical and had a passion for putting ideas and concepts, and even life's activities, into compartments. The Aryans not only divided society into four main groups but also divided the individual's life into four parts: the first part consisted of growth and adolescence, the student period of life, acquiring knowledge, developing self-discipline and self-control, continence; the second was that of the householder and man of the world; the third was that of the elder statesman, who had attained a certain poise and obectivity, and could devote himself to public work without the selfish desire to profit by it; and the last stage was that of the recluse, who lived a life largely cut off from the world's activities. In this way also they adjusted the two opposing tendencies which often exist side by side in man—the acceptance of life in its fullness and the rejection of it.

In India, as in China, learning and erudition have always stood high in public esteem, for learning was supposed to imply both superior knowledge and virtue. Before the learned man, the ruler and the warrior have always bowed. The old Indian theory was that those who were concerned with the exercise of power could not be completely objective. Their personal interests and inclinations would come into conflict with their public duties. Hence the task of determining values and the preservation of ethical standards was allotted to a class or group of thinkers who were free from material cares and were, as far as possible, without obligations, so that they could consider life's problems in a spirit of detachment. This class of thinkers or philosophers was thus supposed to be at the top of the social structure, honoured and respected by all. The men of action, the rulers and warriors, came after them and, however powerful they might be, did not command the same respect. The possession of wealth was still less entitled to honour and repect. The warrior class, though not at the top, held a high position, and not, as in China, where it was looked upon with contempt.

This was the theory and, to some extent, it may be found elsewhere, as in Christiandom in medieval Europe, when the Roman Church Assumed the functions of leadership in all spiritual, ethical and moral matters, and even in the general principles underlying the conduct of the state. In practice, Rome became intensely interested in temporal power and the princes of the Church were rulers in their own right. In India the Brahman class, in addition to supplying the thinkers and the philosophers, became a powerful and entrenched priesthood, intent on preserving its vested interests. Yet this theory, in varying degrees, has influenced Indian life profoundly, and the ideal has continued to be of a man full of learning and charity, essentially good, self-disciplined, and capable of sacrificing himself for the sake of others. The Brahman class has shown all the vices of a privileged and entrenched class in the past and large numbers of them have possessed neither learning nor virtue. Yet they have largely retained the esteem of the public, not because of temporal power or possession of money, but because of temporal power or possession of money, but because they have produced a remarkable succession of men of intelligence and their record is notable one. The whole class profited by the example of its leading personalities in every age, and yet the public esteem went to the qualities rather than to any official status. The tradition was one of respecting learning and goodness in any individual who possessed them. There are innumerable examples of non-Brahmans, and even persons belonging to the depressed classes, being so respected and sometimes considered as saints. Official status and military power never commanded the same measure of respect, though they may have been feared.

Even today, in this money age, the influence of this tradition is marked and, because of it, Gandhi (who is not a Brahaman) can become the supreme leader of India and move the hearts of million without force or compulsion of official position or possession of money. Perhaps this is as good a test as any of a nation's cultural background and its conscious or subconscious objective: to what kind of a leader does it give its allegiance?

The central idea of old Indian civilization, or Indo Aryan culture was that of dharma, which was something much more than religion or creed. It was a conception of obligations, of the discharge of one's duties to oneself and to others. This dharma itself was part of *rita*, the fundamental moral law governing the functioning of the universe and all it contained. If there was such an order then man was supposed to fit into it and he should function in such a way as to remain in harmony with it: If man did his duty and was ethically right in his action, the right consequences would inevitably follow. Rights as such were not emphasized. That, to some extent, was the old outlook everywhere. It stands out in marked contrast with the modern assertion of rights, rights of individuals, or groups, of nations.

Thus in these very early days we find the beginnings of the civilization and culture which were to flower so abundantly and richly in subsequent ages, and which have continued, in spite of many changes, to our own day. The basic ideals, the governing concepts were taking shape, and literature and philosophy, art and drama, and all other activities of life were conditioned by these ideals and worldview. Also we see the seeds of that exclusiveness and touch-me-notism which were to grow and grow till they bacame rigid, octopus-like with their grip of everything—the caste-system of recent times fashioned for a particular day, intended to stabilize the then organization of society and give it strength and equilibrium, it developed into a prison for that social order and for the mind of man. Security was purchased in the long run at the cost of ultimate progress.

Yet it was a very long run and, even within that framework, the vital original impetus for advancement in all directions was so great that it spread out all over India and over the eastern seas, and its stability was such that it survived repeated shock and invasion. Professor Macdonell in his *History of Sanskrit Literature* tells us that, "the importance of Indian literature as a whole consists in its originality. When the Greeks towards the end of the fourth century B.C. invaded the north-west, the Indians has already worked out a national culture of their own, unaffected by foreign influences. And in spite of successive waves of invasion and conquest by Persians, Greeks, Scythians, Muhammadans, the national development of the life and literature of the Indo-Aryan race remained practically unchecked and unmodified from without down to the era of British occupation. No other branch of the Indo European stock has experienced an isolated evolution like this. No other country except China can trace back its language and literature, its religious beliefs and rites, its dramatic and social customs through an uninterrupted development of more than three thousand years."

Still India was not isolated and throughout this long period of history she had continuous and living contacts with Iranians and Greeks and Chinese and Central Asians and others. If her basic culture survived these contacts, there must have been something in that culture itself which gave it the dynamic strength to do so, some inner vitality and understanding of life. For this three or four thousand years of cultural growth and continuity is remarkable. Max Muller, the famous scholar and Orientalist, emphasizes this: "There is, in fact, an unbroken continuity between the most modern and the most ancient phases of Hindu thought, extending over more than three thousand years." Carried away by this enthusiasm, he said (in his lectures delivered before the University of Cambridge, England, in 1882) : "If we were to look over the whole world to find out the country most richly endowed with all the wealth, power and beauty that nature can bestow—in some parts a very paradise on earty—I should point to India. If I were asked under what sky the human mind has most fully developed some of its choicest gifts, has most deeply pondered over the greatest problems of life, and has found solutions of some of them which well deserve the attention even of those who have studied Plato and Kant—I should point to India. And if I were to ask myself from what literature, we here in Europe, we who have been nurtured almost exclusively on the thoughts of Greeks and Romans, and of one Semitic race, the Jewish, may draw the corrective which is most wanted in order to make our inner life more perfect, more comprehensive, more universal, in fact more truly human a life, not for this life only, but a transfigured and eternal life—again I should point to India."

Nearly half a century later Romain Rolland wrote in the same strain: "If there is one place on the face of the earth where all the dreams of living men have found a home from the very earliest days when man began the dream of existence, it is India."

5

THE CULTURAL INFLUENCES OF ISLAM

Modern Indian civilization has developed from the action and reaction of so many different races and creeds upon each other that it is extremely difficult to say which of its features is due to a particular influence. Hardest of all to assess is the influence of Islam, for the various Muslim incursions into India brought comparatively few people of an alien race into India. Even the great Bābur, when he 'put his foot in the stirrup of resolution' and set out to invade India, in November 1525, only took with him some 12,000 soldiers and merchants. Of the eighty odd million Muslims, who today form a quarter of the population, the great majority are descended from Hindu stock, and retain certain characteristics common to Indians as a whole. Yet because the Muslim invaders came as conquerors, rulers, and missionaries they made such an impression, especially in the north, that to many Europeans and Americans the characteristic life and architecture of India must seem to be Musulman. Muslim culture in India, being a blending of two cilivizations, is something *sui generis,* and as such has its special contribution to make to the Western world, as well as to the rest of Islam. The process by which the blending took place is of special interest. A passage in the *Cambridge History of India,* by Sir John Marshall (vol. iii, p. 568), well describes the influence of Hindu and Muslim culture on one another. He observes:

'Seldom in the history of mankind has the spectacle been witnessed of two civilization, so vast and so strongly developed, yet so radically dissimilar, as the Muhammadan and the Hindu, meeting and mingling together. The very contrasts which existed between them, the wide divergence on their culture and their religions, make the history of their impact peculiarly instructive.'

The earliest contact of Islam with India began in the second half of the seventh and the beginning of the eighth centuries of the Christian era, through Sind and Baluchistan. The Arabs, who conquered Sind and remained there, have left a lasting impress on the manners and customs of the people. Later on, another stream of Muslim people came to India, through its north-west frontier. They were racially and culturally different from the Arab invaders, who had come to the western coast. Representatives of various tribes and dynasties of Central Asia, who felt the spell of Islam and embraced the faith, started a long series of invasions of India. It is obvious, however, that invasions like those of Tīmūrlane or Mahmūd of Ghaznī were not calculated to produce marked cultural results or to leave many permanent traces of their influence. These contacts did not last long and offered no opportunities of any intimate relations between the people of the country and their unwelcome visitors from the north. The real contacts began when Muslims began to settle down in the country as their adopted home.

Several dynasties of Muslim kings preceded the establishment of the Mughal Empire in India, and undoubtedly contributed much to the grafting of Muslim culture on the ancient civilization of the country, but there is very little material available for making a definite estimate of their contributions. Attention has to be confined mainly to the Mughal period, which has contributed most to the development of an Indo-Muslim culture.

Some of the influences which have come to India through Muslims may not have been essential ingredients of Islam when it originated in Arabia, but they came to be identified with it in course of time, in its onward march from Arabia to Persia and Central Asia. Of these countries Persia has had a dominating influence on Islam and through it on India. The Arabs conquered Persia, but Persian civilization made such a profound impression on them that the Persian language and literature became a necessary part of Islamic culture in many Eastern lands. The

Central Asian dynasties, which came to India and established kingdoms in it, had come under the influence of Persian literature before they came to India, and the result was that Persian was adopted by them as the language of the Court and of literature. In the time of the Mughals the study of the Persian language was eagerly taken up by Muslims as well as non-Muslims. The Hindus, who possess a great capacity for adaptation in matters intellectual, took kindly to Persian literature, just as they are now eagerly studying the English language and its literature. The Northern Provinces of India furnish many brilliant examples of Hindu scholars of Persian, who could use the language very effectively in prose as well as in poetry. Two classes of Hindu have particularly distinguished themselves in this respect—the Kashmīrī Pandits and the Kāyasthas. Recently a large book has been published containing selections from Persian poems composed by Kashmīrī Pandits. It was through the medium of Persian, which, in its turn, had been largely influenced by the Arabic language and the texts of the sacred books of the Muslim faith, that the best ethical thought of Islam influenced the educated Hindus of the period. One great result of this influence was the gradual prevalence of a widespread belief in the Unity of God and the growth of indigenous monotheistic faiths. The second remarkable result was the creation of a new indigenous language, called Urdū, which was a mixture of Persian and Hindī, and which has become, in course of time, the most commonly used language in India.

These two influences have had far-reaching effects in the past and are fraught with great possibilities in the future. They require, therefore, to be discussed at some length. Other influences are too numerous to be noticed in detail, as they cover a very wide range. You see them in the style of building and houses, in music and painting, in arts and crafts, in dress and costume, in games and sports, in short, in the whole life of the country. We shall have to be content with passing references to these commemorations of a happy blending of two cultures, the streams of which decided, long ago, to take a common course.

Let us first consider religious thought. A large majority of educated people in India, even among non-Muslims, believe in one God, as the Creator and Preserver of the Universe, with no rivals and no euqals. Though this belief is to be found in almost all the great religions of the world, in one form or another, it cannot be denied that no other faith has laid so much emphasis on it as Islam. We have to remember that the systems of belief prevailing among the Hindus at the time of the advent of the Muslims had largely drifted away from the original purity of the doctrines in their earliest sacred books, and various forms of idolatry had been substituted for divine worship. Things have so changed now that, in spite of the fact that orthodox Hindus have still got idols in their temples, their attitude towards the worship of idols is very different from what it used to be. The intelligent and the educated among them declare that idols are only meant to serve as aids to concentration of thought, and that those who appear to worship them are, in reality, offering worship to Him to whom alone it is due. In this greatly changed attitude the influence of Islam can be easily traced, though in recent times the influence of Christianity has been another great force working against idolatry and superstition. It is also noteworthy that forces have sprung up inside Hinduism itself to combat the tendency to worship idols or to blindly follow designing priests. The Ārya Samāj, founded by the late Swāmī Dayānanda Sarasvatī in the Punjab, in the second half of the nineteenth century, may be mentioned as the most striking instance of the revolt of Hinduism aganist idol worship. This movement purports to be a revival of the ancient Vedic faith. Though it sometimes adopts a militant attitude towards Islam, in order to counteract its influence, it is significant that some of its reforms run on lines parallel to the teachings of Islam. Besides condemning idol worship, it denounces priests, it allows the admission of people of other religions into the fold of the Āryan faith, and commends the marriage of widows.

Apart from these indications of Islamic notions, gradually and imperceptibly influencing the modes of religious thought in India, Islam has had a more direct influence in bringing into existence monotheistic systems of faith in

India. The Sikh religion, founded by the saintly Guru Nānak, is a remarkable instance of this influence. This holy man believed in the Unity of God as strongly as any Muslim, and desired to smooth the differences between Hinduism and Islam. The *Granth Sahib,* the sacred book of the Sikhs, bears testimony to the fact that the founder of the religion loved God and loved his fellow men and had great respect for the Prophet of Arabia and other holy men of Islam. A well-known Sikh gemtleman, Sardār Umrāo Singh of Majītha, has recently published a book which clearly shows that the essential beliefs of the Sikhs and the Moslems are very similar to one another. This book is a Persian translation of Sukhmāni, which is a part of the sacred book of the Sikhs and every verse in it breathes the love of God. Sardār Umrāo Singh luckily lighted on the Persian manuscript of this book in the Bibliothèque Nationale of Paris and copied it. He took the copy to India and has taken great pains in comparing the translation with the original and editing it carefully. It is highly regrettable that, for want of sufficient knowledge and appreciation of each other's beliefs, the Sikhs and Muslims have drifted so far apart from one another.

Another great religious teacher who may be specifically mentioned in this connexion is Kabīr, the best exponent of what is known as the *Bhakti* movement. In the words of a recent writer this movement 'recognized no difference between Rām and Rahīm, Kaaba and Kailash, Qurān and Purān and inculcated that Karma is Dharma. The Preachers of this creed, Rāmānanda, Kabīr, Dādū, Rāmdās, Nānak, and Chaitanya, who flourished in different parts of India and preached the principles of Unity of God, were immensely influenced by Islam.'

In more recent times the religious movement that showed the strongest signs of Muslim influence is the Brahmo-Samāj, founded by the late Rājā Rām Mohan Rāy and carried on and strengthened by the late Keshab Chandra Sen. Rājā Rām Mohan Rāy was a good scholar of Persian and very well versed in the literature of Islam. His study of English brought him into touch with Christian beliefs also, and he conceived the idea of an eclectic religion, combining the best points of the teachings of the

Vedas, the Bible, and the Qurān, and holding all the great spiritual teachers of the world in equal veneration, as the best solution of the difficulties of India. The Brahmo-Samāj, as a strictly unitarian faith, shows the predominance of the most essential doctrine of Islam in its beliefs. This Samāj has included in its fold men of the highest intellectual calibre in our country, though, for obvious reasons, the number of its members has never been very large.

LANGUAGE, LITERATURE, AND ART

The Urdū language is another proof of the union of Hindu and Muslim cultures, though it is strange that there is a tendency in some quarters to look upon it as something imported from outside, which might be got rid of as foreing to the soil. This mistaken view is due to want of sufficient information as to the origin of the language and its development. It is gratifying to note a growing recognition of its value even in provinces where provincial languages are spoken. The following passage taken from an article by Mr. Anilchandra Banerjee on Indo-Persian literature and the contributions made to it by the famous poet, Amīr Khusrū, of Delhi, embodies the opinion of a fair-minded Hindu writer as to the place of Urdū in the culture of our country. He says:

'Almost every work in Indo-Persian literature contains a large number of words of Indian origin, and thousands of Persian words became naturalized in every Indian vernacular language. This mingling of Persian, Arabic, and Turkish words and ideas with languages and concepts of Sanskritic origin is extremely interesting from the philological point of view, and this co-ordination of unknowns resulted in the origin of the beautiful Urdu language. That language in itself symbolized the reconciliation of the hitherto irreconcilable and mutually hostile types of civilization represented by Hinduism and Islam.'

The language thus developed by the combined efforts of Hindus and Muslims now boasts of a fairly varied and wide literature, which may be claimed as a common heritage by both, and is gaining every day in importance and strength.

Urdū literature is rich in poetry. It must be admitted, however, that Urdū poetry has been considerably restricted in its scope in the past and it is only recently that effrots have been made to widen its sphere. The most popular form of versification in Urdū was the *ghazal,* consisting of stray thoughts on such subjects as love, beauty, and morality. Each line was in the same metre, and the endings of each line rhymed with one another. This style of writing has found numerous votaries among Muslims as well as Hindus. In the collections of the *ghazals* of many of our eminent writers you can find literary gems bearing comparison with some of the best pieces of literature in other languages, though for the bulk of this kind of verse no merit can be claimed. Hence it was that some of the poets of the second half of the nineteenth century who realized the limitations of the *ghazal* and its shortcomings felt the need of literary reform. In Delhi, Ghālib was the first to realize this, but it fell to the share of his distinguished pupil, Hālī, to inaugurate the reform. He started a new school of Urdū poetry, which has had many adherents among his contemporaries and successors. In Lucknow a departure from the ordinary style of poetry was introduced by two great poets, Anīs and Dabīr, who wrote *marsiyas,* or elegies, about the martyrdom of Imām Husain. Anīs and Dabīr vastly enriched the store of Urdū literature and greatly refined and polished the Urdū language. It is very interesting to note that these two eminent literary men were not only great as writers, but were equally remarkable for the wonderful effect they could produce by giving public readings of their works. They made reading an art, which has since been imitated, but has not so far been excelled in India. Large gatherings of people of all classes, Muslims and Hindus, used to assemble to hear their recitations, and this brought about a cultural *entente* between the two, which still exists. A noteworthy influence of this form of literature was an adoption of the style of the *marsiyas* by distinguished Hindu writers for depicting the charming story of the Rāmāyana, concerning the sacrifices made by the heroic Rāma in the performance of his pious filial duty and the unselfish love of Lakshman, his brother, and of Sītā, his wife. Munshī Jawāla Pershād (*Barq*) and Pandit Brij Nārāyan (*Chakbast*) are among the Hindu writers who have effectively used the style originated by the two great masters of *marsiya* writing.

This reference to the Lucknow school of Urdū literature will not be complete without a brief mention of the famous *Fisānai-Āzād*, a remarkable work of fiction in Urdū, written by the late Pandit Ratan Nāth (*Sarshār*), who holds a unique position among the writers of Urdū prose. He has given graphic pictures of the life of the rich as well as the poor in Lucknow. In this book of his, as well as in many of his other works, the influence of Muslim literature, which he had read widely, is clearly visible.

Among the literary institutions popularized by the Muslims may be mentioned the *Mushaira*, which means a symposium or a meeting for a peotical contest. This contest is ordinarily held in order to judge who excels in writing a *ghazal* in a given meter. The poets joining the *Mushaira* all recite their respective compositions. It is not customary in high-class *Mushairas* for the meeting or its chairman to declare who wins the laurels of the day, but in most cases the audience is not left in doubt as to the merits of the best poem, the indication of opinion being given by the loud applause of the listeners or by expressions of approbation uttered in the course of the recitations by those in a position to judge. This institution, though not enjoying the vogue which it did in days gone by, is still fairly popular and often brings together people of different classes and communities. who manage to forget their differences for the time being, in their admiration for a common literature.

Of all branches of art this has always appealed most strongly to Muslims. One reason is that painting of human beings and animals was discouraged on religious grounds during the first period of proselytism and of Islamic expansion, and the tradition survived for many centuries afterwards. In India the building of mosques, tombs, and palaces was the most characteristic activity of the early Muslim rulers. This allowed great scope both to those artists who came from other parts of Asia, and also to the indigenous craftsmen who worked under Muslim inspiration and orders. They found vent for their artistic genius in drawing beautiful mural designs in letters and figures, and cultivating symmetry and proportion in buildings. Mausoleums and mosques thus became an inspiration to artists in every form of art. They came from every part of the country to take sketches of these buildings. Floral designs adorning the walls of these structures have been copied for embroidery and textile work. It would be impossible to estimate the immense educative value of these buildings in forming and developing the tastes, the standards of craftsmanship, and the imaginative scope of millions of Indians all over northern India, Bengal, and the Deccan. The structure of Indian society tends to make artistic production dependent upon the continuous patronage of rulers and of the very wealthy. This patronage the Mughals, and, to a far lesser extent, the earlier Muslim rulers, were able to provide. They brought not only new ideas, but also a new urge to produce. A modern writer, Mr. Ja'far, in his *History of the Mughal Empire,* had laid great stress upon the influence which the Emperors exerted on their courtiers, and through them on the rest of India.

'Bābar displayed a remarkable taste for painting. He is said to have brought to India with him all the choicest specimens of painting he could collect from the library of his forefathers, the Timurides. Some of these were taken to Persia by Nādir Shāh after his invasion of India and the conquest of Delhi, but as long as they remained in India they exerted a great influence on and gave a new impetus to the art of painting in India.'

As we know, Bābur did not live long enough to carry out his schemes for the development of India. His somewhat unfortunate son, Humāyūn, also had an unsettled reign. It was left to Bābur's grandson, Akbar, to bring to perfection the love of art which he had inherited. He proved a great patron of art in all its branches. According to Abul Fazl, the well-known Minister of Akbar, the Emperor had more than a hundred *Karkhānajāt* (*i.e.* workshops of arts and crafts) attached to the royal household, each like a city. (See *Āīn-i-Akbarī*—Text 9). Interesting details about these institutions have been collected by a modern writer, Mr. Abdul Azīz, in his remarkable book on the reign of Akbar's grandson, Shāhjahān.[1] I am indebted to this book for the following extract from an old historical work of Father Monserrate, who was at the Court of Akbar in 1580-2. He writes:

'He has build a workshop near the palace, where also are studios and workrooms for the finer and more reputable arts, such as painting, goldsmith work, tapestry making, carpet and curtain making, and the manufacture of arms. Hither he very frequently comes and relaxes his mind with watching at their work those who practise these arts.'

The lead given by Akbar in the patronage of art was followed by his son, Jahāngīr, who was himself fond of painting. Shāhjahān was also artistic, and his personal interest encouraged his courtiers to imitate him and thus his influence further filtered down to those who came in contact with them. This tendency was particularly among the nobility of the Mughal Court. Mr. Abdul Azīz, writing about this tendency in the book above mentioned, observes:

'The Mughal nobility constituted a sort of agency through which the ideals of art and morals and manners were diffused among the lower classes......The habits and customs of the people, their ideas, tendencies, and ambitions, their tastes and pleasures, were often unconsciously fashioned on this model. The peerage acted as the conduit-pipe for this stream of influence. The patronage of art and culture followed the same lines; and even where the interest was not genuine the enlightened pursuits were followed and encouraged as a dogma dictated by fashion.'

The merits of the paintings done under Muslim patronage during the Mughal period have been the subject of several monographs. Their value as an aid to history has been discussed in a lecture, given by the late Sir Thomas Arnold, before the Royal Society of Arts. There are considerable numbers of admirable miniatures in various European collections. The India Office in London, the British Museum, and the Bodleian at Oxford have many rare and beautiful specimens of an art which has hardly been properly appreciated by the Western world. We give two specimens of this delicate and wholly delightful work.

Closely allied to the art of painting is the art of illuminating books. This found great encouragement under the influence of Islam in India. Muslims, who could afford to do so, liked to adorn manuscripts of the Qurān and other books of religion or classic literature with gold borders on every page and to have the bindings of books adorned with gold. The taste for possessing such books was shared by their Hindu countrymen. Artists of both communities derived amusement as well as profit from illuminating books of Arabic, Sanskrit, and Persian.

Caligraphy, or the art of writing a beautiful hand, was also very widely cultivated, and though a good many people adopted it to earn a livelihood, there was a sufficient number of well-to-do people who practised it as a relaxation from other pursuits, and liked to copy in an attractive form the books they wished to treasure. It is recorded that the Emperor Aurangzīb was not only an accomplished master of this art, but that he used to earn a livelihood by making copies of the Quran and offering them for sale, as he did not like to spend the money of the State on his personal requirements.

In connexion with the subject of manuscripts, it may be mentioned that paper was brought into India by Muslims. This was a very material contribution to the advancement of learning. It appears that originally the manufacture of paper came to Central Asia from China. There was a great manufactory of it in Samarqand and it was from there that paper came to India about the tenth century A.D.

We may now consider the contribution made by Muslims to another branch of art, *i.e.* music. As observed by Mr. Ja'far, in his *History of the Mughal Empire,* 'Indian music, like other fine arts, proved a new channel of intercourse between the Hindus and Mussulmans. The process of co-operation and intermutation was not a new thing in the time of Akbar. It had begun centuries before. In the domain of music it became distinctly perceptible how the two communities were borrowing from each other the precious share they possessed in this art, and thereby enriching each other. *Khiyāl,* for example, which was invented by Sultān Hussain Shāh (*Sharqī*) of Polpur, has become an important limb of Hindu music. *Dhrupod,* on the other hand, has engrafted itself on Muslim Music.'

Abul Fazl tells us that Akbar paid much attention to music and patronized those who practised this art.

It is significant that though in the beginning of Islam this branch of art had also been discouraged like painting, yet the contact of Islam with Persia brought about a change in the attitude of Muslims towards it, particularly under the influence of *Sūfīs,* or Muslims mystics, who believed in the efficacy of music as a means of elevating the soul and as an aid to spiritual progress. This attitude became more pronounced when Muslims settling in India found that their Hindu countrymen were fond of music and made use of it in their religious ceremonies. The reuslt was that though Divine worship in mosques continued to be performed on the rigid lines of orthodox Islam, without any extraneous aids of singing or playing on musical instruments, music became quite popular among Muslims in India. The fondness of the rich for it made it a favourite amusement, so that it was customary to have musical performances on all festive occasions. The liking which the *Sūfīs* had for music started the custom of semi-religious congregations assembling to hear songs of divine love sung by professional singers. This class of musicians is known as *Quwwāls* and the tunes which they sing are called *Quwwālī* and are very popular.

A number of new musical instruments were either introduced by Muslims or were given Persian names, after some modifications in their appearance. Instruments like *Rabāb, Sarod, Tāūs, Dilrudā,* are instances in point.

The Mughal gardens of northern India are almost as well known in Europe as Mughal buildings. Centuries earlier the Arabs had introduced into southern Spain the idea of the well-ordered garden, as a place in which to find repose, beauty, recreation, and protection from the heat of the day. Water, preferably flowing, was an essential feature, not only to irrigate plants and shrubs, but to bring coolness, and in the plains to bring the illusion of the mountain streams. These would call back memories of their original homes to the Mughals as much as they did to the expatriated Moors. The rediscovery in Northern India of these rather formalized gardens undoubtedly had an influence upon Italy and England.

The Mughals had undoubtedly a great feeling for natural beauty, and a certain nostalgia afflicted them in the dry arid plains of the Punjab, before the days when widespread irrigation had done something to relieve its monotony. At times they eagerly went to distant places in search of natural beauty, incurring great trouble and expense in doing so, at other times they incurred even more trouble and expense in bringing beauty to places where it did not exist before. It is interesting to read in the letters of Abul Fazl an account of the journeys of the Emperor Akbar from Agra to Kashmir, to enjoy the wonderful scenery and climate of that beautiful valley. We are told that he used to go there for the summer, attended by his courtiers and troops, and used to take a new route every time, so that sappers and miners had to go before him making roads where no roads existed. His son, Jahāngīr, kept up this practice and was as fond of the beauties of Kashmir as his father. The famous garden, known as Shālamār, in Kashmir, still exists as a thing of beauty and a joy for ever, and contributes to the pleasure of thousands of visitors every year. So does the other equally beautiful garden there, called the *Nishat*. The journeys to Kashmir are thus instances of Muslim kings going to the beauty spots of India, while the creation of a Shālamār garden in Lahore illustrates their enterprise in bringing to the plains of India the beauties of Kashmir. This garden is, to this day, one of the great sights of Lahore. The stages into which the garden at Srīnagar (in Kashmir) is divided were made possible by the natural situation of the site chosen for it. It was at the foot of a mountain and water gushing down from the hillside flowed into the garden and enriched its soil. The natural ups and downs of the locality easily lent themselves to being shaped as stages of the garden. At Lahore, however, the garden was divided into three stages by artificial means, which added very much to the difficulty of the task. There was no water available near the site chosen for it and it had to be brought by means of a canal, but still the beauties of the garden in Kashmir were reproduced in the heart of the Punjab. I have specifically mentioned these gardens to illustrate the point that the love of gardening displayed by so many Moslem kings in India was a valuable cultural influence and has left a lasting impression on the taste of the well-to-do classes in India, Hindus as well as Muslims. This taste has now had a further stimulus with the advent of the English, who are behind no other people in their love of gardens.

The Emperor Jahāngīr was specially keen on horticulture, and was fond of gaining knowledge and collecting information about trees, plants, and flowers. In his time he imported many new trees and plants into India. A part of Lahore which is known as the *Badāmī Bāgh* was full of almond trees which were successfully planted there. In the private collection of paintings. I have seen an old book, containing hand-painted illustrations of leaves of trees and fruit-plants, indigenous as well as imported, which was prepared in Jahāngīr's time and, presumably, at his instance.

The beauty and tranquillity of the Mughal gardens undoubtedly struck the imagination of contemporary scholars and travellers, as well as of the Indians in whose midst they were placed. They provided a new conception of life and its aims which influenced literature both in India and in Europe. There are poems in Indo-Persian literature as well as in Urdū, which were professedly inspired by the gardens in Kashmir and Lahore. Our distinguished Indian poet, Iqbāl (or to give him his full name, Dr. Sir Muhammad Iqbāl) has several exquisite poems in Persian, which were inspired by a visit to Srīnagar. A famous couplet in Persian, improvised by a Mughal princess, owed its inspiration to the sight of the beautiful waterfall which adorns the centre of the Shālamār at Lahore. She was watching with admiration the sparkling water of the *Abshar* falling on the slope of the marble, which constituted the artificial fall, and was listening to the sound so produced, when the following improvised song came to her lips:

Ai Abshar nauha gar az bahr-i-kīstī.
Sar dar nigūn figanda zi andoh-i-kīstī.
Āyā chi dard būd ki chūn mā tamām shab.
Sar rā ba sang mi zadī o mī giristī.

It is not possible to bring out in translation the beauty of the original, but the words may be freely translated as follows:

Whose absence, O Waterfall, art thou lamenting so loudly,
Why hast thou cast down thy head in grief?
How acute was thy pain, that throughout the night,
Restless, like me, thou wast striking thy head against the stone and shedding tears profusely!

So far we have dealt chiefly with the amenities of life, but the Mughals also brought new ideas of administration into India. Many of these, like the land revenue system, have been absorbed into the ordinary government of the country under British rule. Although much of the Mughal administration had collapsed before the battle of Plassey, there were the rudiments of a postal system, and the Muslims had made roads, dug irrigation canals, and encouraged gardening from wellwater. They had covered the land with *kārāvan serais,* and almost certainly made it easier for Indian or European to travel in India. They had established a rule of law, which was in many ways more humane than that administered in contemporary Europe. The death sentence, which was inflicted for theft in contemporary England, was reserved for far more serious offences under the Mughal administration in India. There is abundant evidence to show that the Bengalis, in the latter half of the eighteenth century, found Muhammadan criminal law much easier to understand than the uncodified and exotic law which was enforced by the English High Court. A famous passage from Macaulay describes the devastating effect of the introduction of the new system. The merits of Muhammadan law have been fully recognized by colonial administrators in Africa.

There is some question as to how far the Mughals initiated and how far they merely adapted the elaborate court ceremonial and etiquette which so struck many travellers. From Milton onwards there are numberless references to this side of Mughal civilization. It is possible that the Mughals, like the English who followed them, believed in the psychological effect of this pomp upon the popular mind. It may be open to doubt whether this impressive show of power and wealth was really conducive to any development of culture. I must say, however, that these spectacles have an irresistible hold on the imagination of the people, and even countries boasting of the highest modern civilization cannot do without them. A peculiar feature of a Darbar in India was that poets used to come and recite *Qasīdas*, or panegyrics, praising the ruler presiding over the function, and used to be rewarded for doing so. This custom is not forgotten yet and prevails in Indian States and to a smaller extent in British territory, where *Qasīdas* are sometimes read in honour of Governors and Viceroys. These poems are not always of a very high order from a literary point of view, but there are instances of *Qasīdas* possessing real literary merit having been presented on such occasions.

The libraries that came into existence in India, as a result of the love of learning of many of its Muslim rulers, had a great influence on Indian culture. It was not only kings and princes who collected rich stores of literature for their enlightenment, but noblemen of all classes vied with one another in owning such collections. Of the Mughal kings, Humāyūn was very fond of his books and the stone building that housed his library still stands in Delhi. It was from its narrow stairs that Humāyūn fell when he died. Among the Mughal princes, Dārā Shikoh, the eldest son of Shāhjahān, a scholarly and broad-minded prince, was a great lover of books and left behind a large library, the building of which survived for a long time and the site of which is still pointed out. The ruin that followed the terrible period of the Mutiny of 1857 swept away most of these stores of literature. A few private collections of that period may still be found in some ancient families in India or in Indian States, but thousands of valuable books were lost or destroyed or sold cheap by those who got them as loot. A large number of them have travelled west and are fortunately preserved in the libraries of Europe. Among these may be found manuscripts bearing the seals or signatures of Muslim kings and noblemen who owned them. They furnish a silent but eloquent testimony to culture of days gone by, when in the absence of modern facilities for propagation of literature and for the multiplication of books, human patience endured great hardships to preserve for posterity the best thoughts of the learned men of antiquity.

REFERENCE :

1. *History of the Reign of Shāhjahān*. It is being published serially in the *Journal of Indian History*.

—*ABDUL QADIR*

6

SHAIKH NIZAMUDDIN AULIYA*

Shaikh Nizamuddin's paternal grandfather, Khwaja Syed Ali, had emigrated from Bokhara and settled in Badaun, where the Shaikh was born in A.D. 1238. While he was yet a child, his father, Syed Ahmad, fell ill and his mother, Bibi Zulaikha, dreamt that a voice was asking her to choose between her husband and her son. With the eternal instinct of the Indian mother, Bibi Zulaikha preferred to save her son, and as destiny would have it, Syed Ahmad died soon after. Bibi Zulaikha was a lady of fervent piety, and her character left a deep impression on the son, whom she adored and managed to educate in conditions of appalling poverty. Mother and son had no means of livelihood except what their neighbours brought to them unasked, and their maid-servant ran away from the starving household. Nevertheless, the Shaikh, who was remarkable for his diligence, learnt all that Badaun had to teach, and, at the age of sixteen, went with his mother and sister to complete his studies at Delhi. The great capital was at that time full of scholars and men of learning; education was practically free; and a student so intelligent as the Shaikh had access to the best teachers. His principal tutor, Maulana Kamaludding Zahid was distinguished by a remarkable independence of character. Sultan Ghiya-suddin Balban, having heard of Maulana Zahid's piety, invited him to the court and offered him the post of Head Imam. "Our prayer is all that is left to us," the Maulana replied, "does the Sultan wish to seize that also?" Balban was struck dumb, and, after offering a brief apology, allowed the Maulana to depart. From such a scholar Shaikh Nizamuddin obtained his final certificate at the age of twenty and, perhaps, also imbibed that indifference towards men of worldly grandeur that distinguished him through out his life.

Though he had hiherto followed the normal course of studies, the Shaikh's mind was already inclined towards mysticism, and he had often told his comrades that he would not for long remain in the atmosphere of their literary discussions. At the age of twelve he had heard a *qawwal*(reciter of mystic verse) praise the piety of Shaikh Farid Ganj Shakar of Ajodhan; ever since then he had developed an extraordinary reverence for that saint and went to see him as soon as his studies were completed. "Every new-comer is nervous," Shaikh Farid remarked on seeing that the young man was unable to speak from fear. Shaikh Nizamuddin shaved his head and was enrolled among the disciples. He was, of course, absolutely penniless; a kindly lady washed his clothes when they became too dirty to be worn any longer, and Shaikh Farid presented him with a gold coin when he was about to leave for Delhi. But it was the last coin of Shaikh Farid's own household, and that very morning Shaikh Nizamuddin discovered that his master and his master's family would have to go without dinner because they lacked the means of purchasing it. The disciple laid the master's gift again at his feet. It was gratefully accepted. "I have prayed to God to grant you a portion of earthly good," Shaikh Farid blessed the young disciple, and then seeing his anxiety added: "Have no fear about it, *for you the world shall not be a temptation.*" The master's discerning eyes had not failed to see the greatness of his successor.

There have been distinguished men in all religions whose lives have been a continuous struggle against the world, the flesh and the devil—who have fought and, to a considerable extent, succeeded in the great battle that is supposed to be constantly raging between the higher and the lower elements of human nature. Shaikh Nizamuddin was *not* one of them. He is not recorded to have recited a surprising number of prayers; he did not, like Shaikh Farid, hang himself by his feet in a well or bring himself to the verge of death by unending fasts. There was no element of asceticism in him, because for him the ascetic discipline was not necessary. He did not exercize the devil by torture or self-mortification, which very often only substitutes morbidity for worldliness, but ruled him out by the quiet joy that inspired his heart. He never married and never possessed a house of his own. People observed that his eyes were red in the morning after his night-long meditation, like one slightly tipsy, and an indescribable happiness shone on his face. There was nothing in the external circumstances of his life to explain this inner bliss.

"I have given you the spiritual empire of Hindusthan," Shaikh Farid had ordered him: "go and take it". But Shaikh Nazamuddin on returning to Delhi, was for long undecided as to whether he should remain at the capital or select a provincial town for his residence. This is the only inner struggle that seems to have taken place in his mind; but ultimately he decided to face his duty boldly by living and working in the great metropolis. There followed about thirty years of appalling poverty. He first stayed in the house of 'Imadul Mulk, Amir Khusrau's maternal grandfather, who was generally known as *Rawat-i-Arz,* but after two years 'Imadul Mulk's sons returned to Delhi and summarily evicted the Shaikh from their house. He sought refuge in a thatched mosque near by, and that very night 'Imadul Mulk's house caught fire and was burnt to ashes. Thereafter, till his final settlement at Ghiaspur, he kept wandering from one quarter of the city to another. He had no means of his own and never condescended to ask anyone for help. "In the days of Ghiyasuddin Balban, the Shaikh used to say in later life, "melons were sold at the rate of one *jilal* per maund, but very often the season passed away without my being able to taste a slice..... On one occasion I had to go without food for a night and a day, and half the second night had passed before I got anything to eat; two seers of bread could be had for a *jilal,* but from sheer poverty I was unable to purchase anything from the market. My mother, sister and other persons in my house suffered along with me. On one occasion we had starved for three days when a man knocked at my door with a bowl of *Khichri.* I have never found anything so delicious as that plain *khichri* appeared to me then. 'We are the guests of God today,' my mother used to say when we had no food left in the house, and an inexplicable joy overpowered my heart at these words. Once I dreamt that Shaikh Najibuddin Mutawakkil, brother of Shaikh Farid, had come to our house, and I asked my mother to get something for him to eat. 'But there is no food in our house,' she replied. Soon after I dreamt that the Holy Prophet was coming with his Companions. I kissed his feet and requested him to visit my house. 'What for?' 'I will place before you and your Companions whatever dinner I can provide.' 'But has not your mother told you just now that there is no food in your house?' the Prophet replied. I felt thoroughly ashamed at my position."

The venerable mother bore everything bravely along with her son, whose peace of mind no earthly misfortune could disturb, but the continued starvation was, perhaps too much for her health. "Whose feet will you kiss next month, Nizam?" she asked him during her last illness when he had placed his head on her feet after seeing the new moon. "And to whose care will you assign me mother?" the son inquired. Before the morning had dawned she called him to her bed-side. "Almighty God!"—she took his hand in hers—"I assign my son to Thy care." And with these words on her lips the venerable lady passed away.

Meanwhile the Shaikh's fame had been spreading far and wide, and everyone who came in contact with him was captivated by the strange joy that radiated from him. In A.D. 1267, Shaikh Farid nominated him his successor and, just before his death, ordered his cloak, staff and prayer-carpet to be conveyed to Shaikh Nizamuddin, to the intense annoyance of his own children, who expected to succeed to the profitable post. Sultan Jalaluddin offered to endow a village for the Shaikh's expense; the disciples who had collected round him protested that they had suffered as much as they could stand, but in spite of their protests the offer was firmly refused. The Sultan next asked for an interview; it was not granted; and when the Sultan resolved to pay a surprise visit, the Shaikh, who had come to know of his intention from Amir Khusrau, avoided the interview by undertaking a journey to Ajodhan. The Shaikh had made up his mind to keep aloof from politics, and nothing could turn him from that resolution. But it was impossible for the teacher, who had opened his door wide to all who came, to keep politicians away. In the beginning of Alauddin's reign the nobles began to visit his monastery at Ghiaspur; the Shaikh was annoyed at their visits, but did not refuse to see them. Gradually their number increased.

Towards the end of Alauddin's reign, the Shaikh's reputation reached its full height. Khizr Khan, the heir apparent, became a firm believer in the Shaikh, and every number of the Imperial family and every servant of the Palace joined the great discipleship. The Sultan himself was the only exception. "What sort of heart was Alauddin's?" the pious Barani remarks: "How indifferent and bold? From thousands of *farsangs* travellors and students came to pay their respects to the Shaikh; the young and old of the city, scholars and common people, the wise and the foolish, all tried by thousands of tricks to present themselves before him; but it never came to Alauddin's mind that he, too, should either visit the Shaikh or invite him to the court." The Emperor and the Shaikh were, in fact, too great in their own departments to have anything more than a distant respect for each other. Alauddin cared as little for saints as the Shaikh did for politicians. In his own erratic way he had made up his mind to bend his sinful knees before God alone.

Thanks to the *malfuzats* of Amir Khusrau and Amir Hasan and the *Siyarul Aulia* of Amir Khurd, Shaikh Nizamuddin, at the fullness of his reputation and influence, is better known to us than any other figure in mediaeval India. "He opened wide the doors of his discipleship and confessed all sinners—nobles and commons, rich and poor, *maliks* and beggars, students and illiterate folk, citizens and villagers, soldiers and civilians, freemen and slaves." Forenoon and afternoon and the hours after sunset were set apart for those who came to consult him; but he was always accessible and seldom kept anyone waiting.

The work of a Shaikh was to educate the people in virtue and goodness, and to this task Shaikh Nizamuddin applied himself with singular devotion throughout his long and useful life. People of every class came to his monastery and he talked to each according to his knowledge and understanding; and everyone who visited the Shaikh felt himself captivated. Besides a thin volume of *malfuzat,* Shaikh Nizamuddin never cared to write anything, and the surviving works of his disciples can but dimly give us the impression of a personality which was as unique as it was fascinating. No Indo-Muslim mystic has left such a deep impression on his contemporaries. "No deed will bring a greater reward on the Day of Judgement," he used to say "than bringing happiness to the hearts of Mussalmans and of men." And yet, in spite of the fact that he was mixing and talking with all who came, people felt that the Shaikh's heart was always "turned towards God as if He was looking at him".

The annals of Hagiology are strewn with the records of meaningless miracles, but Shaikh Nizamuddin was not a miracle-monger of the ordinary sort. He never flew in the air or walked on water with dry and motionless feet. His greatness was the greatness of a loving heart; his miracles were the miracles of a deeply sympathetic soul. He could read a man's inner heart by a glance at his face and spoke the words that brought consolation to tortured hearts.

Khawaja Mubaral of Gopamau used to get a robe of honour from Sultan Alauddin whenever he presented himself at the court, but on one occasion the Sultan only bestowed a white sheet on him, and the Khwaja, greatly pained at this change in the Sultan's attitude, came to see Shaikh Nizamuddin. The latter looked at him tenderly and said: "A kings's gift is a thing of value, be it a gold coin or a shell." "My heart rejoiced at the words," the Khwaja declared later, "and my despondency disappeared."

A young sceptic once presented himself with his friends before the Shaikh, and along with the sweet-meats brought by his friends, he placed a little sand wrapped in paper before the Shaikh. When the servants came to remove the presents, the Shaikh ordered them to leave the packet of sand where it was. "This antimony," he said, "is specially meant for my eyes." The young man trembled and confessed, but the Shaikh presented him with a dress and tried to console him. "If you are in need of food or money," he asked , "tell me so and I will do what I can."

In the period of his poverty the Shaikh once sat down to eat a few crumbs of bread after he had gone without food for two days. But a beggar, who passed that way, imagined that the Shaikh had finished his dinner and very unceremoniously took away the crumbs from his dinner-cloth. "Our sufferings must have been accepted by the Lord that he tries us further."

A visitor, who saw the Shaikh and his disciples starving, offered to teach him alchemy. But the Shaikh would have none of it. "Mixing colours," he said, "is the work of Christians, and accumulating gold is the task of Jews. We, Mussalmans, do not wish for the goods of this world or the next. We live for the Lord alone."

Call such things miracles, if you please, provided, by a miracle is not meant something morally irrational or meaningless. The Shaikh's life was, in fact, the embodiment of what psychological research shall one day prove to be the deerest principle of our human nature: that salvation, or happiness in its highest form, lies not in a war with the attractions of worldly life or in indifference towards them but in the healthy development of the "cosmic emotion", in a sympathetic identification of the individual with his environment, so that the distinction of the *I* and *not-I* disappears in a myscie absorption of the human soul in the Absolute. God is not so much a Creator to be acknowledged as an Existence to be felt—felt not as an abstraction but as a reality embodied in the living and inanimate creatures around us. And thus salvation is not something to be obtained in the world beyond; it is to be attained by progressive stages, here and now, or it will be never reached at all.

The blessing of Shaikh Farid accompanied: his disciple throughout his life. *"For him the world was never a temptation."* When, in later life, presents began to come to Shaikh Nizamuddin from all sides, he distributed them to the needy with a liberal hand, and every Friday the kitchen and pantry were swept clean before the saint went for his prayer. Sumptuous dishes were placed before his visitors, but the saint, who fasted almost every day, dined only on a plain bread with some vegetable. And when a follower remonstrated against his continued abstinence, he replied that "while so many poor and miserable men were standing in the mosques and before the shops in the market, it was impossible for a morsel to pass down his throat."

His sleep was a meagre as his diet; he slept a little at midday and rested a little before midnight. But after midnight, when every one had gone to bed, the Shaikh locked up the door of his bedroom and kept meditating, reading, praying and reciting verses till the morning. "In silence I and the lamp keep each other company till the break of day; sometimes I extinguish it with the coldness of my sighs, at other times I make it burn brighter with the fire of my soul." He had a delightfull time of it. "Every night when the morning is approaching," the Shaikh said once, "a verse comes to my mind which brings me great inspiration and delight. This morning I recollected these lines:—

'The garment by Thy separation torn
Living, once more, once more, re-knit I must.
And if I die, accept my frank excuse,
Alas, the hopes that crumble into dust!'

But when I was reciting the verses a second time, a woman appeared before me and with great humility requested me not to continue the recitation." "Was it a dream?" asked one Qazi Sharfuddin. "No, I was wide awake," answered the Shaikh, "I saw her as clearly as I see you." "Then this woman was the symbol of the world which did not wish you to leave her," the Qazi remarked. "You are right", said the Shaikh.

But in spite of all his efforts, Shaikh Nizamuddin could not quite keep out of the whirlpool of politics. Sultan Alauddin's eldest son, Khizr Khan, was a disciple of the Shaikh, and it was naturally imagined that the Shaikh would favour his succession. But in the intrigues that followed Alauddin's death, Shaikh Nizamuddin kept quiet. Sultan Kutbuddin Mubarak Shah, who ascended the throne of his father after an interregnum of forty days, at first followed a liberal policy and showed no hostility towards the Shaikh; but, while returning from his Deccan campaign, Mubarak discovered a dastardly conspiracy organised by Malik Asaduddin, a cousin of Sultan

Alauddin, and his hand fell heavily on the conspirators. Even the late Sultan's sons, Khizr Khan, Shadi Khan and Shahabuddin, who had been blinded and imprisoned by Malik Kafur at Gwalior, were put to death, and Mubarak felt that he should nurse a grievance against the Shaikh. "He began to speak ill of the Shaikh," Barni tells us, "and displayed open hostility. The *maliks* and *amirs* of the court were ordered not to go to the Shaikh's monastery at Ghiaspur, and the intoxicated Sultan would often declare with his fearless tongue that he was prepared to give a thousand *tankas* of gold to anyone who brought him Shaikh Nizamuddin's head."

Sultan and Shaikh once came face to face at the *siyyum* of Shaikh Ziauddin Rumi, but Mubarak paid no regard to Shaikh's dignity and even refrained from acknowledging his *salam*. Shaikh Ruknuddin was called from Multan in order to turn away the public eye from Shaikh Nizamuddin Auliya; but as he was an old friend of Shaikh Nizamuddin, Mubarak Shah tried to set up one Shaikhzada Jam, an old enemy of Shaikh Nizamuddin, as a sort of antipope.

When people are inclined to quarrel, it is easy to find occasions for doing so. The Sultan build a mosque, called the Masjid-i Miri, and invited the leading men of the capital to the first Friday prayer. The Shaikh refused to go. "The mosque nearest my house," he told the Sultan's messenger, "has greater claims on me." Worse than that, the Shaikh ventured to disregard to custom, which required all men of note to attend the Sultan's court on the first day of every month, and sent his servant, Iqbal, as his deputy. The Sultan naturally resented the insult and finally threatened to call the Shaikh in person by a legal summons as soon as the new moon was seen. But the occasion for it never arrived. On the night of the new moon, Mubarak Shah was assassinated by the Barwars, and Shaikh Nizamuddin was set free from a difficult situation. The murder of the Sultan, the pious Amir Khurd would have us believe, was due to the prayers of the Shaikh, not to the crimes of the Barwars. The decision of such problems is, fortunately, beyond the province of the historian.

The Barwar regime, which followed Mubarak's death, was turbulent and short-lived, But Ghiasuddin Tughlak, who mounted the throne after suppressing the rebels, proved to be an ideal ruler according to the needs of the time. Shaikh Nizamuddin's relations with Sultan Ghiasuddin, however, are said to have been none too cordial; so at least later writers would have us believe. Ferishta, who sums up all that he found floating down the stream of time, gives two reasons for this. Khusrau Khan, in his attempt to find supporters in every direction, distributed large sums of money to distinguished mystics. Three of them refused; others accepted the money but kept it safely in order to give it to the legitimate king whenever he should appear. But Shaikh Nizamuddin, who had been offered 5,00,000 *tankas*—while other mystics only got 3,00,000 *tankas* each—immediately took the money and distributed it to the poor. Ghiasuddin recovered most of the money Khusrau Khan had thrown away; all other mystics paid up, but nothing could be recovered from Shaikh Nizamuddin, for the simple reason that nothing was left. This incident is said to have alienated Sultan Ghiasuddin's mind. He also objected to the Shaikh's listening to mystic verses recited by *qawwals,* though after a learned discussion among scholars the Sultan withdrew his objection.

When returning from the Bengal expedition, Ghiasuddin sent a message to the Shaikh asking him to leave Delhi before the Sultan's return. "Delhi is still far off (*Hanauz Delhi dur ast*)," the Shaikh replied, and the Sultan never reached Delhi. The fall of a mysterious pavilion built for his reception by his son, Muhammad bin Tughlaq, cut short one of the most promising reigns of mediaeval India.

The incident is quoted by shallow critics as evidence of the Shaikh's spiritual power. The truth is more tragic. Shaikh Nizamuddin had already departed for "the world beyond" several days before the Sultan's funeral procession entered Delhi. The story, whatever its moral worth, appears a later day fabrication. Neither Barni nor Amir Khurd says anything concerning the unpleasantness between the two men, who were so eminently virtuous in their different spheres of life.

"I want no monument over my grave; lay me to rest in the broad and open plain," Shaikh Nizamuddin had said before his death, but Sultan Muhammad Taghlaq, none the less, built a dome over it. Six hundred years have elapsed since; empires have risen and fallen; Delhi has been repeatedly destroyed and rebuilt; but throughout all these changes, the mausoleum of Shaikh Nizamuddin has remained the one living spot in the city of desolate and crumbling ruins. It is frequented by Hindus and Mussalmans alike.

NOTE :

* Popular usage nowadays divides Indian Mussalmans into Syeds, Moghuls, Pathans and a fourth, extensive and non-descript class, designated Shaikhs. In mediaeval India, a Shaikh meant an eminent mystic or saint. I have used the term in its mediaeval significance.

7

AMIR KHUSRAU

"The incomparable Amir Khusrau stands unequalled for the volume of his writings and the originality of his ideas; for, while other great masters of prose and verse have excelled in one or two branches, Amir Khusrau was conspicuous in every department of letters. A man with such mastery over all the forms of poetry has never existed in the past and may not come into existence before the Day of Judgment". Thus wrote Zia-ud-din Barani, the contemporary historian.

Zia-ud-din's estimate of Amir Khusrau is fully endorsed by modern critics. Maulana Shibli remarks in his *Shi'‘s-ul Ajam*: "No person of such comprehensive ability has been born in India during the last six hundred years, and even the fertile soil of Persia has produced only three or four persons of such varied accomplishments in a thousand years. To take poetry alone, Khusrau's mastery over all its forms is marvellous Firdausi, Sa‘di, Anwari, Hafiz, ‘Ufi and Naziri are kings in the realm of verse, but the mastery of each of them was confined to one section of it only. Firdausi could not advance beyond the *masnavi,* Sa‘di could not write *qusidas,* Anwari had no power over the *ghazal* or the *masnavi,* while Hafiz, ‘Ufi and Naziri were unable to step outside the circle of the *ghazal.* But Khusrau's comprehensive genius takes the *ghazal* as well as the *masnavi, qasida,* and rubai within its all-embracing fold, together with the minor departments of varsification *mustazad, sana-‘i* and *bada-‘i.* For sheer quantity no one can equal him. Firdausi's couplets amount to about seventy thousand, Sahib has been responsible for over a hundred thousand, but Amir Khusrau's couplets number several lacs."

One wonders all the more, therefore, that a poet who has left such a legacy behind him passed all his life as a courtier. He did not shut himself up for years as Firdausi did to write his *Shahnama,* nor did he like Moliere accompany the court without being a courtier. Our poet had to attend his patrons as a courtier; only when his duties became too exacting he would register a mild protest as he did to 'Ala-ud-din: "If I stand before you day and night how can my mind produce poetry? Without thought surely my poetry will be frivolous and shallow." In a pathetically frank passage he compares his life with Nizami's, who had, Khusrau asserts, no other occupation except writing poetry. "But poor as I am", continues Khusrau, "needy and confused, my brain always boils like a cauldron. All night till day break and from morning till evening I find no respite from my worries. For the sake of my selfish spirit I have to stand on my feet before a man like myself. The wages which they give me they think to be a favour and all my labour is ignored, just as a wretched ass who carries loads of fodder is given some oats with a sad grace." (*Masnavi of Majnun-o-Laila*).

But his busy life may not have been harmful to the poet. Imagination in art consists in knowing how to find most complete expression of an existing thing, not merely to suppose or create that thing. Khusrau not only found it but he represented "the spirit, the form, the language of his time."

To understand his works, therefore, it is necessary to realise the significant details of his life.

II

A Turkish soldier named Amir Saif-ud-din Mahmud settled at Patiyali, a small town in the Etah district, and entered the service of Iltutmish, the second Slave King of Delhi. Saif-ud-din became an army officer of high rank, and married the daughter of Imad-ul-Mulk. Three sons were born of this marriage, of whom the second born in 1253 was called Abul Hasan Khusrau or Abul Hasan Yamin-ud-din Khusrau.

There is a tradition that soon after his birth, his father took him to a saintly person who exclaimed on seeing the baby: "O Amir, you have brought to me one who shall surpass Khaqani himself."

Though like many good soldiers of his time Saif-ud-din was illiterate, he decided to give his three sons the best possible education. But the precocious Khusrau received the greatest attention from his father, so that the future poet might,—as he informs us—"achieve literary proficiency."

Khusrau was therefore sent to a Maktab at an early age, and some private tutors to teach him at home were also engaged. Of his student days Khusrau wrote later: "My father sent me to the Maktab for study, but I repeated only rhymes, and while my learned teacher tried to teach me calligraphy I composed verses about the silken down on fair faces. In spite of the persistent efforts of my teacher, continuous and long like the tresses descending from head to foot on the back of a beauty, I would not renounce my infatuation for the locks and the mole. As a consequence, at that tender age I began to compose verses and *ghazals* that roused the admiration and wonder of my elders."

Fortunately the boy had intelligent teachers who did not smother the natural longings of a poet. One day before he had reached the age of eight, he was taken by his teacher to Khwaja Izz-ud-din, a distinguished scholar. After the boy had charmed every one present by reciting verses, the Khwaja asked him to compose a verse containing the four words: hair, egg, arrow and melon. "In the presence of all the people in the assembly" says Khusrau, "there and then I composed the following verse: 'Every hair in the tresses of that beauty has attached to it a thousand eggs (*i.e.*, grains) of amber. But do not consider her nature to be straight as an arrow for like the melon the teeth (*i.e.*, the seeds) are concealed within'." The Khwaja then gave Khusrau the penname of Sultani, which he has used in some of his earlier poems.

Soon after, at the age of eight Khusrau lost his father. A pleasing trait of Khusrau's character is his filial affection. At the height of his fame he humbly acknowledged the debt he owed his father: "In my clay is the seed planted by him and it is now blooming forth." When he was writing *Majnun-o-Laila* his mother and younger brother died (A.D.

1297). Like a child Khusrau longed for her: "Where are you, O mother mine, that I cannot see you? Have mercy on my tears and come smiling out of your grave! In days gone by I was as insolent as you were loving, and now that I am ashamed of my conduct, how can I ask your forgiveness......." Addressing his dead brother he wrote: "Oh, let me see you; do not turn away your face. Wake up, wake up! You have slept too long. Or, if you are too pure for my physical eye to perceive, at least come to me in my dreams."

The death of his father did not interfere with the life of ease to which Khusrau was accustomed. His maternal grandfather Imad-ul-Mulk rose under Ghiyas-du-din Balban to become one of the chief officials of the administration. Imad-ul-Mulk maintained more than two thousand slaves and one thousand soldiers; fifty to sixty slaves were engaged in offering betel leaves to his guests. It was an age when the Turkish nobles vied with each other in generosity, and mad splendour. Says Barani: "If a khan or malik heard that five hundred persons dined at the table of a certain khan or malik, he bacame envious and tried to feed a thousand at his table. Again if one of them came to know that such and such malik gives as charity two hundred "tankahs" when he rides out, he was jealous and determined to give away four hundred "tankahs" when he himself rode out. If one of the nobles bestowed fifty horses in his wine-party and gave robes to two hundred persons, another noble hearing this would feel jealous and would try his best to give away a hundred horses and to bestow robes on five hundred persons." Khusrau was a child of the age and he voiced its feelings in his advice to his son in *Aina-i-Sikandari*: "Remove the curst of selfishness from thy heart. Give with a pleasant face whatever thou hast. shower thy gifts on all and be not like the cat that withdraws into a corner whenever it has found a morsel to eat. Every silly ass can be generous to his wife and children. The man whose kindness extends to his family only is really selfish."

This condition of society and attitude of mind should be remembered when one judges Khusrau for attaching himself to nobles and kings all his life to earn his livelihood. A modern critic may censure him for trading his poetic genius. Khusrau can vindicate himself by quoting precedents as he once actually did in a letter to 'Ala-ud-din : "The allowance which I get from your Majesty is my right and the reward of my service for I remain always beside the royal stirrup..... But as I want to praise you, how can I write verses without some reward? You cannot possibly be unaware of the generosity shown to poets by other kings, who often gave away a treasure for an ode." Khusrau then cites the examples of Khaqani, Mu'izzi, Firdausi and Unsuri on whom kings bestowed proverbially rich presents and adds: "Grass grows only with rain and poetry with the generosity of kings".

Moreover, he was probably never free from financial worries in order to maintain the standard of living set before his young eyes by his affectionate grandfather. It was however in that noble man's house that Khusrau came across the best scholars and poets of his age. They were naturally delighted to hear the boy recite his compositions and encouraged him heartily. Khusrau was elated and improved himself by reading the works of great masters. Contrary to prevailing custom, he did not attach himself to any famous scholar or poet; his own talent and diligence brought him to the forefront before he reached the age of twenty.

Khusrau seems to have avoided advanced studies, particularly, in scientific subjects. About languages he says in his *Nuh Sipihr* that with his "knowing mind" he had "studied most of the languages spoken by men. I know them, comprehend them, and have composed in them also." Unfortunately, there seems to be an element of exaggeration in this statement, for, elsewhere he retorts: "I am an Indian Turk and can answer you in Hindi; I have not Egyptian sugar (Arabic) to talk of Arabia".

This brings us to the vexed question as to whether Khusrau wrote Hindi. Some Hindi verses are ascribed to him, but some scholars deny his authorship. Khusrau's own position is unambiguous : "I am the parrot of Hind, question me in Hindi so that I may talk sweetly. Elsewhere he remarks :

(7)

"Hindi is no less sweet than Persian," and proves his fondness for Hindi by using many words from that language in his Persian poems. But Khusrau was given to exaggeration where his own qualifications were concerned, and the use of a few Hindi words does not prove much. On the other hand one must remember that he was quite capable of picking up enough Hindi by constant association with Hindi speaking men to write a few verses. But as his essential and natural medium was Persian, this point has little except academic interest.

Another qualification of Khusrau has also aroused some controversy. There is no doubt that Khusrau was very fond of music and was an accomplished musician. He probably took part in musical contests which in those days were very popular, and seems to have been quite familiar with Persian and Indian systems of music. But he is also credited with having invented about twenty new melodies and the *sitar*, which is doubtful. It is quite likely, however, that the popular melodies *qaul* and *ghazal* were first introduced in Indian music by Khusrau. Qawwals all over India recognize him to be their master even today.

III

Imad-ul-Mulk died in 1271 at the age of one hundred and thirteen. Khusrau composed a touching elegy on his grandfather, and in the same year became a disciple of Shaikh Nizam-ud-din Auliya whom he seems to have known since his early boyhood. Probably to his affectionate nature spiritual solace was necessary after his grandfather's death.

It was however, now necessary for Khusrau to find some employment. He therefore attached himself to Malik 'Ala-ud-din Kishlu Khan popularly known as Malik Chajju or Jhujhu. The young poet was lucky, for Malik Chajju was the most liberal patron of that age. "For two years", says Khusrau, "I sang his praises in some of the most ornate verses, one of which it would take other poets one year to compose. I was constantly present in the garden of that cypress (Malik Chajju) and refreshed his court with the soft breezes that blew from the lily of my tongue." Here is an ode he addressed to Chajju:

The radiant glow of amber-coloured dawn
Had just displaied the darkness of the night;
The yellow crescent with its curving horns
And jaundiced looks was sinking out of sight.
I asked the morn: "Where is thy promised sun?"
And Chajju's face shone with its rising light.
I turned next to the starry heaven and asked;
"Say what supports thy panets in their flights?"
It smiled at my vain question and displayed
The Maik's arms that held them all upright.[1]

One day Bughra Khan, the younger son of Sultan Ghiyas-ud-din Balban, came to a party organised by Malik Chajju. With his habitual candour Khusrau describes his performance of the evening and his almost childish glee at the "wonderful scattering of gold". Unluckily, pleased with his "sweet verses" Bughra gave him a plate full of "tankahs" and Khusrau accepted it. This, he says, enraged Malik Chajju, and after trying in vain to appease him, he "bolted away like an arrow". In the *dibacha* to *Ghurrat-ul-Kamal* Khusrau says: "My poetry is not like that of other poets for I have never praised any other than the patron in whose service I have been." Probably he learned with experience.

Khusrau went to Samana where Bughra was the governor and the prince, the cause of misfortune, gallantly took him under his protection. "I began to serve him" says Khusrau, "and everyday I rose higher in his esteem and favour". But his good fortune did not last long. Tughril rebelled in Bengal; Balban took Bughra with him to suppress it, and Khusrau as the latter's protege had to march with the army to Lakhnauti.

To an easy going man like Khusrau the arduous march from Delhi to Bengal during the rains was terrible. But worse followed: Bughra was left as governor of Bengal. But none could persuade Khusrau to stay there. He returned to Delhi and luckily came into contact with Prince Muhammad, the eldest son of Ghiyas-ud-din. Muhammad was the governor of Multan, and there Khusrau stayed in Multan, "watering" he says, "the five rivers of Multan

(Punjab) with seas of my delectable verses". But this glorious life ended tragically.

At this time the duty of the governor of Multan was to check the Mongol raids, and this Prince Muhammad performed very efficiently. Recalling these Mongol raids Khusrau wrote: "Although every year the Mongols come in serried ranks like storks with owlish wings and ominous faces, at the time of their rout under the world-conquering sword of the Prince (Muhammad) they are rent into morsels and are despatched to Kirman." In 1238, however, a very strong force of Mongols entered India and Prince Muhammad hastened to give them battle. The main Mongol army was defeated and fled with the bulk of the Indian army in hot pursuit. Muhammad got down from his horse to offer the midday prayers, when suddenly a band of Mongols who lay hidden nearby fell upon him, and in the struggle a chance arrow killed the gallant prince. Immediately there was panic; the Mongols either cut down or enslaved the rest of the small detachment and marched away to join their main army. Among the prisoners Khusrau found himself.

Though a poet and used to a soft life, Khusrau after all was the son of a soldier. His wit did not desert him in his predicament which he describes with genuine passion: "I was taken prisoner and from fear that they would shed my blood, not a drop of blood remained in my veins. I ran about like a torrent here and there, with innumerable blisters on my feet like bubbles on the surface of a stream, and the skin of my feet was rent. My tongue was parched and dry from excessive thirst and my stomach seemed to have collapsed from want of food. Like a leafless autumn tree the body was naked, and torn into a thousand shreds by painful lacerations from thorny bushes. Tears dropped from my eyes as pearls fall from the neck of brides. The despicable wretch who drove me sat on his horse like a leopard in a hill; a nauseating stench came from his mouth and arm and filthy moustaches hung on his chin.[2] If exhausted I sometimes slowed down my pace, he would threaten me sometimes with his frying pan and sometimes with his spear. I heaved sighs of despair and thought in my mind that I would never be able to escape alive from this situation."

But his lucky chance came soon when they reached a stream. His thirsty captor and his horse drank immoderately as much water as they could and soon after died. "Although I was terribly hot and thirsty, I did not pour oil on my naptha by drinking too much water." Khusrau just moistened his lips to refresh his body, so as soon as his captor died be was able to run back to Multan.

From Multan he returned to Delhi and wrote an elegy on the Martyred Prince. This made him famous among the mass for the first time. Soon after Balban died and the worthless Kaiqubad succeeded. The new king called the poet to his court, but for political reasons Khusrau avoided the king and attached himself to Malik Amir Ali Sarjandar known as Hatim Khan who loaded him with rich presents. Khusrau himself admitted later that if he had not squandered away the money he received from Hatim Khan his children and grandchildren might have lived a life of ease.

When Kaiqubad marched against his father Bughra Khan, Hatim went with him, and thus Khusrau was present at the touching scene which saw the reunion of father and son, the theme of Khusrau's famous historical *Masnavi Qiran-us-Sa'dain*.

Hatim Khan was appointed the governor of Oudh and poor Khusrau had to accompany him there. Oudh then was a beautiful country, and Khusrau describes its charms in a letter to his friend. Still he pined for Delhi, "for," as he put it, "although the rose can live for a while in a flower-vase, it soon dies when away from the parent tree." He was also very anxious for his old mother, so after two years, with the Governor's permission, he returned to Delhi.

Kaiqubad renewed his offers and this time Khusrau joined the court. Since then the Sultanate of Delhi passed through many terrible days, but Khusrau remained the court-poet, serving three dynasties. As has been said he became "a part of the royal paraphernalia that changed hands at the death of each successive monarch and like the black canopy, the crown and the throne, the palaces, the slaves and elephants became the property of the new master."[3]

Thus when after the overthrow of the Salve dynasty Jalal-ud-din Khalji became king, Khusrau was appointed the "keeper of the Royal Quran." The new king, a poet himself, became a great admirer of Khusrau, and, "each night," says Barani, "Amir Khusrau brought new *ghazals* to the assembly of the king." Two fo Khusrau's former patrons, Chajju Khan and Hatim Khan rebelled against the new king, and were defeated. The poet, a finished courtier, congratulated his master.

His capacity to change with changing times was never more striking than when he welcomed to Delhi 'Ala-ud-din, congratulating him on his success, that is, the murder of Jalal-ud-din. In one of his *masnavis* he boasts that he was the first to congratulate 'Ala-ud-din on his accession to the throne. But one should remember before condemning Khusrau, that he did what everyone else was doing. Almost all the Jalali nobles and officers joined 'Ala-ud-din without any protest. Khusrau was a man of the world, and knew the age he was living in.

Khusrau now settled down in Delhi, and the next two decades were the most productive period of his life. Except rarely when he accompanied 'Ala-ud-din on a campaign, he lived in his beloved Delhi. He now developed intimate relations with Shaikh Nizam-ud-din whose disciple he had for a long time. In the doxologies of all his later *masnavis,* he praises the Shaikh and names him even before the Sultan. This from a courtier like Khusrau shows genuine respect and love, and no little courage. 'Ala-ud-din was indifferent, but his successor Mubarak Shah displayed open hostility towards the Shaikh. For some time nobles were forbidden by Mubarak to visit the Shaikh, but Khusrau dexterously managed to keep on good terms both with the King and the Saint. As a matter of fact, Mubarak treated Khusrau much more generously than did 'Ala-ud-din, and Khusrau wrote *Nuh Siphar* (Nine Heavens) a versified history of the principal events of his reign.

Mubarak's reign was violently terminated and followed by the short interregnum when the Hindu convert Khusrau Shah sat on the throne of Delhi. All the nobles at Delhi submitted to Khusrau Shah, but for once the poet abstained from attending the court. With the accession of Ghiyas-ud-din Tughluq Shah however, Khusrau returned.

Tughluq Shah treated Khusrau very kindly; the poet was more prosperous in this reign than ever before. He accompanied the Sultan to Bengal, and a few days before return, Shaikh Nizam-ud-din died. Khusrau's grief knew no bounds. "My end is not far off," he declared, "for the Shaikh has told me that I would not survive him long." So it was. Before six months had elapsed, Amir Khusrau died (1325). He was buried at the foot of his Master's grave.

NOTES & REFERENCES :

1. Translated by M. Habib : *Hazrat Amir Khusrau of Delhi*, p. 12.
2. The irate poet uses a stronger simile, which unfortunately cannot be translated.
3. M.W. Mirza : *The Life and Works of Amir Khusrau*, p. 78.

8

THE NATURE OF INDIAN CULTURE

WHAT IS CULTURE ?

Culture is the spark of immortality that a race wins in its struggle against the power of negation. Life has the seed of death embedded in it. This is also true of the life of a race. Its march towards light is only a small fraction of its culture. The major part of its culture evolves only from its struggles against death.

There is something highly self-contradictory in the roots of life. Whenever life yearns for light and stretches its hands towards it, death comes from behind and imprisons it in its coils. It requires tremendous effort and wisdom to come out intact from these coils. The power of death is not alien. It comes from life itself. Negation is as much a part of life as affirmation. This temple of life is made of light and darkness, of both life and death. The soul is the deity enshrined in it. This deity is all-radiant, pure light and life, without any segment of darkness and death. This seed of immortality inspires life to become like it.

As a result, life ever moves towards more light and sweetness. The bitter element of death gets agitated and holds life back through several artifices, tricks and might. This struggle of life against a seed lying within it, called death, has been characterized sometimes as the interplay of Yang and Yin; sometimes and Purusha and Prakriti or Jiva and Pudgala.

Since ancient days the seekers have been searching for the hidden path which makes life free of the clutches of death. This path has been called Dharma, and Vyasa says that its course is as difficult to trace as that of fishes in deep waters. *Dharma is the art or science, as you will of getting rid of the seed of death, which lives within life.* The trees and flowers, the lakes and houses that grow along this road of Dharma are called culture.

Culture is an attempt to get rebirth from death and darkness. A small part of the light that great visionaries see passes quietly into the consciousness of the common man which is called the racial consciousness. Sometimes great visionaries like the Buddha and Mahavira, Sankara and Vyasa, make special efforts so that their vision and light may become a common possession, a part of the racial consciousness. The suffering of the common man arouses their compassion and they do not cross the threshold till their light enters into the waters of the common man's life and becomes a heritage.

This gift of light accumulates and helps the common man in his struggle against death. *This thread of light passing through millions of pearls, (i.e.people,) is called culture. It expresses itself in the form of music, sculpture, literature, customs, festivals, values and many other things.*

The power of negation is at work everywhere. Where we find life there we find death too. A people sincerely strive for an ideal society and still corruption grows and starts eating its resources like a parasite. A lover and a beloved start on the road to true love and the powers of hatred, envy and corruption start separating them. A young man wants to work selflessly for common ideals and he finds himself helpless. Frustration eats out his vitals. A Bach comes and tries to make life sweeter with his music, but oblivion comes from behind and hides him for over 150 years.

This power of negation is experienced by all of us. It looks clever, malicious and wicked, working as a secret organization. Like a moth, it spreads its network of destruction most cleverly.

Ancient Indians never looked at this power of negation with a hostile eye. They never aimed at its destruction. They knew that such attempts immortalize it. As negation, it was Not-Being. It did not exist. It was *asat,* a name that the Vedas gave it. It has been sent by God, the Brahman, Himself into the world of man, not with any malicious motive. God intends to realize immortality as life. He is immortal as God, Spirit, Brahman. It is possible to be immortal as life. He tries to fulfil this dream through His son, man.

This power of negation has always been looked upon by the West as an anti-thesis to God. It has been given several names—the Devil, Satan, Lucifer, Mephistopheles, etc. The struggle there has been of light against darkness, of God against demons. A different concept has grown in India. The power of darkness or negation is not an anti-thesis of God. It is the Not-Being which has the magical power to project itself as more than the Being. It is Maya which projects its spider-web around life in order to provide it with the darkness, without which it does not strive for more illumination.

It is the virtue of the gods to give and to say always '*yes*'. The word '*no*,' does not belong to the gods. In man the earthly and thc divine elements are synthesized. It is earth which works as the power of negation against the seed. It buries it. It resists its efforts to sprout and multiply. Still the seed knows the secret art of taking rebirth from earth. This rebrith gives it more life.

In Indian culture the power of negation is referred to as the terrible mother. *It is Sirsa, the mother of dragons, from whom Hanuman achieves a rebirth.* She comes to swallow him but his wit and courage help him to change this death into a renewed life. It is Holika, who takes Prahlad into her lap and leaps into the fire to burn him alive. But virtue, courage and divine grace come to help Prahlad. It is the fire-test from which every Sati or the truly existent one has to come out successful.

The freedom to say '*no*' has been given to the Indian people by their culture. To attain the highest a mere (yea) to life is an incomplete utterance. If a Neitzsche dares it, he throws himself to oblivion and madness.

Indian culture teaches us the art of utilizing the powers of both'*no*'and '*yes*'. To deny the expression of '*no*' is to breed the power of negation. A better course is to neutralize it by the other force of affirmation given to man. One who learns the art of neutralizing these two powers, one divine and the other demoniac, is rewarded with that real life-force which fulfils the dreams of Brahma. Culture tells us of this hidden Saraswati. Unless it awakens, life goes waste.

How wise was this course has been discovered by the West after suffering for thousands of years on the straight road to light. The cry of existentialists like Camus is for the freedom to say '*no*'. The basic discipline there has been obedience, '*yes*' to every command. It is this total '*yes*' which is at the base of all public schools. It is in fact at the base of all Christian morality. This rigorous discipline has rendered the Western people incapable of saying '*no*' in a normal way. To say '*no*' means a revolution there, the upsurge of the powers of negation. Indian Culture on the other hand has taught the common man the art of saying '*no*' without summoning the dark powers of negation and destruction. The working of this art can be seen easily in the manner in which the Indian people, silently and without any noise or violence, overthrew the Congress regime. From the Western point of view this is a total revolution.

How could this miracle be wrought? We shall not find anything to wonder in it if we know that Indian Culture has aimed at giving normal expression to our urge to say '*no*'. We have grown in this tradition. Therefore '*no*' has not become the power of negation in our life. It has been as much a means of the flowering of life as '*yes*'.

The gods in us do not get shocked at denial. They have learnt that it is the secret of life on earth. Miguel Serano rightly said that the Indians are a people who got themselves bitten once by the serpent, and that ever since they have been in search of immortality through poison.

It is not possible to define culture in a regular phrase. Some aspects of culture will be considered and discussed in this essay. *Culture is a substitute for waywardness, wastage, cynicism, confusion and darkness.* To say so is certainly to bring all the positive values of life within it. Those who think it to be a set of values and practices, discovered long back, do not define it for life. They make it a precious item of lost days. In the ever-new flow of life, culture evolves naturally and keeps on changing in many subtle ways. Anything that realizes, at a particular crossing of time and space, the highest happiness and elevated expression for a people, is culture. Such happiness cannot be attained without fulfilment. And for fulfilment it is essential that nothing in us remains denied and no aspect of human life gains over the other so much that the other is denied or suppressed. The task of culture becomes difficult since this fulfilment of the whole in us is to be realized without cynicism and on loftier summits. It is never difficult provided there is a will for freedom and a freedom from obsessions. *What we are today is but a moment in our racial consciousness.* Most of us are ignorant of this inheritance because of faulty education, sophistry, pedantry or no education at all. Yet we all share it and are aware of it in some half-way. This awareness has been carried to us by a whole mass of self-filtering beliefs, practices, myths and legends. It is these that form our cradle and many of us continue to lie unwillingly and unconsciously in the cradle.

The anguish in a man's soul is due to confusion in the elements of his soul, all struggling for self-fulfilment and none reaching it. This struggle is enormous and ultimately leads the uninformed individual into a belief that life is futility, confusion and darkness. Those who try to borrow light without suffering to find it develop a false personality. It is no source of joy to them since it only covers inner blankness and sorrow. Their life comes to live on the surface and it is hatred for their exterior and interior, which this type of living generates. They never live to realize the real joys and depths of life.

Since time immemorial there has been talk of the blossoming of life. To put it clearly it is nothing but the expression of the whole, the realisation of the whole, in us. For such people who import a false culture 'the expression of themselves' bears no meaning. They find their selves simply disgusting and a medley of different types of confusions, angers and frustrations deserving no expression. Its cause is their ignorance of their self, and the various suppressions they have registered on themselves in assuming a mask. Any action, howsoever noble, is nothing if it does not come out as an expression from within. Every action which does not grow so is bound to weigh on us, howsoever good and howsoever noble it be.

By knowing the past we realize the various tendencies working in us. Thus we discover a big part of our darkness which we cannot be aware of otherwise. It is inevitable that the consciousness and ways of life known to our heritage should form a part of us. We can deny this only by coming to live on the surface, which would be a denial of life itself. A brave people would never resort to such cowardly and self-negating tactics. Even those who want only to live a full life and want to enjoy the gift of existence will never do so. The constituents of life are naturally fired with such thirst for light that no imposition can be placed on them without losing heavily. Artificial denials or arrangements of these constituents bring only disharmony, cowardliness and confusion. It only makes a tough surface, an outer crust, tense or placid, with the inner side completely hollow.

Persons with such torn personalities and with such falsehood and masks can never understand themselves, nor others. The result is the kind of society where there are only individuals and only an artificial congregation of a society. People under such false conditions often remain concentrated on the surface as a measure of self-defence, to check and prevent the unmasking. Their seeming sense of enormous self-importance is shallow, vain and surface deep. In fact a man who realizes his importance truly, immediately realizes the importance of all life. The stream that unites man to man is underneath, in every human heart. Without discovering that, without reaching it all efforts at understanding and loving others will be artificial, tiring and unsustaining. Love and a feeling of oneness spring only when the inner self, leaving its muddles, rises for the finer and the purer. *Culture is an adventure of the dark towards light, of the low for elevation. It is the noble efforts and vow of man to flood the whole of that which is within with light.* It is not difficult once our love for life comes to be higher than every other thing. *Today we are denying life in our very modern lust for life.*

MATHEW ARNOLD'S DEFINITION OF CULTURE

It would be insufficient to define culture with Mathew Arnold as "a pursuit of our total perfection by means of getting to know on all matters which most concern us, the best which has been thought and said in the world; and through this knowledge, turning a stream of fresh and free thought upon our stock notions and habits..." Perfection is not attained by means "of getting to know on all matters which most concern us." This would mean that perfection is an impossibility. This process of getting to know would never end for there would always be something of "the best which has been thought and said in the world" which we could not get access to. Culture is not a process of stuffing ourselves with outer knowledge. To come in contact with "the best which has been thought and said" is of help only in the awakening of the sleeping self. Surfeiting ourselves with the best thoughts and other forms of knowledge is not end of culture. True culture can never be attained in that manner. It will make us either learned, virtuous or high-brow, but will not bring about that most essential achievement of culture—*total inner freedom and self-realization.* This can come only when there is no stuffing and when all old stuff has been removed from the self. Again, "*turning a stream of fresh and free thought upon our stock notions and habits....*" *would be a very poor gain of culture.* It awakens nothing. It simply makes us wiser to turn the acquired stream of free thoughts on our "stock notions and habits." It is only at an elementary stage that this could be called an achievement of culture. It is not turning a fresh and free stream of thought, developed by communion with the best that has been thought and said in the world, on our stock notions and habits, but self-illumination, the celebration of the birth of light within, the state where all such turning of the stream becomes needless and our stock notions and habits themselves get illuminated from within—that marks the true goal of culture.

Culture is a call of perfect freedom and freedom is a process of constant rise. We have not only to know the best but have also to rise above it when its function is over. Stock notions and habits have to be viewed critically in the light of fresh and free thought; but to stop here is to deny proper ends to culture. Culture is not so much a matter of acquisition as of inner revelation. Acquisition forms a stage of it since by acquiring right thoughts we start the process of struggling against the darkness within. But to hold to this acquired "stream of fresh and free thought" is to prefer another cage, albeit a golden cage. The free bird of self does not rejoice living in any cage be it of iron or of gold. Acquired thoughts have only a function to perform. They are of utility till we are able ourselves to fight our inner darkness. Beyond this they are superfluous and a stuffing of ourselves with them would only be a check against freedom and self-perfection. We have not to acquire and adorn ourselves. We have only to awaken.

Culture thus requires higher sacrifices worthy only of those who do not value any gain more than that of selfperfection and revelation of the inner self. Those who overcome all lures to cross the threshold, in one supreme effort, attain all the ends of this life and the other. They fulfil their destiny as the impossible children of two worlds, the impossible creations of time and eternity. The closed shores of ego are broken and in a flood of light they go to share the life of all, as children, nameless, devoid of ego, and messengers of light and joy.

TRUTH AND CULTURE

The culture of India grew on a firm faith that nothing remains except turth. It prepared the people to face brutal foreign invasions with calm and composure. The Greeks, the Huns, the Sakas and the Mongols came and went leaving no memory in the racial consciousness of the Indians. Whatever they did was not true. It was too brutal to be true. Truth is also good and beautiful. The mere fact that something happened does not make it true. If it is not beautiful and good it is a mere fact. The Indians in their spiritual journey kept facts and dreams at the same level for both are untrue.

The wild orgies and ruthless tyranny of a conqueror are facts. The Indians were taught not to be shocked by them. Truth is never cruel. If somebody enlarged facts so as to pass them for truths, the race ignored him. Only truth lasts. Facts that do not mature into truths are destined to destroy each other. It was believed that all creation devoid of truth is four-faced. Brahma, the Creator, is four-faced. Even so the untrue world is four-faced. One should not get excited at a cruel fact, but rather actively search in the three remaining facts. The moment we correctly find them out they start neutralizing each other. They are destined to destroy each other for they are not truth and nothing lasts except truth.

The number *four* thus has a very special significance in Indian Culture. It signifies the unreal.

It is in this context that the desire for the whole of truth becomes meaningful. The common man does not distinguish between fact and truth. He was advised to know the whole of what he calls truth, which in fact is only a body of facts. When he does so, facts neutralize each other. Truth alone remains in his soul.

Here is a human situation to illustrate this idea. I take the example of disciplining the younger ones. The forerunners of Indian Culture never thought discipline to be a 'yea' to everything taught by the elders. It was only a means to know the soul. The younger ones were, however, expected to obey their elders even if the latter demanded total submission. This was to be done knowingly with a belief that the excesses of the elders would automatically breed their opposites. A fourfold working of the unreal is bound to set in when an ideal becomes larger than truth. Our soul is not supposed to fight it. The exaggeration of a fact is its corruption. It is a shadow. It is *asat*. Three more forms of *asat* are bound to appear to wash it even as six more colours appear along with violet in the rainbow to neutralize all colours into one white ray of light.

The Indian tradition believes that nothing except truth remains. It also says that truth has a tendency to conquer. It is not passive.

If some zealous teacher teaches an excess of 'yea' to the student, it is no cause for worry. The freedom to say 'no' is bound to develop in the student as a reaction to it. The process will not stop here. A third face of Maya will emerge. It is angry criticism on the part of the teacher. He cries out: the twisted tail of a dog does not become straight even it we keep it in a pipe for twelve years. This violent anger will break the personality of the student. On this debris will emerge a fourth face of Maya. It is the loss of all self-confidence on the part of the student. He has been torn away from his roots. He is ready now to be indoctrinated.

Indian Culture teaches us not to be alarmed even at this. Such is its implicit faith in truth. It teaches us to take all these four faces as mere appearances, without any reality. The student should not be misled by the fact that the fourth face looks to be his own face. He should not forget his original and true face. The faith that truth and the soul never die alone helps him here. If he were to take refuge in this faith he would see the four faces as the faces of the unreal. This knowledge will suffice to set all the four on the task of eradicating each other. Thus have the wise in India made the dictum that truth alone survives, a practical reality.

Indian Culture is a way of transforming abstract truths into practical experiences. Einstein said that you get from truth only what you dare. The Indians dared the whole of truth. They have been paying a very heavy price for it. But it is also ture that you find no other people on earth in whose life so many abstract truths live. Generally, nations have accepted a total division between theory and practice for the sake of success. They do not hesitate to say that idealism is theoretical. It is not meant to be practised. Practical life is entirely different.

This is not so in Indian Culture. There is a way to grow the most sensitive heavenly flowers on the body of the rugged earth. Indian Culture aims at teaching the way to do it.

Life has to be an expression of the highest truth. All powers of affirmation, negation, condemnation and total surrender play a shadowy drama on the stage of life. And we have to survive the storm. While we do so we learn how to keep the flame of the soul burning steady and undisturbed even while hurricanes are assailing it.

In India today it appears that we have gradually lost our love for truth—a love which formed such an integral part of our life. Even under the yoke of foreigners and suppression, this love was aflame all through our history. It is in fact this love which helped us above all to appreciate the value of Dharma and light and to live by it with passion and trust. The relationship between truth and culture is profound, for culture is mainly a social and individual reflection of truth. It is the image of truth in the daily business of man. It is a vow to reach the highest light through the very turmoils and oddities of life. In our day culture has lost its appeal to the masses, since its intrinsic relationship with truth has often been ignored by its adherents. They have exhibited a tendency to isolate it as a system of fineries and make it a specialised function. The true touches of life have been denied to it. With this basic denial it has drifted so far that in the cultural achievements of our age one rarely finds anything more than the new, the amusing or the baffling. It is under these fresh conditions that the forces of ruin operate.

The seed of ruin for man is in his removal from the road of life. Culture would be of little use and meaning, if its ground is not life, and if its aim is not the full flowering life. Culture carries within it its own seed of cancellation. When all the circular and lost roads have been linked with the highway, when all that could be attained by turning everything to light has been attained, culture becomes superfluous. An inner urge emerges to grow out of discipline, for life becomes self-illuminated. It is here that culture itself becomes a veil, and for a higher emancipation even this has to be removed. "Remove it O Pushan," one cries like the Rishi in the *Isopanishad*, "so that I may look at the face of Truth." Culture is the last golden disc which we refine from all mixture and finally this itself seeks removal for full realization of the inner significance.

When the aim is to search out the highest happiness and not to subjugate life to any lust, culture appears and grows. It is an incessant search for light and happiness. An isolated search merely for spiritual riches might confuse a people and make them one-sided. True culture does not isolate any part of our being. It is a continuous rebirth form the forces of negation. It is not a straight race towards light. It is the art of returning to the dark womb of nature.

CULTURE AND THE FREEDOM OF THE MIND

There is much talk of a certain coldness on the cliffs. It is said that the winds on the heights are too cold and not bracing. The higher ones often fall prey to depression and gloom and realize too soon the sad scheme of things. The zest goes and life retains nothing interesting. This is a solace to the non-aspiring and a reward to his muddled life. He claims superiority on the grounds of these results and often it is thought that elevations are but moonshine. Man is an earthy creature. He fulfils his life best if he chooses to remain within his confines. The passions that derange his reason—the little reason that keeps him company amidst all pursuits—his desires and psychological conflicts, all are considered to be inevitable parts of his destiny. It should be wise, they infer, if he remains what nature made him; if he does not challenge her scheme by aspiring too high. The call of the beyond and the twilight is said to be a mirage—the work of delusions and too much dreaming.

The ruin and decay of many superior souls on elevations is cited. It is maintained that the human vessel is too limited to discover Truth. Man is condemned to a life of confines and incompleteness. He can work it out best by accepting these cruel facts of Nature.

There is no doubt that the best of men have betrayed chilly sensations and unhappy associations on the heights. Heights brought to them gloomy isolation and an exciting yet arid dry company of thoughts and visions. The inner urge of life is to share life. This first and primary urge gets denied on elevations. One gets doomed to incurable loneliness. Fulfilment does not come. The inner self remains as much thirsty, full of yearnings. It gets thristy even for the common joys of earthly life which no more belong to it. Like a queer stranger to both the worlds— of stocks and of dreams— the higher spirit soars and yet reaches nowhere. It becomes a bird with open wings condemned to fly eternally but never to reach. It should certainly be no gain if we were to relinquish our earthly joys and sufferings for something higher, and the higher should be inaccessible since our nature is incurably limited.

Neitzsche got tired of his heights. For all his persistence he only achieved a shattering of that rare brain of his. In the end he too was prepared for the "Gutterphilosophy", as he cried, to be guttered and levelled with all. The urge to feel again as an ordinary living human being came in pathetic exclamations when the mind had broken and he had no proud check left. If the elevations were fulfilling the question would be, why should there be so much yearning for sharing life, for the sheer joy of participating in the simple chorous of creation, to live and reciprocate the love and feelings of others?

Byron and Shakespeare and Tolstoy had all come to the same wisdom which was a version of profound disillusionment. Everything in life was fleeting, unsubstantial. All was enveloped in clouds and dreams. It was a show in which we participated but could never know the play. We were actors who did not know their roles. Like puppets, though with brains, yet powerless to comprehend, we were in the hands of something. It played us as it willed, systematically sometimes, with reason, compassion and a sense of beauty; sometimes simply with vengeance and mockery. We are helpless and at its pleasure. We know nothing and are denied the very bases on which to stage our opposition or build our own roles. With such dark existence it is in vain to strive for heights. Even the heights are not known. Little do we know, it is said, what height is, what Truth is? The struggle for elevation is merely a wastage like wandarings for love of a ghost.

True, much in life is shrouded in mist and the mysterious. The urge to know never gets satisfied. It seems to be insatiable. But this certainly is no argument against search for elevations. We may not know the origin and end of life. Yet we know something. The little that we know is not little and is perhaps the very clue to knowledge, freedom and light. We know that life has certain inlaid definite distinctions. It has an innate distinction between the beautiful and the ugly, the true and the false, the good and the evil. It is this gift which we always ignore in our dumbness and despair before eternal questions. We never properly asses this gift. We beat the rocks and never touch the only stone-gate. It seems to be a long filtering superstition that the clue and cure to all our miseries is in knowing the 'whence' and the 'wherefore', the age of the planets, and the process of creation. This knowledge should give us enormous clarity. But this too should be little for the realization of our happiness. Our happiness rests with a feeling of inner flowering. The road to happiness is not to be found in search of knowledge, but in rising to a level of spiritual freedom. In this state knowledge becomes self-revealed. Knowledge is no addition to us. It is a removal of all darkness that colours and shades the inner lamp. It is this lamp which is knowledge. The secret of everything is known to it since it is this which alone is close to the heart of nature.

Lao-Tze was right when he said that man has to learn nothing. He has only to remove the coating that wrong, desire-directed thinking has left in his soul. Knowledge is first a matter of moral and spiritual freedom. Our mind acts with its stock notions and directions given by desires. Mind never acts itself. It is always some desire or other that sets it working. All desires misguide and lead us to their limited ends. When desires are conquered and do not guide and mind, another power awakens in us. It is the true power, the power of the soul. This power may not be very clear. Long suppression and persisting clouds may not let us feel it. It rises slowly when mind becomes free of the dictates of desires. This power is the light within, the source and explanation of all creation. When mind recognizes its function to be mere submission to this inner light, waywardness ceases. The freedom of mind does not consist in trackless thinking, refusing all forms of formal thinking and logic. This results in chaos. Freedom of mind consists in making it free of the dictates of desires and passions. It may be said that this would mean inactivity and a state of lifelessness. It is true, but it is so only as long as the inner self has not come out of the clouds and of bondage. When mind, thus freed and calmed, surrenders itself only as an instrument of this inner light, true flowering begins. Gradually the inner-self becomes revealed. All our senses and faculties become its instruments. By our unflinching adherence to it, by our total trust and repose in it, it comes to greater and still greater manifestations. It is not our trust or repose that brings it to manifestation. It is self-manifest and self-illuminated. Our trust and repose only calm down our faculties and prepare them to recognize this light. It is in our ability to recognize that the light exists for us. To develop this ability we need moral and intellectual discipline and true culture. By our submission to these disciplines we train our mind to refrain from false habits of thinking. When it comes to manifestation, all discipline becomes needless. Culture, religion, philosophy and moral discipline no longer mean anything since we have reached their very source.

The road to liberation and true knowledge is laid within. One who dissociates his mind from submission to the inner and attaches it to outer objects with a view to knowing them, derives only the empty satisfaction of half and coloured information. It is not knowledge since all knowledge is a flowering of the inner self.

The confusion and darkness that we find around us is nothing but a projection of the inner state. It is inner darkness which we never think of dispelling. It is the inner call which we always subdue and throttle for petty outer gains. It is the subtle boundage of desires and lust that have fastened the inner self on all sides, denying its freedom and flights. How vain it is to cry, for outer freedom under such conditions!

The tragedy with man is in his often being gripped by the hunger to live by lofty standards without attaining them spiritually. The distinction between good and evil is one such illustration. Often men prefer to call this distinction a mere man-made creation, with no sanctity about it. It is said that much thinking through the ages under religious and moral prejudices have given this. A finer urge is expressed—to be above and free of this distinction. The distinction is ignored mentally and forcibly forgotten. All inner protests are forced down as mere cries of a racial consciousness.

It is true that good and evil are man-made distinctions, and ultimately on the higher regions they disappear like other distinctions. The higher flight would not be complete if this distinction remains clinging. But it is important to know that this distinction has not come to be so strong in us simply from a vacuum or owing to the racial consciousness. Why should these distinctions alone be the strongest elements in our racial consciousness? The distinction is an immediate reaction of the inner self to the mixer, clever and vile state of affairs in the world. This distinction was not known to man in his pure and original state. But with the development of evil, fear, distrust and selfishness, it came as a reaction to the inner light. Those who would desire to be free of this distinction have a tedious and brave journey to perform. To force it down as a remnant of the racial consciousness or a state of the superstitious self is to confound oneself and deny all doors to light. Such aspirants have to rise, rise in their inner journey above vileness and greed, above the bondage of lust and desire, to a state of innocence where such distinction may mean nothing to their inner self. It remains there outside but it has lost all its significance to the inner soul. For only as long as the inner self is bound to things and is clouded by dark designs does it feel this distinction. When it has risen in the light of its lamp and has shattered the bondage of desires and passions, then only does it realize pure illumination and elevation from the discursive state.

As for coldness on the summits, the summits are indeed cold. But true elevation is always a warmth of the heart. It is the inner self which alone is to be the refuge. Our dependence on the outer warmth has to be overcome. It is only in total self-restoration, in faith only in the inner self, that our journey for self-perfection has its goal.

There is another scaling of heights, the scaling by mind alone. The mind has a power to dissociate itself from the rest of our being and to soar. It is this soaring of the mind alone which causes despair. The higher winds are not for weaker souls. It is a strong self, awakened, that alone can feel at home on such cliffs. Those intellectuals who try to reach heights by mental effort alone are bound to face frustration and to get frightened. Elevation is not a matter of meditation, or mental yoga. It is a spiritual, not an intellectual, journey.

Mental concentration can give us enormous powers and access into super-human regions. It would be a delusion to consider such access as elevation. This danger was envisaged long back and the Buddha warned against such degrading attempts to attain powers. They are positive obstructions in our self-flowering. All desire for power corrupts, even the desire for yogic powers. It has repeatedly been said that man has to walk on his road with no external support, with only one support, that of his inner light.

Sufferings and darkness have thus two causes: one an attachment to the impermanent, *i.e.* to wordly things, and the other attachment to spiritual things. "Those who confine themselves to the worldly objects suffer darkness," says the *Isopanishad,* "but those who confine themselves to the other-worldly objects are in a still greater darkness."

The inner self knows no such attachment or confinement. Even though it aspires for the higher regions of light, for ultimate union, its aspiration is not the same as attachment. It is mind that attaches itself till it learns to be an instrument of the inner self. Often it is the higher attachment which people mistake for elevations, and come to distrust them, since it brings them a new darkness.

In aspiring for the higher, the fully luminous and the perfectly beautiful, the self does not attach itself to anything outer. It only aspires to realize its own stage of perfection. It is a future of the self itself for which it aspires. There has never been any crowd on it. Persons whom no earthly or heavenly gain chains, walk on it. It is renunciation not only of the world but also of the heavens. This renunciation is not the same experience that the ascetic knows. The true seeker loses nothing by it, nor does he close himself to earthly joys and heavenly gifts. Rather, with the awakened light within he feels them more keenly and shares them freely. Only he has learnt not to betray the inner light. This saves him from carrying dust on him.

It is in the freedom of the inner self that repose and joy rest. This freedom is the same as self-realization. To make the self free of all desires, outer checks would not suffice. For freedom, the self has to rise to heights. It is only when it freely manifests itself and realizes itself that freedom comes to it.

The desire to share life with others is a misguiding one. We do not share life with others by remaining socially and personally attached to them. We may live with people through a whole lifetime and still remain perfectly lonely within. This experience is a common one and needs no illustration. Sharing is not a matter of living in close mutual understanding even. We may be understanding someone with sympathy and clarity and yet sharing may be distant. Attachment never brings the feeling of sharing. It is only an outer, inconvenient union.

All sharing is a matter of the inner self. As long as we keep it reduced to an ego by several subtle bondages, it remains lonely since it is narrow and finds little like it. When by an uncompromising urge for full flowering and realization we elevate it to the very region of light, it loses the narrow folds and becomes love itself—the same love that is the essence of all life. It does not recognize itself as distinct. The very condition of total self-realization includes oneness with all. This oneness is not realized by intensified desire for it. It is a natural outcome of the journey to light.

CULTURE AND FREEDOM OF THE HEART

Self-perfection does not mean only a search for the perfection of mind and body. The freedom of the mind, as the Buddha said, is half freedom and by itself a dangerous freedom. There is another freedom without which the freedom of the mind remains a misnomer. It is freedom of the heart, which is love. Pursued on its own as in this scientific age of ours where anything that is not scientific is considered primitive and unworthy of human attention—the freedom of the mind is bound to deny man the human warmth and light in which alone, truth, justice and reason work spontaneously. Reason is destined to be debased, dry, ironical, sadistic and self-destructive without the freedom of the heart. The human mind has a tendency to work in abstraction and isolation, to deny the truth of real life in its false love of flights and free thinking. How thin, unsupporting and uncertain reason is without the almost feminine warmth of heart, without the rise of the whole self to it and not only of mind, is known to all who have followed its lines sincerely. The whole of our being has to make the passage towards light, so that when actions and thoughts spring they are not only the outcome of mind, which is half an instrument of truth, but the outcome of an interplay of mind and heart, of the inner self itself, and thus of the synthesis of opposites, of the very truth of Nature and Life.

As children of light and truth we have to the active in our whole being. To steel one against the hard requirements of the other may help in gaining our immediate ends, but the losses incurred will be immeasurable. The loss, ultimately, will be in a total inability to enjoy the very gift of existence. None can express his nature by emphasizing certain fractions in it and denying others. When deluded by the powers and arrogance of mind, we lose sight of this truth and follow the alien and narrow lines imposed by mind in the development of our personality, we do not develop, nor express our nature. We only play with ourselves cruelly in planting ideas, forces and half-truths on ourselves. For the spontaneous expression of ourselves and for the fultilment of our nature the whole is to be taken into account and the whole is an epitome of Nature. Many opposites come to form it. It is not the realization of man against nature or against opposites. It is realization of man and nature in the same process, for in essence the two are not different.

LYRICISM AND CULTURE

Lyricism of a culture is its inner flavour. It is something which the long practice of a beautiful, sweet and fulfilling custom, ceremony or festival brings to the life of a people. It is so even in the case of language or any other form of expression. Lyricism is the inner flavour of life discovered and made intimate to a people through certain forms of expression. The form in itself may be fantastic, imaginary or merely sentimental. It yet has the power of bringing man close to the inner flavour of life. No doubt its expressions are symbolic and for those people they mean much more than an onlooker can make out. The racial memories, faith, myths, the very details of life of a people are intimately linked with the symbolic language of their culture. They are deeply buried in it. In fact apart from intensity, which it derives from sincerity, and the level of spiritual tension which went in its formation, all its filling material is from the myths, lores, history and life of those people. Some phrases owing to the rich associations they arouse in the minds of a people, or owing to their association with something profoundly sacred, joyous or sorrowful in their history and mythology, become fuller in meaning and almost magical in effect. Their dictionary meaning gets confounded before the sense they convey or the associations they arouse. Such expressions form what is known as the lyrical essence of a culture. In their precision, fullness and capacity to cover vast stretches of time and space, of feelings and thoughts, they become symbols of that culture. It is here that the highest aspirations, feelings, thoughts and all that is finest in a people become simple and dissoluble directly in life. It is when the higher achievements in beauty, truth and goodness get dissolved in the common current and are no more distinct and awesome, but have become the sweet murmur and ripple in the waters of life, that lyricism develops in a culture. When people could sing the highest philosophic thoughts as songs and hymns in the Vedas and Upanishads, then alone Indian culture achieved a dimension of deep waters for common life. Spiritual yearning became something common and got mixed in the very blood of the people, because a whole host of superior individuals had taken it to its musical ecstasies. It no longer flowed from them in its intellectual form, but as the very bubbling song of life and soul. In this primal form it could be intimate to every commoner.

Similarly when lack of inhibitions matured and sex established itself as one of the *purusharthas,* its significance dawned upon the common man; not through reason or philosophic discussion, but only when rhetoricians and poets and artists drew it and chiselled it, without reserve, and yet with that fine sensitivity of soul which was free of sinful craving—as in the writings of Kalidasa, Bhartruhari and others, the sculptures of Konarak and Khajuraho—that sex achieved lyrical qualities and came to form a new dimension in the life of the common man. It was no longer merely a lustful action, shameful joy or a burden of procreation.

Lyricism in fact is a quality which grows in a culture the more it discovers closeness to common life. Culture begins with flights and often proceeds towards the abstract. It is when all things of value attained from this abstraction are brought back to life, through animistic realization in the heart, that a culture becomes lyrical. It is this which determines the ability of people to combine the things of earth and heaven in one. It is in direct proportion to such ability that a people realizes the hidden song of life. The inner flavour of life is never known as long as there is bifurcation between the two worlds—the world of facts and the world of vision. All joy that we experience is only a coming closer of the two. The closer they are, the grester the ability of a people to combine them in one feeling, the greater the prospects of fulfilment and joy. This power rises among the common people only when greater men realize this closeness in their exalted person so fully that it reaches every commoner as a simple song through them.

In its lyrical form, culture becomes a part of the soul of a people and a perpetual joy and enrichment to them. This lyrical element is not always precise and brief. It was given to the genius of Veda Vyasa and Valmiki to make whole epics and make many, many heroes lyrical for our people. One has no need to go to books on culture or to art products to assess the extent to which the lyrical has been assimilated in the common life of India. Each man and woman carries those imprints, and the ancient waters of life as seen by Vyasa run deep in our life to this day.

The drawings that Hindu women make on floors or walls on different festivals may be simple floral or geometrical patterns, or unskilled expressions of the observation of their surroundings. But the very brass cups filled with colours, the drawing, the feeling behind it, have a meaning for the Indian which cannot be comprehended by an onlooker. It is that superstitiously ignored and misunderstood part of a culture which not only works for intensity but also for the other vital hunger of life, fullness. It is this hunger which is completely missed by those who link culture with pure rationality. When the moon is worshipped by women with homely songs—woven round human hopes, love and fear, or water is offered to the rising sun, Indians are not to the told of their significance. To suggest that they are superstitious may be true from the viewpoint of a merely scientifically trained mind. Such a suggestion will merely be shocking. It will be known to be superficial, a truth from an uninformed. standpoint—and nothing unfamiliar. The rational aspect is not calculated here. It is an expression of the urge in life for saturation, for fullness, to have the very shining disc of the moon placed among the wonders of the heart. One of the essentially great elements of Indian Culture is this courage to bear the burden of irrational longings. It is an attempt to bring irrationality to light and light to irrationality.

To the pure rationalist, it may be rather shocking, and yet revealing, to see even an educated woman on a particular night looking for the reflection of the moon in a bronze plate full of water before accepting her meals. It is not fear or mere hope of gain which moves women to such strange actions. They spring from the colours of a heart demanding to share life with the whole universe. It is the demand of the heart for fullness.

It is understandable when the poet Raghupati Sahai Firaq says that a sense of fullness came to him from the two earthen pitchers that he used to watch as a child in the courtyard of his house. That water was used for no purpose and yet everyday the pitchers were washed and filled with fresh water. Similarly, he says, he developed an intimacy with nature in those early days when, as a child, early in the morning, he followed his mother to the Tulsi plant which she used to water and worship.

These simple everyday rituals have developed powers for the Indian mind quite incomprehensible to a narrow scientific onlooker. They have gone deep to form the Indian's being and have the miraculous effect of immediately drawing him out of his narrow individuality.

These rituals give him a temporary feeling of oneness with nature, with the various powers manifest in the sun, water, moon, wind and time, ancient lores, myths and the roll of ages.

It is in vain to depend solely on the scientific method and ignore a vital part of life owing to a rigid scientific outlook verging on superstition. It is true that the modern age has advanced in its use of the clear and purely rational method of science, but this also is true that science method of science, but this also is true that science and its method have developed new cages for the soul of man by restricting his vision, by making him blindly dependent on them. Science has become a kind of religion and has greater blinding power over modern man than any religion ever had. Whatever closes our vision is a fetter, a veil. There are many ways to the inner light of man and life revels in groping through them all. It is in discovering the light within through all the clouds of darkness, and laying the milky way to truth that the hope of freedom rests. We cannot be happy by clearing only one road and ignoring others. The cry of the inner soul is for light, light that burns and revels in burning out all darkness. By denying this full right to light none can hope for happiness. The higher our demands on life, the more darkness cries out for the touch of light. It is for culture to take into account this whole of man. The aim of culture is not to negate but to understand, to illuminate everything. The achievement and glory of a culture lies in making even the unclear and irrational in life an expression of the same light.

FOLK ART, RELIGION AND CULTURE

It is not wrong to say that our culture is identical with our religion. To understand it properly we must first know what religion means to the ordinary man in India. It is not a set of injunctions. We have in fact no Bible. Largely it is an unwritten religion. It is a common saying that religion is in each one's heart. Sometimes people call kindness or compassion their religion. They are more inclined to call a human feeling, like love or piety, their religion. They are all in fact *Nirgranthas, i.e.* those for whom religion does not come from the scriptures. It grows in each soul. Christ is born in every human heart.

The Indian word for religion is dharma which means a natural and spontaneous way of doing things. Therefore even a dance could be a religious act here. To go further, even a courtesan could claim to be religious if she gave her body to all irrespective of their beauty , age and *varna*. The first couplet of Valmiki was a religious act, even though it spoke only of sexual love between two birds. The contemplation of beauty by a poet was a religious act. Religion defined so widely can very well be the same as culture.

It is true, whatever its implication, that the strongest moving force in India has been religion. This may appear a little unwholesome to the secular and scientific reader. However, the matter will not appear so unpleasing if it is correctly understood. What, then, did religion mean to Indians? From the very beginning, religion has been to the Indians more of an inner force than external. True that various codes of conduct were prescribed, and the life of the individual was showerd with ideals and precepts and that modes of behaviour were laid down. It has often been inferred from this that religion, *i.e.* dharma, governed the life of people as an external force. In fact the results achieved were very different and it may be said that those results were in no way accidental and different from the desired ones. The desire was not to make dharma the external guide of people but to arouse their inner self. In the course of years the term *Swadharma,* came in use to express, perhaps, this somewhat complex aim of Hindu society. Dharma was only a discipline to prepare them for the acceptance of the inner truth. It was for the creation of such cleansed conditions under which alone the inner voice could be heard. In any case, in order to understand the constitution of Indian society, it ought to be understood that somehow this evoking of the inner truth came down, as a direct message to the common man. Even while adhering strictly to the injunctions of dharma and following all that was prescribed for practice, he knew that this was of little avail unless he could refer to the inner truth. It was known even to the common man that the true gain of dharma was the awakening of the inner self which would render dharma and its discipline superfluous.

It is this which explains the vast sense in which the term dharma has been used in this country. It also explains the queer mixture of religious tolerance and fast adherence to religion.

Religion, thus, was not a set of injunctions, a few do's and dont's, to be imposed upon life so that a life in accordance with the words of the scriptures might be lived and saved from evil. It was the creation of such conditions as would be helpful in the blossoming of truth, of *Swadharma,* of joy within. As injunctions, religion could fight several forms of darkness and cleanse much that persists with individual ignorance and lust. But again simply as injunctions it could hurl us to another kind of darkness. Even those injunctions were nothing sacred ultimately. A constant search, dharma, was to be of a condition where no bondage remained and life could express its inner truth without shame or lust or evil.

Since the flowering of the inner truth also required freedom from all cleansing material, the injunctions, dharma ceased to be what its synonym religion stands for.

It is in this way that throughout the ages dharma responded to the call of life. When in the *Mahabharata* Vyasa said, "the course of dharma is as difficult to trace as that of fishes in deep waters," he was speaking of the same truth which saved these people from identifying dharma with a few prescribed lines of conduct. For a slavish mind such religious tolerance and diverse developments within the same religion would be impossible. Dharma came to a continuous discovery of the road leading to truth. It indulged in experiments too. As the need of individual souls required, at times it was faith, blind faith, superstition, at times purely objective, rational enquiry and at times a sacrifice for the cleansing of the inner self. When a king administered justice with the best of light within, it was an act of dharma. When a poet contemplated beauty or a beloved her lover, a geometrician his figures, it was dharma in each case.

Thus dharma could never force the life of the people into any narrow fanatic mould. Nor could it thus make their life one-sided, denying other facets of their personality. It was the flowering of the whole, even of the *kama* and *artha* (sexual and worldly) aspects of their personality. It is because of such a vast and comprehensive understanding of dharma, that the people of India did not require another phrase, *i.e.* culture, to cultivate the various other virtues of life which, if not expressly denied by religion, have no room in it.

The tragedy with modern India is that shedding this vast, embracing sense of dharma and under the powerful impact of western civilization, people have chosen the same narrow meaning of religion for it. The lyrical charm that dharma had for the Hindu has been very much minimized. The various small details of several ceremonies, profusing life with rhythm and lyricism, are left in a skeleton, and in higher society are completely missing. At every step dharma intended to bring the individual close to nature and to the rhythm of the life around. It was not aimed at making the individual seeking dharma an isolated figure seeking grace. The fulfilment of dharma was not to take away a person from the joys of life and nature. Rather he was brought through acts of dharma more and more close to life and nature so that one day conditions might be evoked to realize truth not in pious words but in the daily face and mirror of life and nature.

During every small festival women could be seen making patterns and colourful drawings on floors, doorsteps and the walls of their houses, with a passionate faith. It was not the faith of a pagan in the mystic powers of his signs or drawings. Something deep, the mixed-up earthy and spiritual longings of the heart; something of a force from the very fountain of life was the impetus behind this act. They were no mere ceremonies or tiring rituals, but a kind of symbolic language through which millions of illiterate women had learnt to express all the treasures of their soul. It had required millennia of faith and heartful adherence to reach this state.

Rivers were worshipped, mountains and animals were worshipped, on some occasions, a tree as well. This was not merely the attachment of a pagan for these objects. It was not the awe or fear of these forces alone or the hope of gaining their favour that was at the root. For millions of illiterate people the pagan faith has always been there.

The primitive savage soul of man has not departed completely. The majesty and awe with which the faces and powers of nature impressed the soul of the primitive man remain a strong part of our heritage. Perhaps the very base of our innate association with it is laid in the primitive soul. With the growth of rationality however, this soul did not ignore the wider truth of human nature by rejecting, out of vanity, such an attitude altogether as pagan and primitive.

With the powers of reasoning reaching their highest level with the Upanishads, the Buddha, Nagarjuna and Samkara, Indians never ignored these vital urges of life simply to satisfy the partial and deceptive demands of the mind. Deeper implications were analysed and understood, and an improved form was given, more acceptable to man, at a higher stage of mental activity. The relation of man and nature became more intimate. It was only a dual manifestation of one essential Truth. It is the river, the earth, and corn that from our body. The sun gives us energy. Thus with vegetation and the entire animal kingdom and the objects of nature, a living intimacy was discovered. Through worship, offerings and holy baths this contact was kept alive lest the common man forget this basic link with all nature and revert back to the primitive, frightened condition of man or to the arrogant lonely condition of the modern scientific man.

The world of man was crowded with the living images of nature, gods and other forms of existence. In the Jataka tales, in the Panchatantra, in various Puranas and the two epics, in art, literature and sculpture, this basic link between all existence has been stressed. The life of an ordinary Hindu could never be confined and narrowed down to himself inspite of ignorance. Through rituals and the details of daily life, he was constantly in touch with the whole of life and nature. A child would grow up watching his mother nurse with tender care and intimacy tiny plants in the courtyard, respect and honour life even in animals and birds and perform rituals of the most sensitive and varied kinds relating to the various forces of heaven and earth.

All these details and rituals of life are fast dying out as they are considered shameful expressions of an unscientific and superstitious soul. The modern Indian, in his new scientific rationalism, is seeking dissociation from nature and life. But the destiny of life is not fulfilled by reason alone.

Perhaps for the first time Indians have chosen the agonizing path of the western individual. Dissociating himself from everything, the young man of today is moving towards oblivion. The growing listlessness and darkness, are no warnings to him. Little do we know that the end that lures us so greatly today has already brought the whole of the West to disillusionment. Frantic in their unbearable and arid purity and hardness of consciousness, men and women in the West are rushing madly towards the doors of life through which they stepped out into a purely scientific individuality and which immediately after seems to have closed for ever. What a paradox that Indians should be seeking the same lonely, monstrous ends, away from the all-embracing warmth of life, when the West itself, tired of its luring grandeur, should be helplessly trying to retrace their steps.

It is difficult for an outsider or the crudely scientific person to comprehend or realize the power and importance of the various drawings and patterns that form a part of Indian festivals and religious ceremonies. They may attract modern man on account of their geometrical designs. They may be found amusing as somewhat primitive forms and representations of life and nature. The modern artist may find them wonderful because of their simplicity and boldness or brilliant colours. But in order to understand the real meaning of these drawings, one must enter into the heart of the woman who draws them with a naive urge for self-expression. She has not become detached from them under the sway of sophistry by taking only the modern woman's delight in them—a delight aroused merely by something curious, or by the conceit of observing an ancient custom simply to appear more cultured and deeply suffused in tradition. Making use of those drawings with a genuine urge has given a curious moving power to those lines and colours. To the simple woman, to draw them or to watch them has provided a deep relief and self-expression. Those figures, drawn by unskilled but true hands, had developed the power to draw out the full expression from the heart of woman. For centuries they have been relieving them of an emotional burden. They are also symbolic representations of the world as experienced by every ordinary woman. It is difficult to overrate the importance of such a medium of self-expression.

It is through these patterns that women conveyed artistically their experience to men. These patterns worked towards the day-to-day fusion of their two worlds of experience. It was this medium that gave meaning and sense to all that was vague, dreamy, very feminine and an inevitable part of their nature. It proclaimed a vaster sympathy for life and an understanding of it which rejoiced in such total expression.

This common form of expression kept art close to life by linking it with small day-to-day details. Art was essentially linked with all kinds of rituals, ceremonies, festivals and religious offerings. Art was not accepted merely as an item of pleasure to while away leisurely hours or just for special cultivation. It became a function of life and as such informed and guided ordinary life. Sensitivity towards the delicate sensations of sound, touch and sight became essential requirements of normal living. With this developed a natural urge for communion with all life; life even in the animal and vegetable kingdom. Trees and animals crowded the world of these symbolic drawings. Man was never left to enter into rituals or enjoy his festivals all alone. A whole atmosphere and imperceptible sense of intrinsic communion with other attributes of life and nature helped in curing that bitter touch of isolation and non-communicability that we moderners feel so often.

Our life, which demands so great an involvement in the profitable and bread-earning pursuits, has every reason to seek expression through such forms in order to remain in touch with all life and thereby achieve a sense of fullness within. The absence of such a sense of fullness has brought our age, inspite of so much advancement, to an unspeakable gloom and vacuum.

Discrimination and the exclusion of all that is not of the nature of light, joy and compassion, forms an important stage in the development of a person. But were we to remain at this stage culture would be nothing but a higher isolation. The pathos of the distance thus achieved is certainly no gain.

CULTURE AND RACIALISM

Life is a whole. It is not divided into individuals and nations nor into past, present and future. All these divisions are but creations of the mind. It is impossible to live fully without realizing this intrinsic oneness. All joy in fact springs only when such oneness is realized. Culture is nothing but that which traces our course back to this intrinsic oneness. Culture does so by breaking the false barriers of beliefs, prejudices and races. Thus culture ultimately negates its own self.

To a consistent mind, the few references made to culture thus far will appear inconsistent. It will be said that these references do not form different facets of the same thing but negate each other. It may further be thought that to hold that culture, at one and the same time, is both the racial consciousness of a people in its various living elements, as well as that which breaks the barriers of thoughts and racialism in retracing the course to the intrinsic oneness of life, is highly confusing and contradictory. If the evocation of the element of racial consciousness is necessary for a life of culture, how then can the demolition of the racial barriers be its end? Both these statements in fact form different stages of human consciousness and are not in the least contradictory. To give expression to the various unknown elements of racial consciousness is essential for a flowering of life, for nothing that forms life should be denied proper expression. To suppress would only confuse and make us estranged from life. Such suppression creates a division within ourselves. To say that true culture breaks all racial barriers and restores life to its intrinsic oneness, means that after realizing the racial consciousness the process of struggle for life does not come to an end. There will be new darknesses and at that elevated stage the very level of culture attained will appear to be a form of darkness. The supreme urge to mingle with the whole of life and realize that deathless oneness with all and not only with one racial group, is felt here. At this level, the urge for a higher culture finds previous achievements insufficient, and the soul takes a higher flight. This pursuit of new summits goes on till life discovers the road to intimacy with all life. At this stage perhaps culture becomes superfluous and the full blossoming of life is unfolded .

Ultimately the task of culture is nothing other than that of religion, science, philosophy and knowledge. Culture performs its task more effectively without creating inhibitions and by pointing to a road wider in scope and freedom.

DOES CULTURE CREATE DOUBLE STANDARDS ?

Ancient culture is a symbol of something great achieved in the past. As a piece of art, or as action or literature, it comes to remind us of the truly lofty and great state of life. Thus nostalgia sets in as if we are touched by the half-calls of a dream, remembered after waking, and we work to attain that state. These achievements in culture help us. So do religion and philosophy and art. Our rigorous training in them dispels the false coating on our soul caused by false impressions, false education and insincere surroundings. We come to be more and more natural. We lose tensions and finally become ourselves. This becoming ourselves is nothing but getting ourselves freed of various fears and impositions. We feel its throb. Its voice comes clear to us. When this stage is reached the old symbols of culture religion, art, etc. no more fascinate us. They have no purpose for us since a return home has been celebrated, and as with all such returns the first passion is of productivity. A whole treasure is discovered within which seeks to express itself. The soul thus realized no more requires the old symbols but has acquired a new thirst to approach light and seek it all by itself. Thus the lover in the soul comes to cry like the seer in the Upanishads for the uncovering of the fine veils of culture, religion and all other known symbols which have been handed down to posterity. It is not that the symbols have been found false, or that a revolt against them has occurred. Their truth remains since they helped the human soul to be itself, to reach and feel itself. Only they are no longer of any use, since the craving for light is of the soul, not of the mind for the lost soul. There are no longer any clouds on the soul, perceived painfully by the mind. The soul cries for light, and like all things original it directly approaches the original source of light instead of feeling satisfied with culture, religion and other expressions of it. It does not condemn them, but before its subtleness and deeper freedom they too now appear only as veils. The dance of Salome is at an end, and the seventh veil is being removed.

It is in this sense that even culture comes to be dropped at the highest stages. We become free of its fascination. Culture develops direct intimacy with truth and light so that it does not bind us with its lustre in the same way as the falling plumes do not bind a peacock in his dancing ecstasy. We admire culture but we have crossed the stage when we were obsessed by it, the stage when our soul was not developed enough to have direct communion with light, and knew only culture as the first representative of light.

Life is nothing but a continuous winning of different stages of freedom. It is by gradual winning and submission, by achieving victories through noble disciplines, in the light of the best calls of our soul, that we reach a stage where all fineness, all great symbols and reminders of light become all too familiar. The only true condition of life is constant emancipation, a continuous rise from the subtler to the still subtler. It is thus that our soul becomes free of weight and grossness, the causes of cynicism and decadence. We rise to attain our lost homestead and finally come to be one with the very light that permeates and explains all.

Culture cannot be anything except the movement of everything in us towards light. We have not only to cleanse the conscious but also the unconscious in order to be true children of light. The various types of barriers among persons are often due to the various kinds of suppressions and divisions between their conscious self and the unconscious. When these barriers are broken, the waters flow and in the light of truth they become understandable. If culture were to be only the preparation of an outer crust of consciousness according to certain ideals and notions of perfection then it would be nothing but a hopeless life-long exercise, not bringing any gains to life. Whenever we withdraw application of these external ideals, we shall degenerate into barbarians. On the contrary, if our effort is to inform ourselves in the very depth and to unfold ourselves, we shall not find life so heavy and unpleasant but an ever new expression of the finest and the most subtle.

Living in society man has an implicit urge to measure upto its expectations. Often those expectations are ruthless and not formed on a proper and sympathetic understanding. They are creations of double standards. Those expectations only embody the cherished notions of a higher life. The well-meaning individual comes and sacrifices himself for them only to gain bitterness and disintegration of his personality. He suppresses that within him which does not conform to those expectations. Such suppression never brings us to any happiness or fulfilment. It is possible for the individual to attain even higher ends than those embodied in the expectations of society. But this can be done only by realizing a freedom within, so that values and the urge to realize them may grow within. This harmony between the inner and the outer self is the first achievement on the road to true culture.

The first and foremost task of culture is the creation of an integrated personality, by bringing everything to expression and by raising everything at the same time to the eternal and the supreme.

One of the biggest tragedies of modern life is the creation of split personalities on a vast scale. There are several reasons for this. One, of course, is the peculiar and unnatural condition of our present-day over-technical society. The second important reason is the willing surrender of the individual to this society, a desire to accommodate himself in it rather than question and trust his inner self. We run for the primitive people and seek company among people belonging to a lower degree of mind and spirit, because in our broken image we find only horror and hollowness, and in them we find the charm of a natural warmth. The real cure for the modern man is to attain harmony within.

The disintegration of the individual has given rise to so many false systems of values, vitiation of tastes, and unnatural and unbalanced standard everywhere. The values represent one of the two selves which torments the other. On the one hand we have become rigid adherents to purely abstract ideas of rectitude and morality, living with no real sympathy with actual life. On the other hand we simply revolt against everything and indulge in a shameless display of vulgarity and cynicism.

Culture aims at bringing this cleavage to a close. It is as integrated wholes that we become the epitome of nature, the proper recipients of its joys and sorrows, which lie spread in the common objects of daily life.

TO REMOVE THE GOLDEN DISC OF CULTURE

It has already been said that the highest ends of culture are attained in making itself superfluous. This is not a negation of culture, as celebrated by the modern freedom lovers, who have come to cast away every bondage and to consider everything, except the uninformed will, to be a bondage. The superfluity of culture comes as a natural sequence to its highest fulfilment. It is only when we have attained all the possibilities of culture in our spontaneous flow towards light and joy that culture becomes superfluous.

The highest achievements of culture would be poorer if they were understood to be perfection of our mind and behaviour alone. Such perfections are only grounds for a fully evolved and cultured life. Culture above all is a life-long struggle for freedom and light. Away from the crowd of theories and confusing alternatives, culture brings us back home. Till one has reached the stage where one can again open the confounded fountains of love and compassion, it would be vain to think that culture has been attained in any essence. To be lost in the fineness and artistry of culture itself is another snare so beloved of intellectuals, which every well-meaning individual has to conquer.

Culture is the restoration of the natural self and the attainments of its true aspirations. It is possible only when we are ourselves. It requires a higher effort to be always ourselves, in our most natural state. If love and oneness with all life are urges and ideals of the highest and most basic type, it is because they have their springs within. They are not impositions.

It is not the stuffing of ourselves with external material, howsoever lofty and fine, that is the work of culture. Anybody who thinks so is thinking of secondary and superficial ends. It is only the unfolding of the natural treasures within, allowing the natural urge to scale all the heavens in our thirst to reach out to heights that is aimed at by true culture. It is thus that culture carries within itself the seeds of its destruction. Ultimately we have to stand naked before light, not even under the fine veil of culture. It is wrong to think of culture as a fine coating on our rough nature. It is in fact the dispelling of all coatings. In its course it has to negate several false coatings with its finer and truer ones. But finally dissatisfied with all such coatings, it removes them too. Rather all such coatings vanish of themselves when the false colours are destroyed. This is attained through a gradual course with an answering call for light, more light. Anything attempted artificially and falsely would only result in the undoing of all attainments. Truly said the Isopanisad: "The face of truth is covered with a golden disc. *Hiranmayen patrena satyasya pihitam mukham.* Uncover it, O'Pushan, so that I the lover of Truth and Dharma may behold it. (*Tat tvam Pusan apavranu staya dharmaya drastaye.*)"

It is not only the alloy discs, discs of many mixed and corrupted metals, that cover the glorious face of Truth. Ultimately it is even the finest discs, the discs of pure metal, of gold itself, that have to be removed, It is dharma, culture, knowledge, all that is finest within man, that has to be removed at the highest stage. But how?

All elevated men prefer to submit to the bondage of culture even after realizing it to be merely a form, *i.e.* a face of *asat.* This discipline is necessary, for forms are also very important for life. If we discard the sweet and illuminated form, *i.e.* culture, we put life in the hands of oblivion. On the surface life is a play of desires. To subject desires to culture is the same as to infuse ideals and noble thoughts into it. This makes desires capable of fulfilling life. They do not lead it astray.

This golden veil of culture is woven out of the best fabric of space and time. Our greatest men, even those who crossed the threshold, the crossing-Makers and the Buddhas, always advocated the retention of this veil. The

Eternal Light has its own laws. Even if some soul realizes it, it cannot be expressed for the benefit of the common man without the help of a form. The finer that form the better equipped it is to convey the inner experience. In the West, the aspirants to the higher life, after encountering Reality have often had an obsession to tear off all veils for they hide the Real. But the experience of men like Neitzsche proves that it is unwarranted. This in fact landed them into insanity. The veil that is hiding the Real also serves as its medium. To remove the veil altogether is to deny expression to the Real. Culture as the finest veil, being ever refined, is to be cherished and valued. Only we must not mistake it for the Real.

Even as a veil, culture is of supreme importance to man. It brings Reality in soft undertones and whispering shadows to us. It dilutes Reality to the extent our mundane existence can absorb it.

Besides, culture fulfils the inherent anthropocentric urge in man. Man's soul comprehends nothing except in the human form. Culture is man's attempt to humanize God. It is no pollution of Reality for this humanization cannot go beyond the form. None can corrupt God. Man has been trying for centuries, rather millennia, to understand the Real. This has given brith to culture. The more he uses his medium with an increasing awareness of its limitations, the more our culture grows. In India this subtle task has been performed by a countless number of selfless visionaries. It is only a foolish generation that will throw away this great gift, this wonderful web, this golden disc, *i.e.* our culture. It is our line of communication with God. It is the language that our finest men have developed to converse with God.

To remove the golden disc is therefore also to replace it immediately after. The seekers go beyond this disc to know the Real and utilize the disc in the way in which it can be of benefit. The great ones in India never tried to destroy all veils that cover the Real. Their knowledge never presumed that it could improve upon God. The veil is there because it is part of the divine scheme. All that we can do is to keep it clean. We can change it at times and colour it to meet the requirements of the day, of space and time.

9

TULSIDAS

There can be no comparison between the polished phraseology of classical Sanskrit and the rough colloquial idiom of Tulsidas's vernacular; while the antiquity of Valmiki's poem further invests it with an adventitious interest for the student of Indian history. But, on the other hand, the Hindi poem is the best and most trustworthy guide to the popular living faith of the Hindu race at the present day matter of not less practical interest than the creed of their remote ancestors—and its language, which In the course of three centuries has contracted a tinge of archaism, is a study of much importance to the philologist, as helping to bridge the chasm between the modern tongue and the mediaeval. It is also less wordy and diffuse than the Sanskrit original and, probably in consequence of its modern date, is less disfigured by wearisome interpolations and repetitions; while if it never soars so high as Valmiki in some of his best passages, it maintains a more equable level of poetic diction, and seldom sinks with him in such dreary depths of unmitigated prose. It must also be noted that it is in no sense a translation of the earlier work: the general plan and the management of the incidents are necessarily much the same, but there is a difference in the touch in every detail; and the two poems vary as widely as any two dramas on the same mythological subject by two different Greek tragedians. Even the coincidence of name is an accident; for Tulsidas himself called his poem, the *Ram-charit-manas,* and the shorter title, corresponding in characer to the "Tliad" or "Aeneid", has only been substituted by his admirers as a handier designation for a popular favourite.

The earliest notice of our author, as indeed, of all the other celebrated Vaishnave writers who flourished about the same period, *viz.* the 16th and 17th century A.D., is to be found in the *Bhakta-Mala,* or "Legends of the Saints," one of the most difficult works in the Hindi language. Its composition is invariably ascribed to Nabha Ji, himself one of the leaders of the reform which had its centre at Vrindavan; but the poem, as we now have it, was avowedly edited, if not entirely written, by one of his disciples named Narayan Das who lived during the reign of Shahjahan. A single stanza is all that is ordinarily devoted to each personage, who is panegyrized with reference to his most salient characteristics in a style that might be described as of unparalleled obscurity, were it not that each such separate portion of the text is followed by a *tika,* or gloss, written by one Priya Das in the *Samvat* year 1769 (A.D. 1713) in which confusion is still worse confounded by a series of the most disjointed and inexplicit allusions to different legendary events in the saint's life.

Professor Wilson, in his most valuable and interesting "Essay on the Religious Sects of the Hindus," gives the following notice of Tulsidas, and adds that he had derived it from the *Bhakta-Mala:* "Having been incited to the peculiar adoration of Rama by the remonstrances of his wife, to whom he was passionately attached, he adopted a vagrant life, visited Benares, and afterwards went to Chitrakut, where he had a personal interview with Hanuman, from whom he received his poetical inspiration and the power of working miracles. His fame reached Delhi, where Shahjahan was emperor. The monarch sent for him to produce the person of Rama, which Tulsidas refusing to do, the king threw him into confinement. The people of the vicinity, however, speedily petitioned for his liberation as they were alarmed for their own security, myriads of monkeys having collected about the prison and begun to demolish it and the adjacent buildings. Shahjahan set the poet at liberty and desired him to solicit some favour as a reparation for the indignity he had suffered. Tulsidas accordingly requested him to quit ancient Delhi, which was the abode of Rama: and in compliance with this request the emperor left it and founded the new city, thence named Shahjahanabad. After this Tulsidas went to Vrindavan, where he had an interview with Nabha Ji; he settled there and strenuously advocated the worship of Sita-Rama, in preference to that of Radha-Krishna."

In addition to his great work, Tulsidas composed at least six other poems, all of them having the one object of popularising the cult of his tutelary divinity. They are the *Ramgitavali,* the *Dohavali*, the *Kabil-Sambandh*, the *Binay Patrika* the *Satsai* and the *Ram Agya*. All of these have been published, either at Lucknow or Benares, within the last few years, and all now for the first time, excepting the *Binay Patrika,* which was printed in good type by Sri Lallu Ji for the use of the college of Fort William as far back as the year 1826; but copies of this first edition are now very scarce. The list is not unfrequently extended by the addition of the following minor works, as to the genuineness of which there is considerable doubt, viz., the *Rama-Salaka,* the *Hanuman Bauka,* the *Janaki Mangal,* the *Parvati Mangal,* the *Karka Chhand,* the *Rora Chhand* and the *Jhulna Chhand*. An autograph manuscript of the *Ram Agya* was preserved in the temple of Sita-Ram at Benares, which Tulsidas had himself founded, till the Mutiny, but was then lost.

His theological and metaphysical views are pantheistic in character, being based for the most part on the teaching of the later Vedantists as formulated in the *Vedanta-Sara* and more elaborately expounded in the *Bhagavad-Gita,* Which is the most popular of all Sanskrit didactic poems. The whole visible world, as they maintain, is an unreal phantasm, induced by ignorance or illusion, and it is only by a concession to conventional speech that it can be said to exist at all. The sole representative of true existence is the supreme spirit, Brahman, conceived as an absolute and unchangeable unity; invisible, eternal and all-pervading, but having no relation to the world—since that would involve a notion of daulism—and for the same reason void of cognition, will, activity and all other qualities; a potentiality, in the ordinary use of language, rather than an actual entity. All phenomena, whether material or spiritual, including even the gods of Vedic mythology, are simply fictions of the mind. But the worship of the inferior divinities and compliance with the external ritual of religion, are considered to purify and prepare the intellect for the reception of higher truths. They are, therefore, salutary and even necessary practices during the early days of the soul's progress towards perfection. If a man is overtaken by death before he has advanced beyond this preliminary stage, he is born again either into this or into a higher world in some different form, the dignity of which is determined by the aggregate merit or demerit of all actions in all his previous births. The highest reward for devotion to any special god is the exaltation of the soul to his particular sphere in heaven. But this blessedness is not of permanent duration: on the expiry of a proportionate period the burden of mundane existence has again to be undergone. It is only on the attainment of perfect knowledge that final emancipation is complete and the individual soul is absorbed for ever into Impersonal:

A spiritual star—wrought in a rose
Of light in Paradise, whose only self
Is consciousness of glory wide diffused.

Except to a theosophist, the promise of such an ultimate destiny is not a very attractive one, nor is it conducive to popular morality. For good deeds and evil deeds and the god that recompenses them, all alike belong to the unreal, to the fictitious duality, the world of semblances; while the so-called Supreme Being is no proper object of worship, being a mere cold abstraction, unconscious of His own existence or of ours,and devoid of all attributes and qualities. To correct this practical defect and supply some intelligible motive for with standing temptation and leading a pure and holy life, the supplementary doctrine of *Bhakti,* or Faith, was developed. Some one of the recognized incarnations of the Hindu pantheon was no longer regarded as a partial emanation of the divinity, but as exalted into the complete embodiment of it. A loving devotion to his personality was then enjoined as a simple and certain method of attaining to endless felicity; not the transitory sensual delights of Indra's paradise, nor the mere unconsciousness of utter extinction, but the conscious enjoyment of individual immortality in the immediate presence of the Beatific Vision.

The late introduction of this crowning dogma of Faith in an incarnate Redeemer and its marked similarity to Christian ideas have induced several scholars to surmise that the brahmanas borrowed it from the early Christian communities in Southern India. The notion is favoured—if not, indeed, originated—by the fact that in the *Bhagavad-Gita* it is Krishna who figures as the embodiment of the Supreme Being, and both in the name and in the legends of Krishna there is a superficial resemblance to the name of Christ and to some of the incidents recorded of Him in the Gospels. As I have shown more fully elsewhere, there is no historical basis for the supposed connection, while the similarity of name is demonstrably accidental. The doctrine appears to have grown up as a natural sequel to the purely indigenous school of thought in which we find it established, and an exact parallel can be traced in the history of Buddhism, where the nihilism of Nirvana was practically abrogated by the gradual deification of its teacher. In selecting Rama as his ideal of the divine in preference to Krishna, Tulsidas has certainly improved upon the teaching of the *Bhagavata*.

The tendency of modern scientific thought is setting strongly in favour of the Vedantist theory; as declaring the existence from all eternity of a personal God to be simply unknowable and referring all phenomena to a strange mysterious energy, or will, that pervades all nature, that produces all the work done on the face of the earth, and is probably at the root of life itself; invisible and insensible, and exhibited only in its effects. Such a theory—as we see from our author's own case—is by no means incompatible with a belief in a divine incarnation: the difficulty is to establish by historical proof that such and such a character—Rama or Krishna, or whoever it may be—was really born out of the ordinary course of nature, really performed the marvellous acts ascribed to him for the deliverance of the saints the overthrow of the wicked and the establishment of righteousness, and having accomplished them was again taken up into the heaven from which he came. The whole of Tulsidas's *Ramayana* is a passionate protest against the virtual atheism of philosophical Hindu theology.

The problem that confronted him is the very same that now most exercises the thought of the nineteenth century. If the Supreme Being is a personal God, he must be limited by the conditions of personality, and can neither be omniscient nor omnipotent. If, on the other hand, the Deity is an omnipresent, all-pervading impersonality, how can any special relation be developed between such an abstraction and the individual soul? The difficulty is one that has its root in the nature of things; and no solution of the mystery can be found but in the recognition of faith and reason as two distinct human faculties, with the infinite and the finite as their separate provinces. In the words of Saint Ambrose *non in dialectica complacuit Deo solxum facere populum suum* (God would not be adorable if he were not incomprehensible): and a religion that does not transcend man's understanding is not, strictly speaking, a religion at all. A just discrimination of good and evil and a sound code of morality are not beyond the compass of natural intelligence; but the rites and mysteries of religion can only be learnt by a direct revelation from God and through the action of His grace. Their acceptance by faith, even when they seem to conflict with reason, is a part of our earthly probation and a meritorious confession of our dependence on the Supreme.

The final purpose of the Incarnation, like the idea of any revelation whatever from God to man, is above comprehension. The fact of the divine message having been sent may be reasonably established by historical evidence, but the tenor of the message transcends argumentative discussion, and demands nothing short of implicit and absolutely unquestioning submission. For the dogmas of revealed religion must, *ex-hypothesi*, be incomprehensible mysteries. If they were ascertainable by the ordinary processes of reason it would not be consistent with the economy of the universe to communicate them by the special vehicle of revelation. A professedly revealed religion, which is demonstrable and intelligible throughout, stands self-convicted as a human invention.

The words "Blind are the eyes which deem the Unmanifested manifest" emphatically condemn the worship of any incarnation, on the ground that it involves an inadequate conception of the Deity. Tulsidas, on the other hand, insists that they derogate from the divine perfection, who divest it of personality and reduce it to an abstraction. Against such theologians he hotly protests as when he cried (VII *Chhand 5*)—"Let them preach in their wisdom who contemplate Thee as the Supreme Spirit, the Uncreate, inseparable from the universe, recognizable only by inference and beyond the understanding; but we, O Lord! will ever hymn the glories of Thy incarnation." Nor does he want supporters even in this nineteenth century, who give the same answer to the old question "Can the attribute of personality be ascribed to the Absolute?" Thus Lotze, in his *Outlines of the Philosophy of Religion,* argues as follows: "If all the predicates of unconditionateness are to be valid for the highest being, then one condition of this validity lies precisely in the addition of a last formal predicate, viz. that of personal existence. All hindrances of perfect personality we can imagine as not existent in the Infinite Spirit. On this account we conclude with the assertion—which is exactly the opposite of the customary one—that Perfect Personality is reconcilable only with the conception of an Infinite Being; for finite beings only an approximation to this is attainable."

The introductory portion of the first Book of the *Ramayana* is curious as containing the author's vindication of his literary style as against his critics, the pendants. They attacked him for lowering the dignity of his subject by clothing it in the vulgar vernacular. However just his defence may be, it has not succeeded in converting the opposite faction: and the professional Sanskrit pandits who are its modern representatives, still affect to despise his work as an unworthy concession to the illiterate masses. With this small and solitary exception, the book is in every one's hands, from the court to the cottage, and is read, or heard, and appreciated alike by every class of the Hindu community; whethere high or low, rich or poor, young or old.

The second Book is more generally read than any other part of the poem, and is the most admired by Hindu crities. The description of King Dasharatha's death and the different, leave-takings are quoted as models of the pathetic, and in a public recital there is scarcely one in the audience, who will not be moved to tears. The sentiments that the poet depicts, and the figures that he employs to illustrate them, appeal with irresistible force to the Hindu imagination; and, if for no other reason than this, they would be interesting to the English student for the insight they afford into the traditional sympathies and antipathies of the people.

The Hindi *Ramayana* has many passages that are instinct with a genuine poetic feeling, which appeal to universal humanity, and which it is hoped will be dimly recognised even through the ineffectual medium of a prose translation. The characters also of the principal actors in the drama are clearly and consistently drawn; and all may admire, though they refuse to worship, the piety and unselfishness of Bharata; the enthusiasm and high courage of Lakshmana; the affectionate devotion of Sita, that paragon of all wife-like virtues; and the purity, meekness, generosity and self-sacrifice of Rama, the model son, husband and brother, "the guileless king, high, self-contained and passionless—the Arthur of Indian chivalry."

In the later Books, the narrative is generally more rapid than that in the earlier part of the poem, and several incidents are so casually mentioned that, without the explanatory references to the Sanskrit *Ramayana*, a literal rendering would convey no meaning to the ordinary reader. It is to some extent a literary defect that the role of poet is so often dropped for that of theologian; and the frequent hymns of Rama, who is apostrophized under every conceivable name that can help to realise to the mind the mystery of incarnate divinity, soon become wearisome. But the object that Tulsidas had in view is his sufficient excuse. By the course that he has adopted, fitting his special doctrines of faith, individual immortality and the like into the familiar frame-work of ancient legend, instead of inculcating them by a more strictly didactic method, he has succeeded in popularizing his views to a far greater extent than any of the rival Hindu reformers, who flourished about the same period. It was their object also to simplify the complications and correct the abuses of existing practice, but the only result of their preaching was to establish yet another element of dissension and augment the disorder which they hoped to remove. Tulsidas alone, though the most famous of them all, has no disciples that are called after his name. There are Vallabhacharis and Radha Vallabhis and Maluk Dasis and Pran Nathis, and so on, in interminable succession, but there are no Tulsidasis. Virtually, however, the whole of Vaishnava Hinduism has fallen under his sway; for the principles that he expounded have permeated every sect and explicitly or implicitly now form the nucleus of the popular faith as it prevails throughout the whole of the Bengal Presidency from Hardwar to Calcutta.

10

CHAITANYA AND MIRABAI

In the fourteenth century, the classics and the philosophies receded into the background. Even the Puranas by themselves did not meet the requirements of the people. And the cult of *bhakti* became the most potent factor in the Puranic movement, stimulating an intensely devotional attitude towards the gods and particularly Sri Krishna.

I

Sri Krishna was the first to become the centre of a great devotional impulse. He occupies the highest place in the Indian pantheon; in poetry, the supreme love; in religion, he is God himself; and in philosophy, the all-pervading Over-soul, Parabrahman. He is the One who delivered the message of the *Bhagavad-Gita,* the most popular and profound scripture in a land of conflicting scriptures, which has inspired the life and thought of great Indians from Shankara to Tilak, Sri Aurobindo and Mahatma Gandhi, among the moderns. He has fired the imagination of almost every Indian poet since the *Bhagavad* was composed (c. 8th century). And as the very embodiment of triumphant manhood, he has brought inspiration and solace to millions for centuries.

In the *Rig-Veda,* Vishnu, the Sun-god was the omniscient, *trivikramo visvasya,* and Varuna, the Sky-god, was the king of heavens, *bhuvanasya raja.* Later, *Aitareya Brahmana* elevated Vishnu to the position of the greatest of gods, and the Vedic myths connected with other gods were transferred to him. *Taittiriya Aranyaka* identified him with Narayana, an ancient Rishi, who, as an incarnation of Vishnu, was worshipped by a sect known as Pancharatra

When the original *Bhagavad-Gita* was composed, Sri Krishna, the Yadava hero, had already been accepted as the avatar of Vishnu who had revealed his macrocosmic form (*virat-svarupa)* to Arjuna. All these different attributes came to be transferred to one deity, the god Vasudeva, whose worship was common even in the days of the grammarian Panini (e. B.C. 500). Bhagavan Vasudeva's devotees came to be known as Bhagavatas; such a one was Heliodoros, the ambassador of a Greek king, who came to India (c. B.C. 200). The Gupta emperors were styled *Parama-bhagavatas,* the great devotees of Bhagavan, and the worship of Vishnu and his spouse Lakshmi was popular in the Gupta period.

The Vaishnava mystics and saints known as Alvars were apostles of *bhakti* before the rise of Shankara (c. 800), who refers to the worship of Parabrahman in the form of Bhagavan Vasudeva. The *Vishnu Purana* had for its object the glorification of Vishnu as Vasudeva. The God was great, the devotee, weak and helpless and prayed to his Master with humility.

This *bhakti* was invested with all the attributes of earthly love. Narada, in his *Bhaktisūtra,* defines it as of the nature of intense love. Sandilya, in his *Bhaktisutra,* explains it to be attachment towards God, which was amplified by the commentator, means love "characterized by horripilation and other signs of worldly love, like the love felt by Shakuntala for Dushyanta". The new *bhakti* was an emotion which impelled the *bhakta,* the devotee, to worship the Lord, to seek him everywhere, to yearn for him, to quarrel with him, to remove the distance which reverence implies, in short, to love him passionately as one would a human lover. This new emotion led the national imagination, before c. 800, to create Radha, the eternal bride of Sri Krishna, more human and lovable than the majestic Lakshmi or Rukmini of the Puranas. In *Dhvanyaloka* (c. 850) she shares the incense with Krishna; about 980 she is mentioned as his spouse in an inscription of king Amoghavarsha of Dhara.

In the *Bhagavata Purana,* composed sometime between c. 600 and c. 800, prominence is given to the intense lovability of Krishna as a superb child, youth, lover, statesman and seer, being God Himself. This was an epoch-making work; it soon acquired predominant influence in the country, as much through its being the gospel of the new emotion as by its rare literary charm. Its sentiments and turns of expression were soon carried to the doors of every villager by the *pauranikas* in all provinces. Puru *bhakti* is beautifully expressed in the *Bhagavata*:

"As the wingless nestlings wait for the mother, as the hungry calves long to be suckled, as the love-lorn damsel waits for her lover, so lotus-eyed, does my mind yearn for thee.... To hear about Vishnu, to sing of Him, to remember Him, to fall at His feet, to worship Him, to bow to Him, to serve Him, to be His friend, to dedicate oneself to Him, is the nine-fold *bhakti*."

To the *gopis* (says Krishna): "The nights when I, their lover, went about with them in Vrindavan, were like flitting moments, but when I left them, their nights were endless as cycles....In this way, hundreds who knew not My real Self loved Me only as their Lover, and attained Me, the Parabrahman."

The literary range and richness of the *Bhagavata Purana* at places reaches the inspired directness of the *Bhagavad-Gita*. Its powerful influence can be traced over the religious and secular art and literature of the whole country. The *Panchadhyaya,* the five chapters of the *Dashama Skandha* describing the sports of Krishna with the milk-maids, is a song of everlasting joy and found expression not only in literature, but in every form of art.

The great revolution which the *Bhagavata Purana* made in the cardinal doctrine of Vedanta "was to transfer the emphasis from knowledge, yoga and surrender to God to the passionate and intense love for Sri Krishna who, is human form, was not an incarnation but God Himself". It is one of the greatest devotional scriptures of the world.

Thus, the Puranic movement, leavened by *bhakti*, captured the religious thought and sentiment of the age.

II

Long before the tenth century *bhakti* had taken hold of the South. Temples had been raised to Vishnu and Sankarshana. The twelve Vaishnava mystics and saints, known as Alvars, were wandering singers "mad after God"; one of them was a prince, another a beggar, a third a woman, a fourth an untouchable. According to the *bhakti* of Narayana which they followed and taught, God was accessible by intense love and complete selfsurrender to all, irrespective of rank or caste or even culture. Their devotional songs became popular under the name of the *Vaishnava Veda*, the scriptures of the Vishnu cult.

After the Alvars came the Acharyas, who gave it a philosophic basis. In c. 1000, Yamunacharya propounded the doctrine of *prapatti,* surrender to God; his great-grandson Ramanuja, who succeeded him, gave a complete philosophic background to the movement, and elevated it to the level of a monothistic religion. The influence of the *Bhagavata,* after the *Ramayana* and the *Mahabharata* the most potent source of inspiration in India, led to the foundations of different schools of *bhakti* under five great saints. These great philosopher-saints, by their learning, devotion and dialectic skill, founded new schools of thought; and the linguistic and intellectual unity which Sanskrit imparted made it easy for them to introduce a new outlook in the religious and moral life of India. To them we owe the ubiquity of Krishna-consciousness in the country. About 1150, Nimbarka founded a new school in Telangana stressing the pure *bhakti* of Sri Krishna and Radha. "We worship," says he, "Radha, the daughter of Vrishabha, the goddess who joyfully adorns the left lap of the great deity Sri Krishna, as beautiful as Sri Krishna himself, surrounded by thousands of damsels. She it is who fulfils all desires." Madhwa (c. 1199-1278) laid the foundation of a yet more vigorous Vaishnava cult.

Vishnuswami, said to be a teacher of Juaneshvara and accepted by Vallabha as his guru, appears to be a powerful teacher-saint of the Radha-Krishna cult though little is known about him. The Maharashtra school of *bhakti*, however, headed by Jnaneshvara, Namdev, Eknath, and later Tukaram, worship Krishna and his spouse Rukmini. Their *bhakti* has for its symbol the pure and serene love of the husband and wife (*kanta bhava*), not the temptations of love of Krishna and Radha (*madhura bhava*). Chaitanya was as much the producer of *bhakti* as of the latest Buddhistic influences in Bengal.

In the tenth century, decadent Buddhism under the influence of Kahna Bhatta, a great scholar and poet of Bengal, preached illicit love and complete bodily and mental surrender to the teacher as the only way to emancipation. The Radha-Krishna romance had already obtained a hold over the popular mind through folk-songs and festivals. Both these currents combined to strengthen the *bhakti* of Sri Krishna. Umapati, in the eleventh century, and Jayadeva, the author of the *Gita-Govinda*, in the twelfth, wrote highly artistic and sensuous poems of Sri Krishna. The linguistic, rhythmic and sentimental graces of *Gita-Govinda* caught the imagination and all *bhaktas* in the country, and within a century of its composition, it was recognised as a classic.

III

In the 15th century, the Sultanate of Delhi was spreading destruction in the holy places in the North. Still, in Vrindavan, where Shri Krishna spent His childhood with the *gopis*, the heart of India was throbbing. Wherever the songs of Radha-Krishna were sung—and they were sung in all parts of India—or, wherever Vishnu was worshipped and the *Bhagavad-Gita* or the *Bhagavata* recited, Vrindavan was the living symbol of joy in this life and of salvation in the next.

Pilgrims were drawn to it from all parts of the country from generation to generation, particularly in the holy month of *Bhadrapada*,—in north India (Shravan in western India)—in which Sri Krishna was born.

In the fourteenth century, at Navadvipa (Nadia) an ancient centre of learning in Bengal, some schools of the later Buddhism preached love as the one avenue leading to Final Emancipation. That part of the country also rang with the passionate love-songs of one of the greatest of Indian poets. Chandidasa.

During the reign of Sikandar Lodi, Madhavendrapuri, a *dashnami sannyasi*, and a disciple of Madhwa, came with the lyrics of Chandidasa ringing in his ears to Vrindavan. On the banks of the Yamuna, in the sacred groves, hallowed by the divine romance of Radha and Sri Krishna, the learned sadhu wandered like a maiden in love, singing songs and seeking His love.

Madhavendra's ardent love fused his learning and devotion into a flame and gave new vitality to the devotional schools of Bengal. He built a temple in Vrindavan which attracted *bhaktas* from Bengal.

IV

Vishvambhara or Nimai, as he was affectionately called, was born in February 1486 to a pious and learned brahmana of Nadia. As he grew up into a handsome, impetuous and brilliant youth, he evoked universal admiration. He married and settled down, running *a tol.*

A few years later, when Nimai went to Gaya to perform his father's obsequial ceremonies, Ishvara Puri, a disciple of Madhavendra, initiated him into the mysteries of *bhakti.* Nimai was stirred to his depths; mystic visions awoke in him the love of Sri Krishna. Pride fell from him and so did he lure of the world. "Leave me," he said, "I am not of the world. I will go to Vrindavan and meet my Lord."

Like a love-lorn, heart-broken maid, pining for Sri Krishna, he sang of the Lord, danced for Him, fainted, overborne by the pangs of separation, often went into an ecstatic trance. His mother thought he was mad. But the devotees knew better. "He was a God," they said.

A band of devotees soon gathered round this young, god-like saint and went with him from place to place. He led the devotional *kirtans* in the course of which he and his followers sang and danced ceaselessly to the accompaniment of music. Nimai became intoxicated with God and his followers saw in him Sri Krishna Himself.

Nimai took *sannyasa* in 1510 under the name of Krishna Chaitanya and sent his follower, Lokanatha, to make Vrindavan the centre of *bhakti.* After a short stay at Puri, he went on an all-India tour, visiting the shrines and holy places dedicated to Sri Krishna. Wherever he went, his inspiring presence and flaming love for Sri Krishna set fire to the hearts of those who came to him.

Wherever he went men followed him. Scholars wedded to Vedanta became his devotees; rich men provided him and his party with every facility and kings built temples wherever he halted.

Ultimately, in obedience to the wishes of his mother, he went to live at Puri. From time to time congregations of his followers thered there from all parts of India. Chaitanya's *kirtan* parties led through the streets of the town became the great attraction.

V

Two eminent officers of the Nawab of Gaud—Sakar Malik and Dabir Khan—met Chaitanya on one of his tours and were so much impressed by the saint the they left their positions, their wealth and their faith, and, by the orders of the Master came to live in Vrindavan under the names of Sanatana and Rupa.

In about 1506 Vallabhacharya Goswami, who was more of a scholar than *bhakti,* founded a shrine of Shrinathji in Vrindavan. He established the cult of *Pushtimarga* which was later to inspire the poetry of the eight poets, headed by the immortal Surdas.

On April 27, 1526, Babar made Delhi the seat of his newly conquered kingdom, and the holy places of India saw comparative peace.

In 1556, Akbar the Great became the Mughal Emperor and a new age dawned on India. The foreigner became a national monarch, establishing those eatholic traditions which brought the *Bhakti* Renaissance into spring-time bloom.

With unparalleled statesmanship, Akbar removed the disabilities under which the Hindus had been suffering. He visited Vrindavan, and Man Singh, his favourite general, became the disciple of Jiva Goswami, the nephew of the Goswamis, Rupa and Sanatana. It was under his inspiration that the temple of Govindji was built—a temple which still stands intact as a symbol of the power which was Chaitanya and a living testimony to Akbar's greatness.

VI

Mankind has never seen such love as was Chaitanya's. The individual love of Sappho, Mira, Helois and Laila, are but faint echoes of his. None of them had such a love-lorn heart. To none was the lover—in his case Sri Krishna—so ever-present. His emotion had the quality of giving power, light and feeling to whatever it touched. Dances and songs, prayers and *kirtan* dedicated to Sri Krishna, swept the country with an emotional flood, which was as lyrical as it was ennobling.

Chaitanya never taught and but rarely entered into philosophic discussion; nor did he make efforts to gain disciples. When he died in 1533, it was his personality and experiences rather than his teachings which became the inspiration of the *bhakti* movements. They released new creative forces in Vrindavan; in the rest of India their influence opened the flood-gates of a sweeping religious urge, by direct influence, or indirect impact.

Like a mighty flood, *bhakti,* as reintegrated by Chaitanya, surged round the love of Radha and Krishna. It entered deep into the popular consciousness, intensifying the emotional awareness of fresh joys. It won liberalising triumphs of the heart over the bondage and suffering which political slavery and social rigidity had imposed upon the country. It imparted freshness to life, creative power to literature and richness to human relations, till poets in many parts of India echoed to the sentiment:

To Vraja alone shall I hie;
But never to Heaven:
For there I cannot meet
Nanda's son, my Darling.

Even now, as we know, in many parts of the country men and women congregate, join with song, music and dance, in the *kirtans* to experience the ecstatic glow of a joy which knows neither sin nor suffering.

VII

Thus, *bhakti* grew into the most creative force in the country, bringing joy to every home and revitalising the Aryan culture. The new *bhakti* impulse spread from Vrindavan into Gujarat in the sixteenth century, and, perhaps, the two greatest *bhakti* poets of Gujarat, Mirabai and Narasimh Mehta, were influenced by the sadhus and *bhaktas* of this seet.

Mirabai, the greatest poetess of Western India, was a grand-daughter of Rau Dadaji, Chief of Medta, a small principality in Rajputana. She was born about the year 1500, and her grandfather, a devout Vaishnava, influenced her mind from her earliest years. She was married to Bhojaraj, the son of Rana Sanga of Chitod, but he died c. 1517. In 1532, Sanga's younger son, Vikram, came to the throne of Chitod, which was then suffering from the after-effects of Sanga's unsuccessful was with Babar, the founder of the Mughal empire.

The widowed princess forgot the world in the worship of Krishna. Surrounded by sadhus and *bhaktas,* she prayed incessantly, singing devotional songs composed by herself. Her association with sadhus offended the Rana's sense of propriety, and he tried to put a stop to it by persecution. But Mira's attitude was unyielding.

"Girdhar Gopal is mine and none also. I have left mother, father, and brother; in company of saints, I have lost all sense of shame. I run to welcome saints; I weep, looking at the world. I have reared an immortal creeper of *bhakti*, watering it with tears of love..... The thing has gone forth; every one knows it. Mira, the slave of Girdhar, says what was to happen has happened."

And in one of her beautiful *padas* she addresses the Rana thus:

"Ranaji! What can I do? My love for Krishna is eternal. Rana of Mevad! What can I do? I am so tempted. My heart is at peace only when I worship my Rama; otherwise, I cannot even sleep. The double rosary on my neck is to me a lovely ornament. How can I forget my Lord, my bridegroom in all my past lives?"

The Rana even made an attempt to kill her. Rajput standards had condemned her as a disgrace to the family. In her waking hours, she was a love-lorn cowherdess, beloved of her Lover, living in the imaginary world of Vrindavan.

"No one knows the pain I feel. No, none. The wounded and the suffering alone know the plight of the wounded. Like a fish, I am dying for water. I lie on a bed made of throns. Mira's pain will cease only when the physician, Samala, Dark One, comes."

Krishna is a living lover to her. She visits Vrindavan and yearns to see him. She hears the flute as its notes rise to the sky. He stops her on the way, taking the toll of curds as from other *gopis*. She plays with him, dances the *rasa* with him. She pines away; she is reminiscent. "I am mad with love and no one knows it." She is fascinated with Krishna's face.

"I love your face. Enchanting one, I love your face. I saw your face and the world has become repulsive. My mind has been different since then."

Her longing is acute.

"Kanhu does not know of my love—my virgin love for Him. We went to fetch water from Jamuna, he sprayed us with water there. And the spray was all about us."

The Beloved held a *rasa* in Vrindavan; he pulled off the raiment of sixteen hundred *gopis*. And the raiment was torn to shreds.

"Kanhu! I am mad after you; you have shot your arrows at me; and the arrows have pierced me through and through."

Bai Mira says: "Lord Girdhar, Kanhu has burnt her to death; He has thrown her ashes from a high hill. And the ashes are flying about on all sides."

Again she sings:

"My Girdhar, my Lover, my beloved handsome Dark One! Do not forsake us. You have gone to dwell in Mathura, but do not be curel..... Your flute is still heard; its echoes are about us. Without you the pathways of Vraja are hateful."

So many stories are told about her that it is difficult to ascertain the facts. But one of her *bhajans* sums up her adventures.

"Govinda is my souls. The world repels me; I love only my Ramaji—I know no other. Saints devoted to Hari live in the palace of Mira. Hari lives away from the deceitful; but He lives beside my saints."

Ranaji sends a letter. "Go, and give it into the hands of Mira. 'Leave off the company of sadhus; come and live with me."

Mirabai sends a reply. "Go, and give it into the hands of Ranaji. 'Let go your throne and kingdom; come and live with my sadhus'."

Rana sends a cup of poison, "Go, and give it into the hands of Mira." Mira drank it as if it were nectar; the Lord of the Universe protected her.

"Camelman! Get the camel ready. I have to go a hundred *koshas*. It is sinful even to take water in the kingdom of the Rana." Mira left Mevad and went to the west. She gave up all, for her mind was not with the world.

Mira is the beloved of Hari; she lives in the service of His saints. She likes the company of the holy; her heart is a way from that deceitful person.

Thus Mira came to live at Dwaraka in Kathiawad. After her departure, Chitod fell on evil days. Its throne changed hands at short intervals. Ultimately, the ruling prince traced its misfortunes to Mira's departure from Chitod, and begged her to come back. Mirabai declined to return; but the unfortunate prince wanted her back at any cost. The brahmanas entered upon a fast in order to induce her to come. Moved by this, Mira went into the temple to ask leave of her Lord; she did it with tears in her eyes, singing her songs; and as she sang, she was merged in the idol of her Lord (c. 1547).

Mira is claimed by Gujarat; Rajputana and the whole of the Mathura region and recently the Hindi speaking world as a Hindi poet. But, during the century in which she lived there was only one language in these parts, Old Gujarati or Old Western Rajasthani, and it is no wonder that her *padas* are now found in all the different present-day varieties of that language. She has not left any long poem; a large number of the *padas* which bear her name are not authentic; but some definitely bear the impress of her pure, noble and loving personality. Her language is simple and appealing.

She has only one thing to say, and, in consequence, her range is limited. Her poems have elegance and delicacy rather than variety. Her heart is capable of deep feeling, but its expression is limited by her comparative ignorance. Mira is not ego-centric, only intense: not voluptuous, nor profound.

But passion, grace, delicacy, melody—Mira has all these gifts. Her longing is exquisite; it seizes all hearts, penetrates all souls. Her poetic skill possesses the supreme art of being artless. Sometimes she brings natural beauty to aid sense and sound in producing harmony. An untranslatable harmony characterizes the following:

"The peacock's notes are shrill. Radha! the peacock's notes are shrill. Peacocks call; *papaiyas* call; *koels* sing;

the sound fills the air. Lightning glistens; dark clouds thunder. Drizzling rain pours gently; and as I come to meet you the fringe of my sari is wet. Bai Mira says, this is the charm of my Lord Girdhar; My Lord has stolen my heart."

Mira's *padas,* some of which are *garabis,* have been very popular throughout Rajputana and Gujarat, and have considerably influenced the literature of succeeding periods.

11

KABIR

The fifteenth century, which covers the main period of Kabir's life, was marked by disorder and great social agitation.

Mohammad bin Tuglak (1325-1351) left the Moslem Empire in India in a state of chaos. Reducing the people to a state of great poverty and misery through his maladministration and fanatical religious intolerance, he left behind him a country in the grip of famine, plague and rebellion.

In *1398 Timur Invaded India* and put to the sword thousands of innocent men, women and children, and carried away most of the wealth of the country that he could lay his hands on. The beautiful city of Delhi was reduced to ruins; Meerut was sacked and everywhere in the north of India, through which the Moslem conqueror passed, there was nothing but ruin and chaos.

Hindu India was not shown the beautiful side of Islam. The great personality of the prophet of Arabia remained a sealed book to them. It can be imagined what they thought of Islam.

F.E. Keay gives the following account of India under Moslem rule, immediately before the birth of Kabir: "During the period of the Sultanate of Delhi, the Hindu religion had been exposed to constant danger. The more ruthless sovereigns, or governors of provinces, often carried out wholesale massacres and destroyed Hindu shrines, while even milder rulers often used force to bring about their people's conversion. The *Jiziya*, a tax on non-Mohammedans, was generally enforced......Yet in spite of persecution, Hinduism flourished....."

The destruction of their temples and the outrages on their sacred traditions by the north-western invaders did not shake the faith of the Hindus in their religion. In many instances, it was a period of great religious upheavals. The *bhakti* or devotional school of thought acquired strength and a great wave of devotion of the heart of Vishnu or Hari swept through the land.

Shankaracharya, the supreme exponent of Hinduism, had stressed the importance of *bhakti* as a means to purify the heart; but his main theme was knowledge or gnosis which alone, according to the Vedic doctrines, leads to the inner enlightenment and ultimate deliverance of the soul from the bonds of nescience.

Ramanuja (A.D. 1100), a southern teacher of great erudition and a monk of pious character, developed the school of Devotion in his commentary on the *Upanishads,* the *Gita* and the *Vyasa Sutras.* His doctrine is called *Vishishtadvaita* or qualified monism, according to which the Universe is the body of God, and His spirit animating the Universe is the Essence of man. Even in the final re-union with Hari, the spirit retains its individuality. *Sri Krishna,* the teacher of that most wonderful scripture, the *Bhagavad-Gita,* and the cowherd of Vrindavan, is regarded as the supreme incarnation of Vishnu. Rama, the ideal man and king, is also regarded as an incarnation. Man loves his personality and clings to it with tenacity. In Krishna and Rama the Hindu mind found the very ideals of perfection and wisdom that it loved.

Northern India adopted the *bhakti* school of thought, and the bleeding soul of the Hindus of that time found consolation in the wisdom of compassion, benevolence and self-surrender to Krishna or Rama. Men, women and children found aesthetic, moral and spiritual food in the personality of Krishna and received the spiritual upliftment and ecstasy which made them forget the horrors of their environment and in some cases brought real and abiding peace to their hearts. What more does the spirit of man need?

Poets of outstanding ability and of a cosmopolitan outlook on life sang of Krishna and Rama in their sweet and immortal songs in the Hindi language, the language of the masses.

Many of these spiritual singers were contemporary with Kabir, and it is certain that the child Kabir, born in 1398, heard these sweet devotional lyrics when he was rocked in the cradle by his mother.

Vidyapati, Umapati, Mirabai and others poured forth their burning love, pure as the waters of the Ganges and the Jamna, and men of every walk of life took up these songs and sang of Radha-Krishna and Sita-Ram.

The school of *bhakti* abolished the rigid caste rules, and it was commonly held that anybody who worshipped God belonged to God—irrespective of his caste and birth.

Jat pant puchhe na koi
Har Ko bhaje so karka hoi.

A shoe-maker, Rai Das, was hailed as a saint and worshipped by all on account of his self-transcending love of God.

The Hindu saint whose influence moulded the life of Kabir was Ramananda (1400-1447). A great teacher was Swami Ramananda. His body life was a source of inspiration to many. Among his disciples were numbered Sena, a barbar, Dhanna, a peasant, and Rai Das, a leather worker.

Having travelled through Northern India teaching the doctrine of devotion, *karma,* reincarnation and personal piety, Ramananda lived in the holy city of Kashi (Benares) when Kabir was a child. Hundreds flocked to him every morning to join him in his devotion.

One of the results of the contact of Hinduism and Islam was the development of the Sufi school in Islam, which was free from fanaticism and had a close resemblance to the system of Ramanuja. The Sufi singers mixed freely with the Hindu *bhaktas* and fraternised with men of other cults.

Though the India of the time of Kabir was characterised by misrule and chaos, yet there was great religious activity and literary upheaval in the vernacular.

Benaras has ever been the seat of learning and religious fervour in India. Its gorgeous temples, the slow current of the Ganges, the processions of monks, the debates of schlors and the stately flights of steps cannot but impress the mind of one who lives there as well as even the casual visitor. Kabir is said to have passed his boyhood in this city of Shiva, in which Shakya Muni Buddha "turned the wheel of Law" some 1500 years before Kabir.

Like the lives of other great religious teachers of the past—excepting Mohammad—the life of Kabir is full of legends. The following account may be taken as reasonably correct. A.D. 1398 is the traditional date of the birth of the Saint Kabir. According to tradition, Kabir was born in Benares itself, though the Benares Gazetteer gives Belhara, a village in the district of Azamgarh, as the place of his birth.

A Brahmana virgin widow is said to have given birth to the child who was subsequently called Kabir. The birth is said to have been miraculous. All followers of Kabir admit that Kabir was brought up in the house of a Moslem named Nur Ali or Nura, a weaver, whose wife was named Nima. It is said that a Hindu monk named Ashtananda, who had a knowledge of the real parentage of Kabir, took care to teach him Hindu ideas and ideals when he was a child.

Kabir was a precocious child. He was sent to a Moslem teacher. But he was not satisfied with the teachings given and left him.

From his childhood the religious quest seems to have been his favourite pursuit. The traditional accounts of the birth of Creation and other such matters did not satisfy him.

Kabir Kasauti, an old work taken as authentic by the followers of Kabir, says that in his childhood he did not identify himself definitely with either Hinduism or Islam, and gave offence to many. While playing, he often cried: "Ram, Ram". or "Hari, Hari". The Moslems warned him and said that he was a kafir, an unbeliever. Kabir replied saying: "He who uses violence or rules others, who drinks intoxicants or seizes the goods of others is a kafir."

He put the *tilak* (the sacred mark) on his forehead; and used the *janeu* (sacred thread). The Brahmanas expostulated; "This is not thy religion. Thou hast made thyself a Vaishnavite and callest on Vishnu, Narayana, Hari, Govinda; this is our religion." He answered one of their leaders: "On my tongue Vishnu, in my eyes Narayana, and in my heart Govinda dwells.....My meditation is with Hari."

When Kabir was hardly a youth, Ramananda was preaching his doctrine of absorption in God through pure devotion and benevolence. Evidently Ramananda Swami was a Magnetic personality. He had thousands of selfless disciples and was held in great esteem by those who knew him. Ramananda was in love with rituals and preached *bhakti* as the means to God-realisation.

Kabir heard him in the streets of Benares and was profoundly impressed with his teachings and personality. Knowing well that a teacherless mystic is not fitted for a life of higher devotion and contemplation, Kabir applied to Ramananda for initiation. It was after hesitation and trial that Kabir was accepted as a disciple by Ramananda.

It is stated by some writers that Kabir was a Sufi and a disciple of some Moslem teacher. Professor Wilson, a great authority on the subject, does not hold this view.

Kabir served his teacher personally with devotion, and learned from him not only the theoretical side of the Hindu doctrine, but also the mystic Yoga which he seems to have practised with great patience. Kabir was not a pundit; probably he did not know Sanskrit at all. Having listened to the philosophical controversies that were held between the Benares pundits and his guru, Kabir acquired a thorough knowledge of Vedanta and Sankhya.

In his private life Kabir continued to work as a weaver, spending a part of his earnings on charity and hospitality to the sadhus and part on Nura.

Once he mysteriously disappeared for a while, then suddenly reappeared, full of light, peace and joy.

Kabir married a woman named Loi. Her name figures in many of his songs. We see a reference to Kabir's marriage in the *Adi Grantha,* the Sikh holy book :

His first wife was ugly, of low caste,
of ill-boding feature.....
The present wife is beautiful, intelligent,
of auspicious features, easily child-bearing.

(Quoted by G.H. Westcott)

There are several references by Kabir in his songs to his son (Kamal;) some traditions credit him with two sons.

During the early days of his devotion, Kabir encountered much opposition from his family. His mother often reproached him with neglecting his work and insisted on his giving up his religious devotions and study. His outspoken criticism of the rituals, of both Hinduism and Islam, brought on him the wrath of his fellow-citizens and caused annoyance to his family. After his father's death the burden of supporting the family fell on Kabir. His mother opposed him and wanted him to mind his family affairs only.

Kabir's household affairs undoubtedly suffered on a account of his devotion to religious contemplation and service of his teacher. In a verse he refers to this and says:

O thou art ever compassionate to the poor,
I have put all my family into the boat which is
under thy care.

In another verse, Kabir makes the following reference to his mother:

Kabir's mother is distressed and
weepeth, saying, O God, how
shall I support my children?
Kabir hath relinquished weaving and
has made God's houses his only support.

We find Kabir in the company of a Moslem teacher. Taqi of Jhusi, near Allahabad, participating in his devotion. Taqi gave his full spiritual blessings to Kabir and kept friendly eye on him throughtout his life, they say.

Kabir's wife, Loi, suffered for want of rice and vegetables in the household, her husband having neglected them. In fact, Kabir was passing through those mystic experiences in which the worldly objects seem to receive no attention from a mystic. She complained of the monks in whose company he passed his time. To this complaint, Kabir replied:

These devotees are the support of the drowning,
hear, O mis-guided Loi!
Kabir is under the protection of these devotees.

Kabir obtained the full inner illumination "by the grace of Guru Ramananda." Now all doubts were gone and he saw one Infinite Reality within and without. He became a saint, a liberated being. He had seen God as his own spiritual Self.

Kabir lived a life of voluntary poverty and simplicity. Having seen the eternal beauties of the inner world, the spiritual life, he was in perfect peace and joy. Nothing could add to or subtract from the spiritual joy of his God-vision. He found in the life of contemplation, as Aristotle says, all he needed. The following song is noteworthy:

Kabir says, I have neither a thatched roof, nor hut,
Neither have I a house nor a village.
I think Hari will ask "Who art thou?"
I have neither caste nor name.....
I have never been acquisitive; Thy name
alone
O Hari, is enough for me.

Kabir says : "My heart is full of happiness....." Though Kabir lived in poverty he treated his uninvited guests with hospitality. Sometimes Loi borrowed salt and rice to feed a guest. Anybody who knocked at his door was received with joy and given hospitality.

To a certain section of the people Kabir was an impostor and they treated him with contumacy.

Sometimes Kabir was called a thief pander and dancer He says:

O Ram, thou art my only refuge
I have no need to bow to any man!
I am free from fellowship or partnership
with any one.
Honour or dishonour are just the same to me.
Kabir says, the honour of Hari is
real.
O give up all, and praise only Ram.

Among the disciples of Kabir, his wife Loi, his son Kamal, and one Dharam Das are prominently mentioned. One Surat Gopal Sahib is also mentioned as one of his chief disciples.

Kabir was summoned by Sikandar Lodi, the reigning sovereign of Delhi, to answer to the charges of infidelity preferred against him both by Hindus and Moslems. The Moslems complained that the weaver outraged the ears of the faithful Moslems with his cries of "Ram, Ram," in the streets. The Hindus complained that he unlawfully used the *tilak* and *janeu* (sacred thread).

When brought before the king. Kabir refused to make obeisance.

After a short conversation, the king was convinced of the innocence of Kabir and let him go. But his enemies remained unsatisfied. They approached Taqi, who had influence over the court, and Taqi pronounced Kabir a political danger, hated both by Hindus and Moslems. Charges of moral turpitude were also made against the saint. It was said that he associated daily with low caste reprobates and women of bad character.

Kabir was again brought before the king and it is said that a few of his close associates were among his accusers. Kabir was fearless and without any bitterness towards them. Death or life is the same to one who has known God. Kabir's answer to the charge of immorality is as follows in his own words :

That I know all to be one, what cause
of grief is that to others?
If I am dishonoured, I have lost my
own honour others need pay no heed.
Mean I am, with the mean I would
be numbered.......
For honour and dishonour I care
not; he whose eyes are opened,
he will understand.
Kabir says, honour is based on this:
renounce all else, sing only Ram.......

(Quoted by Admad Shah)

The doctors of Moslem law (Qazi) demanded that Kabir should live as a true Moslem and threatened death if he did otherwise. Kabir was not to be daunted. He had overcome all fear of death. He answered: "Know only One Lord animating the hearts of both Hindus and Moslems. He is not the monopoly of either of them. I worship Him in any form I see Him."

They asked him why he called himself Kabir which, in Islam, is one of the names of God. Kabir answered:

My name is Kabir; all the world knows this.
In the three worlds is my name, and happiness
is my abode.

Water, air, the seasons, thus I created the world.
The unstruck wave thunders in
Heaven, and Soham keeps time.
I made manifest the seed of Brahma
.....God, men and rishis (sages)
do not find my end. Kabir's
saints alone can find it.....
Hear, O Sikandar, I am a pir of
both religions.

Kabir was condemned as a heretic, and having been bound with chains was thrown into the river. The tradition says that "the bonds could not hold him nor the water drown." He was thrown, bound in chains, before infuriated elephants. But the elephants did not hurt him as Kabir "was protected by the power of the name of Hari."

Kabir lived to the age of 120, and voluntarily gave up his body in a town near the holy city of Benares. "Ram is in Benares and also in every other place," said Kabir when his disciples asked him to go to Benares to die.

Tradition says that a dispute arose as to the disposal of Kabir's body, between the two rivals—Hindus and Mohammedans. An appeal to arms seemed imminent. A passing holy man appeared and bade the rivals to raise the sheet that covered the saint Kabir's body. They did so, and to their great surprise, found beneath a heap of fresh and fragrant flowers.

Kabir wrote in Hindi, as off-shoot of Sanskrit. Evidently he was not versed in Sanskrit—which was, long, long before Kabir, a highly-developed language. Kabir's Hindi is simple and his style is attractive. He invented many new metres and wrote verse in so graceful and flowing a language that we can call him one of the fathers Hindi poetry. The great Hindi poets, Keshav Das, Sur Das, Tulsi Das, and Behari Das, who compare favourably with Dante and Shakespeare, were indebted to Kabir.

Most of the verses of Kabir are hymns of devotion, mysticism and discipline. He seldom uses flowery language. Like the great Chinese poets of the Tang and Sung periods, Kabir is a poet without making efforts to be one. In his simple, natural way poetry flows from him like water from a fountain.

Kabir was a great singer. Dressed as a poor wandering devotee, drunk with the love of God, he used to go about with a hand-drum, pouring forth his heart in his songs. He composed thousands of songs, many of which are orally known, but not yet included in any anthology.

Kabir had four chief disciples and eight more to whom he imparted his inner teachings. Each of them has composed songs, attributing them to Kabir. It is, therefore, not easy to say which of the songs credited to Kabir are by him. *Sukh Ni Dhan* (Treasure of Happiness), *Guru Mahatmya* (Greatness of the Guru), and *Amarmul* (Root of Immortality) contain the spiritual teachings of Kabir, but they are not his compositions. Dharam Das, a disciple of Kabir, is perhaps the author of one of them. The dialogue between Kabir and the great Hatha Yogi teacher, Gorakhnath, containing many deep spiritual truths, is not Kabir's composition as the language is more modern and the style not so simple as that of Kabir.

The basis of Kabir's teachings is the strict monotheism of the Upanishads. He places the Lord of the Universe in the heart of man as his higher Self, where alone the soul can discover Him.

Kabir is a follower of the pure Advaita school of Vedic thought as interpreted by the greatest of the Indian philosophers, Shankaracharya. Kabir worshipped the self-conditioned aspect of the attributeless God, through His own power called Maya. He held that the worship of the self-conditioned leads to the contemplation and realisation of the Absolute. Kabir describes Him as compassionate, most lovable, omniscient and the saviour, with whom man can hold intercourse in his being. Kabir says:

He himself is the tree, the seed, and the form.
He himself is the flower, the fruit and the shade....
He is the breath, the word, and the meaning.

Kabir admits Maya, the principle of limitation which, though unreal, yet is the root cause of the false knowledge of daulity.

Kabir finds Love or *bhakti* the easiest way to realise the Infinite within one's own Self. He is positive that God can be seen only in the being of man and that then the whole Universe becomes a mirror reflecting the bliss and beauty of God.

Many of the most beautiful hymns of Kabir are the expressions of his heart's devotion to the Lord immanent and yet transcendent. The name of God dearest to Kabir is Ram. He sometimes calls Him Hari and when he speaks of His mystic names uses the sacred word *Om*. The repetition of the name of Ram, according to the saint, removes all the sins of man and makes him fit to see God in his heart. Kabir says in his *Bijak*:

Hardly a friend have I at all :
What more shall I say, O brother.....
Sitting in the air, studying Yoga,
Vedas, rites and astrology, they
are demented.
....Kabir says the hope of the Yogi
and the Jangam is withered.
If they repeat, like the bird Chatrik,
the name of Ram, their abode in
bhakti is sure.

Kabir called compassion the greatest virtue, and non-attachment to sense-objects the key to inner tranquillity in which Ram is mirrored as our soul. Mind, free of all earthly desires, devoted to the service of the guru rises to the divine state, through love of Ram.

Without the guru there is no release.

Kabir loved his guru Ramananda as God and he recommends this practice to his disciples.

Where Spring holds sway the twelve
months through, few have conceived
the perfection there.
Where light as rain pours down in
ceaseless streams, where the forest grows
green in all its eighteen
regions—
Where unrestrained the waters well up
within, and the cleansing air bears
away all foulness—
No trees are there, yet heaven is
bright with blossoms.
Shiv and Brahma desire to drink its
perfume.

Unlike other Hindu saints, Kabir condemnsidol-worship and sees no meaning in rituals and pilgrimages. He has little patience with asceticism either. No wonder he incurred the hostility of the orthodox by his sharp condemnation of the outer practices of Hinduism.

Kabir condemns the caste system of the Hindus. To him a Brahmana who reads the Vedas and a cultivator who tills the ground are equal. All mankind is one family and God is the supreme head of it.

The doctrines of Karma and transmigration, the basic Hindu teachings, are upheld by Kabir:

The soul assumes many forms,
according to its merits.
After birth and death it again comes to a body.

Kabir believes in man's ability to see God, in this very life. We can see from his words that he claims to have soon God, the fountain-head of all Joy, Truth and Beauty. Here is the personal testimony of Kabir as translated by Tagore:

I have known in my body the Sport of the Universe:
I have escaped from the error of this world.
The inward and the outward are become as one sky;
the Infinite and the finite are united; I am drunk with the sight of All......................

In another song quoted in the *Adi Grantha* of Nanak, Kabir says :

I have met God who dwelleth in the heart.
When a stream is lost in the Ganges,
It becometh the Ganges itself.

Kabir is one of the rare Hindu saints who speak the language of the Quran and he quotes, approvingly, many of its teachings. His acquaintance with Islam is not superficial. He often mentions Adam and Eve and his referances to the Moslem customs are significant. He disapproves of the rite of circumcision and discourages pilgrimage to Mecca.

They fast all day, at night they slaughter the cow.
Here murder, their devotion; how can this please God?
O Qazi, thy One God is in thee, thou beholdest Him not by thought and reflection.

Though gainest nothing by reading and study,
O madman,
since thou redar'st Him not in thy heart.....
What availeth thee thy pilgrimage to Mecca?

Whether Kabir founded the order called Kabir Panth is open to doubt. He was most anxious to see the unrighteous and the ignorant restored to the path of devotion and compassion, and he often said that the chief duty of a holy man is to help others to the path of virtue and unity with God. Kabir was indifferent to wealth and loved simplicity. The order called Kabir Panth rich and the life of its chief is far from being simple.

There are two main sections of the order: one has its headquarters at Kabir Chaura at Benares, and the other at Chattisgarh, in the Central Provinces of India.

There are two shrines to Kabir in the Benares headquarters; one is in the custody of the Hindus and the other is in the hands of Moslems. There is a shrine dedicated to Kamal also.

The order of Kabir is above the caste system of the Hindus and he who joins the fraternity gives up all caste prejudices. The Shudras, or the untouchables of India, are welcome to the order and the order has done much to elevate the lot of these unfortunate followers of the Hindu Dharma.

The followers of Kabir are strict vegetarians and abstain from the use of alcohol.

The influence of Kabir is noticeable in many sects of India. The Sikhs of the Punjab, the noble followers of Guru Nanak, perhaps one of the disciples of Kabir himself acknowledge Kabir as one of the great Mahatmas and sing his hymns daily. The Vairagis, the Udasees and others are all lovers of Kabir and read his literature. Kabir is quoted by the Moslem Sufis freely. In the mystic circles of the Yogis he is regarded with reverence and his exposition of the Chakras is used by them.

Kabir was an *avadhut.* Having realised God as his Self he lived in ecstasy and like Sur Das his songs welled forth from his being, without any conscious effort on his part. Men like Kabir are not in favour of orders and are alive to the future contradictions and inconsistencies that such orders are likely to create.

There are fifty articles of the Kabir Panthi doctrine, a few of which are quoted below:

1. One must devote oneself to the contemplation of the One all-pervading, attributeless Brahman, called Sat Purush. Brahman is known only by means of the Sat Guru.
2. Brahman and Kabir are one. If anyone thinks that Kabir and Brahman—Guru and God—are not one, he will not find God.
3. One ought to serve one's Guru with body, mind and wealth, place reliance on his word and obey him. He who thinks there is any difference between Guru and God will find that all his devotion and meditation will be in vain.
4. One ought to love and serve one's fellow Satsangees. All devotees of God are worthy of great respect.
5. One ought to count all living creatures as one's own body and treat them with kindness. One ought to refrain from giving any pain, at any place or any time, to any living creature.
6. All intoxicating drinks are forbidden.
7. The only way to salvation is the Essence of the Word (Sar Sabda).
8. Without true love, devotion is fruitless.
9. Without liberality, no one can attain salvation.
10. Do not curse any one, nor speak evil, nor think unkindly of any one.
11. So long as one thinks much of one's body, and nourishes it, as if it were real, one cannot give full obedience to one's Guru.

Let me conclude this short article on Kabir with the following Sakhis:

My song is new: none understands the strain.
Whoever has perceived this word; he is a King of Kings.
O Kabir, deck Thyself in the garments of love, and dance,
To him is given honour, whose body and soul live Truth.

12

PERSPECTIVES OF INDIAN CULTURE

A CASE STUDY OF THE KURAL POLITY IN THE MODERN CONTEXT

India has a rich political and cultural heritage. The Kural Polity is a unique example in this context. Yet we accepted a Euro-centric Polity at the time of independence. This paper is an attempt to examine the essence of the Kural Polity in the modern context.

The subject of Indian Polity has been extensively researched by both Indian and foreign scholars. Unfortunately our modern political culture remains unaffected by it in both letter and spirit. Some of the leaders of the Independence movement, notable among them Annie Besant, and some others during their period, made some attempts in this direction.

Today we seem to suffer from a type of neurosis resulting from cultural disintegration. Science has relieved us of grinding poverty and mitigated the torture of physical pain. Yet we suffer from an inward loneliness.

The roots of our modern polity can be traced to the last decade of the nineteenth century and first half of the twentieth century. While the western world had come full circle, and had started realizing the travils and tribulations of their materialistic existence and examining the spiritual aspects of human existence, Indians looked for western ideals to bring about political change. English manners, English behaviour and English language became the means of their salvation. English ideals dominated their lives and thoughts. Immorality, licentiousness and riotous living were the order of the day. Denationalizing emasculation was the prevailing characteristic. Young men took delight in wounding the religious susceptibilities of their countrymen and in cutting their way to salvation through ham and beef and wading their way to liberalism through tumblers of beer. This became the basis of our modern political culture.

THE KURAL

The significance of the Kural of Tiruvalluvar has been equated with that of the Bhagavad Gita and the Dhammapada by scholars. How exactly one should conduct oneself to lead a good life is the central idea of this text.

The work is divided into three sections and covers 133 chapters. We are told that it is a composition of the first century BC. It deals with moral and ethical principles and with the ideals to which the Tamil Aham held on through the ages. It lays down the code of conduct of good life. Known to the Tamils as '*muppal*' it is concerned with three aspects of life viz., '*aram*', '*porul*' and '*enbam*'. Like the Trivarga concept of the Sanskrit epics and of works on polity, it stands for '*dharma*', '*artha*' and '*kama*'.

In the first section of the book the author instructs the people in the path of virtue and truth. The main stress has been on the second part dealing with '*artha*', laying down the duties and responsibilities of the king and his officials. The keynote of the Kural Polity is that the practice of righteousness is entirely, or to a large extent, dependent on the proper performance of his duty by the king. The conception was that but for a well-ordered state in charge of a righteous ruler there would be no society and no state.

A detailed account of the duties and responsibilities of the king, his officials and their functions has been provided as a necessity for peace, prosperity and welfare of the people. The Kural is thus a logical presentation of the values of life and the ways and means by which to realize them. It is not a sectarian but a cosmopolitan work with lessons for all countries and all ages.

The root of Kural Polity was '*dharma*' or '*aram*'. "Aram enapparate livalkkai", *i.e.* virtue is nothing more than a good family life. A good family life was considered as the basis of a good society. Love between individual and society and discipline, resulting in a harmonious coordination between the different spiritual and moral standards resulting in material and moral progress was a sacred duty of the king and his officials. All classes of the society were to observe their duties. *Dana* (gift) and *tava* (penance) were stressed and selfishness was condemned and selflessness exalted. The State was to:

(a) ensure good life of the people by securing wealth and utilizing it generously and properly on things which would aid people in their onward march.
(b) inculcate healthy restraints in the enjoyment of pleasures of life, and
(c) cultivate a detached view of life with advancement in age.

Human nature being what it is, the Kural stresses the need of superior power of the king to enforce rigorous discipline among his subjects.

The form of government advocated is a constitutional monarchy based upon the will of the people who acquiesce in the selection of the monarch, though it was generally hereditary.

THE KING

1. The king is at the top of the state.
2. He is all powerful yet constitutional.
3. Tyrannizing over the subjects would lead to ruin of the king's family.
4. He should avoid vices of different kinds and be a man of good character.

The vices mentioned are :

a) extreme indulgence with women (Two chapters)
b) drinks, and
c) gambling.

The Arthasastra Polity speaks of a seven limbed kingdom (*Saptangam raiyan*). Kural Polity points to six limbs of the kingdom:

1. The army
2. The people
3. The treasury
4. The ministry

5. The allies, and
6. The fortification.

While other texts include the institution of monarchy as a limb of the state, Kural Polity excludes the monarch from the limbs of the state and thus assigns him a more important place. It was not enough that a monarch possessed these institutions to aid him. They may be supplementary or complementary to the discharge of his responsibilities. It was expected that a ruler of excellent character devoted to the duty of protection of his subjects, should:

a) be wise with tremendous courage and energy,
b) be liberal,
c) be learned and vigilant,
d) avoid wasteful expenditure and enrich his treasury, and
e) consult his advisors before taking a decision.

Such a king was regarded as a god among men. "God is impartial and just to all the people and protects the world from disaster. So also the king by his just rule shields his subjects from the unrighteous path".

Kural Polity lays stress on the importance of perfect learning for a monarch. Learning and wisdom are considered the foundations on which a monarch carries on the ship of his state. Knowledge is considered as real wealth which should be enriched by the habit of listening to the wise. This adds to his wisdom to enable him to discriminate between right and wrong, good and evil and gives the king foresight to see things ahead. Emphasis is also laid on the fact that learning and righteousness would flourish in a kingdom where the king is learned and righteous, because "It is not the javelin but the scepter that glorifies a king and his kingdom".

The king must be easy to access of his people and he must patiently listen to their grievances and bring succor to them. He should never use his position for his own selfish ends. The king was god on earth, and a reign of terror or a tyrannical rule was abhorred. So the Kural advises the ruler to do justice tempered with mercy so as to earn the goodwill of his subjects; otherwise, he invited destruction on himself.

Enthusiasm and not illness should be the guiding spirit. Sloth is a canker that should not find a place in a king. It is the birth place of poverty and disease to the different limbs of a kingdom. Courage, persistence, a divine composure and a spirit to fight even against fate will bring sunshine of prosperity and illuminate his kingdom. The king should be learned, impartial and farsighted.

MINISTER

He works out the details of an undertaking, studies the pros and cons of achieving it, waits for the opportunity and commences it, when the right movement presents itself. A minister must:

a) be of indomitable will and noble character,
b) have inexhautible energy,
c) be well-versed in the laws of the kingdom,
d) be wise and clever, paratical and persistent, and
e) be a diplomat

The minister, above all, must be eloquent and must possess command over language. He must be precise in his expression and must endeavour to create public opinion in his favour. He must be bold and dauntless debater.

He should not resort to foul means in achieving his objectives. By clean fight he should remove obstacles. By walking in the path ordained he should advise the king to act up to the laws of the land. He should endeavour to command the respect of the world by following the policy of his predecessors and by firmness of action. Vacillation at a time of action will bring him down in the estimation of the people. Before he comes to a decision, the minister is asked to deliberate calmly and deeply, and when once the decision is arrived at, he should execute without losing a single minute, for delay is dangerous. For instance, a minister can advise a declaration of war only after taking into consideration the following resources: weapons of war, the opportune moment, the nature of action and the place of battle. In every enterprise he should follow the method of deliberation and decision (Ch. 66-68). But at the same time it will spell disaster to a state if the minister proves dishonest and wicked and goes to the length of plotting the downfall or ruin of the king. A vile minister is said to be worse than a host of enemies(639).

THE KINGDOM

We shall now examine the other limbs of the state. One of them is the *nadu* or kingdom. The Kural says (Ch.74) that alone is a kingdom where a contented peasantry, wise men and wealthy people live. It should have boundless natural resources which provide abundant supply of foodstuffs, notwithstanding a drain in time of pressing need. It should have plenty of water supply and natural fortresses which ensure defence. It is concluded that happy is the kingdom where peace and harmony prevail between the ruler and the ruled. It should be free from the ravages of pestilence and famine. It must be a country where people live in amity and harmony, free from all civil and religious dissensions.

ARMY

The necessity of a disciplined army was insisted upon. The soldiers should be valorous and loyal. They should summon all their courage and fight to the finish. The army should be contented and well paid. It must fight to the finish but be chivalrous to the fallen and defenceless.

AMBASSADOR

He should be highly connected, learned and skilled in debate. He must be a statesman of the highest order and gentleman of winning personality. He was expected to deliver his message as briefly as possible and to persuade the alien king to his way of thinking by his eloquence and wit. He was to answer to the points raised calmly and with an eye on the time, place and circumstances of the case for which he was sent of a mission. Even under the threat of torture, he should not utter any word that would leave a stain on his king and kingdom.

THE SPIES/INTELLIGENCE

They were one of the two eyes of the monarch, the other eye being the established law of the land. They were to report day-to-day happenings and the public opinion. Purity and efficiency of the government departments and its servants was fully ensured.The information was often tested by indepenent testimony. These secret agents were not be honoured openly. Most trustworthy servants were generally appointed as ambassadors and spies.

TREASURY

An organised treasury with an unfailing stock of riches was deemed essential. Such a treasury should not be built by foul and unscrupulous means. It should be acquired by righteous methods causing least dissatisfaction among the people at large. The king should be discreet in acquistion of money and its expenditure. That alone would ensure his happiesss and welfare of his subject.

WHAT A KINGDOM SHOULD REALLY BE

A happy land is where the intellectuals, the commercials and the peasantry live side by side in concord and peace. It should be free from communal wrangles and squabbles and should be full of community life based on the comunalistic principles. Mere political unity was not enough; there should be social unity as well.

NOTE :

Summary of Sir William Meyar Lecture delivered on February, 13-14, 1995. University of Madras.

—DR. RAJ KUMAR

13

CULTURAL INTERACTIONS IN SOUTH INDIA (1400-1800)

The Period from 1400 to 1800 has been one during which South India witnessed the arrival and installation of two important alien groups namely the Muslims and the Europeans. This part of the country which has till then subjected only to influences from within India was invaded by cultures altogether different. This led naturally to various internactions of culture. Some of them faded away after a short while, some blossomed during the period itself and yet some others which sprouted during the period developed further in the subsequent centuries. Travellers and missionaries (through their letters) made South India known to Europe particularly to Portugal, Netherlands, France and England. Some far sighted foreigners started colecting manuscripts which they sent to their respective countries. Others happened to be employed by local Prince as Ministers, Generals and Doctors. Changes happened in various fields like religion letters, law, architecture, warfare where foreign influences are still noticeable. I shall confine this note to three fields namely religion, letters and law and that too in the Tamil speaking area at that time.

RELIGION

Religious shock was very important during the period. Mohammedan religion and Christian religion diverged totally from the religions practised by the people. Even though the country experienced several religious fights, those fights were between the different brands of Indian religion which had some basic tenets in common. Further these two foreign religions which had no adopts here necessarily resorted to mass conversions. Mohammedan religion relied more on force than persuasion. Christian religion had rather recourse to preaching, medical care and social service. However when European Companies became powerful enough, Christian missionaries enticed them to use their physical strength to facilitate and consolidate the conversion. All this naturally caused to local population a considerable trauma.

It is to be emphasised that the first Christian missionaries, especially the Jesuits, used persuasion to a great extent. Those missionaries started living like Bhramins. They abandoned wine and drank only water; they adopted khavi dresses; they donned the sacred thread, the wooden foot wear like Hindu Sanniyassies; they ate only the food prepared by Bhramins; they changed their names Jesuit Father Nobily who made the strat, changed his name into *Thathuva Podagar* and Father Beschi changed his name into *Veeramma Munivar.* The latter used to travel in palanquin with men proceeding with umbrellas of purple and fans of peacock feathers. He had a tiger skin to sit upon. Some of the external paraphernalia was a matter of strategy which succeeded whilst other attempts failed. But those noble Fathers have come to realise that austerity (which was not unknown in Europe but was not practised to the same extent) was befitting the religious persons and they have adopted it wholeheartedly. They remained vegetarians even during the lapse of the time they spent at Lisben.

The Jesuit Fathers found also that in order to be successjul they should know thoroughly the religion followed so devoutly by the people. They therefore learnt Indian languages, studied Hindu religion and got acquainted with the religious practises of the country. They even took part in controversial disputations where enigmatical theological questions were debated, in order to prove the superiority of the Christian theology. With these methods they established themselves very strongly at Madura and around and were able to convert a large number of people. According to Francois Martin there were in the year 1694 three lakhs of Christians in the Madura

Mission and there were also Bhramins among the converts. He has also recorded that Jesuits fathers were very careful to see that the aspirants were fully instructed of the mysteries of the Christian religion before being baptised which, he say, was not case in respect of other congregations. The missionaries after deep study of the practises and traditions associated with the religion allowed the people to continue those practises, when such practises were not repugnant to the basic tenets of Christian religion. They some time made adaptations; for instance people were induced to celebrate Pongal on the day of Epiphany and the preparation of sweets which mark Deepavali got shifted to Christmas Day.

Whereas missionaries took care of studying and respecting as far as possible the local customs, the other Europeans were full of contempt for the Hindu religion and practices. They used to say that the people in Asia were not able to understand the subtle mysteries of Christian religion and they condemned without appeal the tenets of Hindu and other religions. The French King-Louis XIV who made Catholic religion the State religion in France, much to the dismay of protestants who then left the country, issued an edict in the year1711 for curbing the religious manifestations of Hindus in public at pondicherry. He was induced to take that step by the missionaries. The local administrators hesitated to promulgate the edict and to implement it. They had to yield to pressure, and this provoked a sharp reaction from the people. The Hindus closed their shops and work-shops; some of them started leaving Pondicherry. The Administrators had to retrieve their steps and to restore the status-quo-ante.

Even though the Muslims and Europeans were contemptuous of the local religion and religious practices they adopted some para-religious Indian practices bordering on superstition. So when the country was devastated by small-pox they resorted to all the practices familiar to the Hindus like typing Margosa leaves in front of the door in order to keep away the evil sprit. It would not be difficult to guess that the conversion to Islam or Christanity was more or less deep according to the process of conversion and the instruction which the converts were subjected to before and after conversion and the association in professional and social life that the converts had with the Muslims and Europeans masters.

Untouchables remained so even after their conversion to catholicism, caste catholics not willing to mingle with them. They were allotted a separate place in churches with even a separating wall some times and that practice remained alive till the middle of the 20th century.

There were also individuals for whom religion was a way to achieve success in life. Francois Martin quotes the example of one Veeranna who has propelled himself to the status of the first merchant of the British Company in Madras. He was originally the slave of a Christian and was baptised. He shifted loyalty to the Muslims who thought he was a Muslim and then he lived among Hindus which religion he practised overtly.

Hindu prices and saints necessarily reacted to this coversion waves. Hindu religion was projected more vigorously. Naik kings took tremendous interest in promoting and protecting Hindu religion. Temples with tall gopurums were built in many places. Mutts were established to protect and promote Hindu religion. So the number of conversion affected only a small fraction of the population, but the new religions more especially Christianity had other effects on the whole population by the values they contained and which they propagated through education.

LETTERS

Changes witnessed in the field of religion had their impact in the field of letters. Works extolling Muslim religious features appeared in all the literary geners in which there were works in Tamil language regarding Hindu religion. The most noteworthy of the literary work relating to Muslim religion is the *Seerapuranam* (17th century) by *Umaru Pulavar.* It is a biography of the prophet in the epic form. In that epic the landscape is not the one found in the middle-east but very much the landscape with all the trees and gushing waters as found in Tamilnadu. Similarly, the characters in the epic also appear and act with all the habits and practices of Tamilnadu. In the description of

Mecca one can recognize that of Madurai. This epic is very much liked even now by the Tamil Muslims of Ceylon. Almost at the same time Father Beschi composed his *Thembavani*, an epic on Jesus Mary Joseph, according to Tamil literary tradition, one distinctive feature is that there are not many love sequences. Here also nature and people are not those of Israel but those of Tamilnadu. Names also have been modified; Joseph becomes Valan, John becomes Karunayan; there is even one character called Sivan.

European missionaries wrote profusely in Tamil which had the effect of introducing new literary generes in Tamil. They stated translating their books on theology, sermons, prayers and rituals in Tamil. Then they wrote directly several books on religion in Tamil. The two versatile writers were Father Nobily and Facur Beschi. Father Nobily has the distinction of being the first great prose writer in Tamil. Parallely, essays on Hindu theology began to appear in larger number. Though this was not entirely absent in the previous period, the stress so far was on mystic works. Now the emphasis shifts towards Theology. The most important works in Hindu religion of that period are on Saiva Sithantham. The culminating work being Sivagnanabotham of Meikandar. In the middle of the 18th century the idea emerged that all religions are valid that there should not be struggle-one against the other, but that on the contrary, peaceful co-existance should prevail. The Tamil poet who spearheaded this new trend was *Thaiyyumanavur.*

In order to buttress Hindu religion all important Puranas in Sanskrit were rendered in Tamil, the most important being *Skanda Puram and Bharatham.* The Sthala Puranas also make their appearance. The genre became so popular that each temple, even the humblest one, wanted and got its Sthala Purana. The most important of this Sthala Purana is *Thiruvilayadal Purunam* relating to Madurai temple.

Another genere worth mentioning is diary writing. The first available diary which is at the same time the most important in Tamil literature is that of *Ananda Rangapillai* in the 18th century. Since no earlier diary was found, the question arises whether this is not an imitation of the

Europeans who at that time were very keen in keeping their diaries. At any rate, it is the availability of paper coming from Europe which made possible the writing of the diary in detail like the one of *Ananda Rangapillai.*

During this period Tamil language, especially the prose, underwent fundamental changes. Formerly, literature consisted essentially of poetry. Prose was not used on large scale; it was also an elaborate and eloquent language accessible only to learned persons. During this period words in prose became more and more abundant. At the time a new prose four got shaped. Two currents are manifest. There was a movement in favour of teaching Sanskrit in Tamilnadu on large scale or at least of rendering accessible the Sanskrit works to Tamilians. For that purpose a new language was devised, called *Manipravalam*; it was a mixture of Tamil and Sanskrit. Under this influence, the new compositions and especially translations from Sanskrit works were made in Tamil language, replete with Sanskrit words. This had been so much in vogue that even a poet like *Arunagiri Nathar* in his mystic work on *Lord Muruga*, who is essentially a Tamil Deity, used profusely Sanskrit words, the second current is provided by the missionaries. Their aim was to reach the people and therefore they started writing in a language more akin to the spoken language of the common man. But they could not escape the prevailing trend of Sanskritisation of the language.

Tamil literature underwent complete changes under foreign influences. At the same time the treasures of Tamil literature and the niceties of Tamil language were made known to others. Missionaries were the most active in this respect as well. The first translations are from Tamil to Latin. Father Beschi provided a number of translations, the most important one being the translations of the first two parts of Thirukural. A curious event is that a catechism was written in Tamil language by Father Nobily and then translated in Portuguese. It is also to be noted that the missionaries were the forerunners in the art of teaching Tamil to foreigners and have composed several works for that purpose.

Tamil language was learnt not only by missionaries, but by almost all the Europeans who settled down in this part of the country for commercial or administration purposes. That was not a period when the Tamils learned European languages, but it was the other way round.

The literary activity of the period would not have been possible without printing. Printing machines were brought to India in the middle of the 16th century. The first printed work is in Tamil language but with Roman characters. It is reported to have been printed in 1554.

The first book with Tamil characters is said to have been printed in1578. The first casting types in an Indian language are in Tamil and were done at Goa. Both are on Christian doctrine. More printing machines were then established at Tranquebar. This gave an impetus to printing in Tamil language. In the course of 18th century printing has taken deep-roots. The first printing machine brought to Pondicherry in 1758 by the Counte de Lally was not put to much use. It was lotted by Coote at the time of destruction of Pondicherry in 1761 and taken to Madras. That marked the beginning of printing in Madras.

In the History of printing, another mention worth being made is that Father Beschi brought about some slight modifications in the Tamil alphabet prevailing then in order to make printing easier and more economical.

To facilitate the study of Tamil language by Europeans especially the young missionaries, dictionaries were composed. The introduced the art of lexicography in Tamil language. Of course, in old times there were poems called 'Nikkandus' in which synonymous words were grouped in verses. But the alphabetical method of lexicography was introduced by the missionaries. Father Beschi alone has composed three dictionaries Latin-Tamil, Portuguese-Tamil, French-Tamil. Books on Tamil grammar were written in the Latin tradition. Though grammar writing was a very old practice in Tamilnadu, the foreigners could not grasp Tamil grammar easily since the classifications are quite different from those they were familiar with. Therefore, grammar in the Latin tradition proved very useful to them and Father Beschi provided two such grammars one for the classical language and the other for the colloquial language. The latter was the first book of grammar ever written in respect of colloquial language. Books of Tamil vocabulary were also produced.

LAW

It is a generally accepted principle that criminal law should be the same to all and will be the law of the ruler. This was asserted by the Muslim rulers and after them by the Europeans. But they could put that principle in practice only in places where they were administratively well established and had full control over the population. With the advent of Muslim law, punishments consisting of mutilations got introduced in a large scale. Europeans added enslavement in the Isles of Bourbon (in the Indian ocean). According to the principle enunciated above old punishments which were in practice in that area which were unknown to Muslims and European laws should have been abolished. On the contrary they had been allowed to continue for the sake of efficiency, like penal sevitude and whipping in public. the latter punishment was meted out invariably along with other punishments. Even at the end of the 18th century there is one record of a woman being punished for the offence of adultery to have her head shaved and smeared with cowdung mixed with water, to have her mounted on a donkey and chased out of the town and the suburbs of Pondicherry with beating of the drums.

As far as Civil law is concerned, all European powers have proclaimed that the oustomary law will continue to apply and they have endeavoured to respect their undertaking Whenever they constituted courts they took care to have special courts to decide matters of Civil law as regards Indians. They were manned either by Indians or with the help of Indians. However in some cases like Sati, they tried to interfere and to prevent it. Franco is Martin in his memoirs reports that he successfully persuaded one woman to refrain from immolating herself. He reports also that all his attempts to foil Sati being committed by another woman proved useless. He naroates in detail how the lady with determination and a sense of self-realisation, after settling all details meticulously, mounted on the pyre to take her place by the side of her deceased husband.

There are other cases in which local customs underwent a change at the hands of the European Administrators. This happened in the case of bonded labour which got transformed into slavery. Bonded labour has been in existence here for a long time. There is an attestation of the custom in the *periya Puranam* of sekkizhar (12th century). The formula used is "I undertake and also bind my progeny to serve generation after generation." But the Europeans who were at that time practising slavery on a large scale assimilated this bonded labour to slavery and officially called the bonded labour slaves. There is also reference in the memoirs of Franco is Martin that slaves are people who surrendered themselves on account of the misery. There is a vast difference in law between bonded labour and slavery. According to the European conception, slaves are things, they do not have jurstic personality, they do not have jurstic personality, they are properties of the master. In the case of bonded labour, though in practice there may be a great similarity they remain juristic persons and in case they are able to pay off the debt they would become fully free. It is worth mentioning that slavery was abolished for the first time in Pondicherry by the Colonial Assembly which was constituted at the time of the French Revolution.

Conversion to Islam or Christianity did not have full effect on customs in matter of law. There are reports of two cases which were dealt with by choultry court in Pondicherry where adoption by Muslims was pleaded and confirmed much against Muslim law. What is note-worthy is that they were not mere cases of fosterage but real adoptions creating a family realtionship effected through declarations before the Cazy, the Muslim religious authority However in the course of time adoption by Muslims at least in such official form appears to have withered away. But there is another Hindu custom to which the Muslim converts clung persistently, that is co-parcenary. Of course in Mohammedan law there is nothing which could compare even remotely to the Hindu co-parcenary. This custom survived for a long time. Eyssette, a French Judge, writing at the end of the 19th century states that there was innate propensity towards co-parcenary among the Muslims who were Hindus converted to Islam, that it was well fitted to them.

As regards Christians the conversion did not bring about any change except in matter of marriage. When

Kanakaraya Mudaliar (a christian dubash of Dupleix) passed away a dispute arose between his widow and brother regarding the right to the estate. All the arbitrators chosen by Dupleix to adjudicate the dispute were Hindus. Hindus law continued to apply to christian converts till the end of the French period in Pondicherry. The situation was the same in British India during the peirod under review and special laws were enacted for Christians only in the 19th century. However, as pointed out earlier the Hindu marriage ceased to have validity and was replaced by the religious marriage celebrated in the church. But the prohibited degrees of kinship did not undergo a change. So the provisions of Cannon law were circumvented by way of exemptions which were granted liberally by the church authorities. Thus the practice of marriage between uncle and niece and cross-cousins remained very common among Christian converts.

The most important change in matter of law is witnessed in the form of law. This part of the country had a law different from the Hindu law followed in North India. This is attested by Father Bouchet, a French Jesuit Missionary who lived for a long time in Madurai. In a letter to a Chief Justice, in France, he gave detailed informations on the administration of justice in South India in which he categorically states that customs prevails over anything else. This is confirmed by a French Judge, Leon Sorg, and John D'Mayne, a forerunner in the studies of Hindu law. What is important for our purpose is that this law, special to South India, remained oral all the time. The Tamils who were well versed in writing, and who have left several treatieses in other subjects and who used written documents to record their dealings and produced them before courts had refrained from couching their law in writing. Father Bouchet who was intrigued by the situation enquired about the matter and found that this was a delibrate attitude and he attested also that the essential rules of the Tamil law which remained oral were well-known to the people.

But the European powers who were accustomed to administering justice with the help of written law found themselves helpless and could not rest content with taking the help of Indian assessors. The one who conceived first the idea of reducing to writing the Tamil customs is the Governor General of Dutch India. The *Dissawe* of *Jaffina Pattinam* was requested at the beginning of 18th century to collect and consolidate all the rules of law which the inhabitants of the province have been observing on the subjects found to be the most important. The *Dissawe* took up the work in all earnestness and he completed very rapidly the work with the knowledge he possessed already on the subject and by enquiring 12 *Mudaliars*. On completion of his work, he requested that his collection be translated and circulated to another set of 12 Mudaliars at the choice of the Governor for the purpose of ascertaining its correctness. When that body also decided that the text presented to them were in confirmity with the usual customs of the locality, the collection was approved by the Governor on 16th December, 1707 and was called Thesavalamai, the Tamil law became thus a written law. A further step in that direction was taken when the British became masters of Ceylon. The Chief Justice tested again the correctness of the collection by personal enquiry. He distributed copies in Tamil to the Heads of the village with a direction to explain it to the population. Had the population forgotten its customs once it has been reduced to writing or has the Chief Justice forgotten that it was nothing else but a collection of customs obtained from the population for the use of the foreign judges ? In any case, the British declared that the *Thesavalamai* will have the force of law and placed it in Volume II of the Legislation Enactment of Ceylon. What was a collection of customs, became statutory law. Steps were taken later by the French and the British to have a written law at their disposal. Thus the Tamils were deprived from the oral tradition of their law which they have preserved for centuries. It has drawbacks of course but has got also obvious advantages.

The period 1400-1800 is a very important one in as much as it witnessed important cultural internations many of them with lating effects deserving to be studied in detail.

—JUSTICE DAVID ANNOUSSAMY

14

INDIA'S EPOCHS IN WORLD-CULTURE

There are academicians, philosophers and publicists, both in East and west, who cannot feel happy unless they make a distinction between culture and civilization. The present writer is not one of them. In his vocabulary culture and civilization are identical terms. The distinction is generally made in Germany where *Kultur* is taken to be more profound, more creative and more substantial than civilization. In France, as a rule, scientists and *les hommes des lettres* fight shy of the word 'culture'. To them the sweetest word is *la civilisation francaise.* Italians are like the French in this respect. Italy does not care for *la colture* so much as for *la civilizzazione.* In English thought the custom continues to be more or less French although the German term and ideology were introduced by Matthew Arnold among others. American intellectuals have not gone in difinitely for one way or the other. They use culture and civilization indifferently. Those contemporary Eur-American sociologists or philosophers who want to exhibit their upto-dateness in German vocabulary, especially the ideologies propagated by Spengler, have to refer to the distinctions observed in Germany by way of preliminary observations. But they virtually ignore them as they proceed unless they happen to be exponents of the Spenglerian or some allied thesis.

To the present author culture or civilization is nothing but the Sanskrit or virtually all-Indian *Krișți, Samskriti or Sabhyatā*. It is a synonym for the creations of man whatever they are, good, bad or different. No moral significance is to be attached to the word. Culture or civilization is entirely unmoral, carrying no appraisal of values, high or low. We have just a term describing the results of human creativity. It is desirable to be clear about it at the very outset.

Any creation of man being culture, the most important item in it is the force behind culture, the culture making agency, the factor that produces or manufactures culture. The analysis of culture or civilization is nothing but the analysis of man's creative urges, energies or forces. It is the will that creates. It is the intelligence that creates, and perhaps likewise it is the emotion that creates. The first thing that counts in the human personality, in the individual or group *psyche* is the desire to create. And the second thing certainly is the power to create. In culture or world-culture we are interested in this desire of man and this power of man to create.

It is the nature of human creativity to be endowed with interhuman impacts, good or bad. Social influence is to be postulated or creation as such. Every creation exerts automatically an influence upon the neighbourhood. The influence may be beneficial or harmful. The creation is perhaps only the production of a food-plant a cave-dwelling, an earthen pot, a song, or a story. But the creator influences the neighbour as a matter of course. His work evokes the sympathy or antipathy of the men and women at hand or far off. It thus dominates the village, the country and the world, be the manner or effect of domination evil or good. Creation is essentially domination. To create is to conquer, to dominate. No domination, no creativity.

The desire and the power to dominate is, then, the fundamental feature in every creative activity, in every expression of culture. In every culture we encounter the desire to dominate and the power to dominate. The quality, quantity and variety and men and women who have the desire and the power to dominate set the limits of the culture-making force in a particular region or race. In order to be able to make a culture or possess an epoch in world-culture a region or race must have a large number of varied men and women effectively endowed with this desire and power to dominate.

The term 'world' in world-culture is not to be taken too literally so as to encompass all the four quarters of the universe and all the two billions of human beings. The smallest environment of an individual is his world. As soon as he has created something his culture has influenced the neighbour. It may then be said already to have conquered the world and made or started an epoch. It is clear that the words, conquest and domination, are not being used in any terroristic, terrifying or tyrannical sense. There is nothing sinister in these words, nothing more sinister at any rate than in the world, influence or conversion.

Once in a while, or very often, it may so happen that while A's creation or culture is influencing, converting, conquering or dominating his neighbour B, B's creation or culture is likewise at the same time influencing, coverting, conquering and dominating A. This sort of mutual influence, mutual conversion, reciprocal conquest or reciprocal domination is a frequent, may, an invariable phenomenon in inter-human contacts. Hardly any religious conversion of a large group in the world's history has been one-sided. It has as a rule led to a give-and-take between two systems of cult. Acculturaion or the acceptance and assimilation of one culture by a region or race of another culture furnishes innumerable instances of this mutuality in domination or reciprocity in conquest. But that the essential item in culture is influence, conversion, conquest or domination is however never to be lost sight of.

The position is, then, very simple. Whenever this man over here or that man over there, be in a position to influence another man, his neighbour, it is to be admitted that the other man has been coverted or conquered by this man. Whenever we find that one group of human beings has made an invention or a discovery and when that invention or that discovery has been accepted by another group as an invention or a discovery that is likely to be useful to itself, we understand that the first group has made an epoch in world-culture.

This position may be described in the words of some of the forefathers, the fathers' fathers, and greatgrandfathers of our Iddian races. It so happens that this attitude in regard to culture, world-culture and the making of world-culture is the mentality of young India during the Vedic period. One of the *Riṣis*, one of the nearly thousand poets of Vedic India, has a passage, a verse like the following. Man (*Puruṣa*) is describing himself to the Earth (*Dharitrī*) in the following manner:

Ahamasmi sahamāna
Uttaro nāma bhūmyām
Abhīṣādasmi viśwāsād
Āśāmāśām viṣāsahi

This is what a poet of the *Atharva Veda* says about man's place in the world. "Mighy am I," says Man to the Earth, "Superior (*Uttara*) by name, conquering am I, all-conquering (*Viśwāsād*), completely conquering every region."

This is the present writer's conception of culture,—the urge, the force, the spirit behind world-culture—the agency that has brought about epochs in world-culture. This conception appears to have been prominent in the mind of one of the oldest poets of the Indo-Aryan world.

This conception of the making of epochs was also shared by no less a world-figure than Śākyasimha the Buddha. The Pali *Sutta-nipāla* has a *Sela-Sutta*. Here we find Buddha declaring himself as follows: 'A king am I, the king supreme of righteousness. The royal chariot-wheel (*Chakra*) in righteousness do I set rolling on, that wheel that no one can turn back again." Buddha was but employing the vocabulary of his contemporaries, the statesmen who were attempting to become *Rāja-Chakravartins* or *Sārva-bhaumas* (world-rulers) in the political domain. His creative imagination or will intelligence and feeling was harnessed to *digvijaya* (the conquest of all directions). He was self-conscious enough to understand that his creation, the wheel, had encompassed the world. Buddha is thus seen continuing the tradition of the Vedic *Riṣis* in regard to the making of culture.

Ou poet Kālidāsa can also be quoted as an illustration of the point of view that is maintained by the present writer as regards culture and the making of cultures. Let us look at the wonderful heroes of Kālidāsa's *Raghuvamśa*. What were Raghu, his ancestors and successors in Kālidāsa's imagination. They were

Āsamudrakṣitīśānām
Ānākarathavartmanām.

Kālidāsa's creations were nothing sort of

Lords of the lithosphere from sea to sea
Commanding the skies by chariots of air.

They were, in one word, world-conquerors, rulers of rulers, bent on and capable of establishing *Pax* Sārvabhaumica (peace of the *Sārvabhauma* or world-monarch) corresponding to the *Pax Romana* of those days in the West.

The Vedic *Riṣi,* Buddha and Kālidāsa, all thought alike. Their mentalities are being exhibited here simply as illustrations or specimens from Old India of the present writer's idea of culture as a function of the desire and power of man to dominate the world.

MILITARY-POLITICAL IMPERIALISM

In this vocabulary domination or conquest, be it repeated, is not a dangerous category. It is akin to conversion or influence. Let us then proceed with the analysis of domination as a social fact, as an historic phenomenon in the relations between individuals or groups. If we begin to classify the dominations or conquests known in the history of the world, it appears that they can be grouped in two different orders. The first is the physical domination of one race by another. To it belongs the military conquest of one country by another, the political subjugation of one people by another. The government of one country by another country is one kind of domination. This is generally known as imperialism, imperialism of the political-militaristic order.

Now there is another kind of domination, imperialism or empire-building. And this consists in the conversion of a people that has a particular system of ideas to another system of beliefs, ideas, etc. It is a conversion, a sunjugation of one set of ideas and ideals by another. It consists in a transformation of the morals, manners, sentiments, laws, etc., of one people, race or region by the moralities, spiritualities, arts and sciences, etc., of another people, race or region. This is also an imperialism or domination.

Thus there are two kinds, orders or systems of imperialism. One is the political-militaristic, the other is the ideological world-domination. The making of epochs in culture can belong either to the one or to the other system of imperialism. Illustrations of both these types of imperialism are to be found among the experiences of the Indian peoples, as among those of certain other peoples in the world.

In regard to the military-political imperialism we shall take up the Western world first. We have been taught to believe, in schools and colleges and through the journalistic world by political leaders, that the Western races do not make slaves among themselves and that they but conquer the East. The militarist-political domination of one people by another is not alleged to be in the European traditions. Europeans and Americans are supposed to be peoples who have never known the subjugation of one race by another, the millitarist-political domination of one country by another and so forth. This is the exact opposite of historic reality.

We shall give only one illustration. Let us, for instance, take England. The people of England was conquered by foreign peoples oftener than once. England was a foreign-dominated country for hundreds of years. England is in Europe, and the peoples that conquered England were the peoples of Europe. The history of England for nearly a thousand years was off and on the story of the government of one people by another. England belonged to the race of subject nations, to the group of slaves who could be governed by foreigners as a "cattle farm," to use an expression from the British philosopher, John Stuart Mill. For a quite a long time, as everybody will recall, England was a slave of Romans. This Roman rule in Britain was an illustration of imperialism of the militaristic-political type. To be precise, the Romans ruled Britain for nearly three hundred and fifty years. The "Barbarian" or Teutonic conquests also were foreign conquests, and followed hard upon the Roman domination. The Danish rule was likewise a foreign rule. During the eleventh and twelfth centuries, again, it was the French people who ruled England. This island was the colony of western France from the Somme to the Pyrenees. The Norman and Angevin Dukes or zemindars of Western France who were the "vassals" of the Kings of eastern France were the rulers of England.

Hundreds of similar instances can be quoted. From the earliest Greek and Roman times until today Europe has ever been a continent of races or peoples governed by foreign races or peoples. Militaristie-political domination has been an eternal feature in the destiny of Europe.

Europeans have not always been used to respecting the liberties of other Europeans. The tug of war between European peoples for the military-political domination of European territories is one of the permanent items in the history of world-culture. The peoples of Europe have also known for quite long centuries the militaristic-political subjugation by non-European, *e.g.,* Asian races, peoples or nations. The domination of southern and eastern Europe by the Arabs, Mongols and Turks is too patent a fact in the annals of civilization.

Let us now come to the East. In regard to Asia also we have been taught to believe that imperialism of the militaristic-political type was unknown in her tradition. Our forefathers on the banks of the Ganges and the Godavari, the Indus, the Tigris, the Euphrates and the Nile, the Hwangho and the Yangtsze are alleged to have been non-militaristic in their outlook and view of life. Many of us have been seriously believing that the Orient has never known the subjugation of one people by another people. Such beliefs are so palpably untrue to facts that they should be treated with contempt as but hallucinations. The present writer's mentality is the furthest removed from such beliefs. The historic reality is that Asians were as adept and happy in establishing militaristic political domination as Europeans. There was no difference between them on this score.

Well, what about our own country, India? It is said that we here in India are used only to *ahimsā*. This notion is being preached from house-tops by certain sections of Indian philosophers, Indian statesmen and Indian historians. If some one were to declare that for five thousand years from the epochs of Mohenjodaro and the

Rig Veda down to Tipu Sultan, Baji Rao and Ranjit Singh, our fathers, grandfathers and great-grand-fathers were only counting beads and cultivating *ahimsā*, The tendency among a large body of intellectuals in India to call him a philosopher of the first rank would be very obvious. Not to fight, to be worthless in secular matters, to fail in worldly wisdom were the characteristics of ancient and medieval Indians according to these philosophers of the first rank. This is the mentality also of a very large number of European and American scholars known as Orientalists, who try to din into the ears of their victims at Oxford, Cambridge, New York, Berlin and Paris that Indians were wonderful metaphysicians exclusively interested in "the other world" and utterly incompetent to manage the things of here below. One is at liberty to cultivate this mentality. But let us have a little bit of our factual history.

We shall draw attention only to one or two periods of Indian life from Mohenjodaro down to 1850, to see whether any generation was unsecular, unmilitaristic and unpolitical. The wars of the Vedic period are too well-known. If the *Riṣis* of ancient India understood any thing they understood killing, burning and destroying. They were the last persons to cultivate *ahimsā*. Lets us come down to the Maurya Empire (313-185 B.C.). This was estabilished 160 years after Śākyasimha (Buddha) who is known to have preached the cult of *ahimsā*. This empire was, as is well-known, larger than the British Empire of India today. But do we once in a while realize—those of us who are philosophers and metaphysicians—that this empire was the domination of one race over many races? Do we ever try to understand that this empire was nothing but the subjugaion of different peoples and differnt regions by one particular people and one particular region? Yes, it was a domination, a foreign domination, from top to bottom as long as it lasted. We know quite well that the Maruya Empire is older than the Roman Empire. Thus it is clear that it is our forefathers, the Hindus, who, inspite of 160 years of Buddha's teachings, preceded the Romans and all subsequent Europeans in the matter of establishing domination over foreign peoples and countries.

Imperialism of the militaristic-political type belongs to the irreducible minimum of ancient Indian culture.

Let us, then, take one particular sovereign of thid Maurya Empire, our great, beloved and enlightened monarch Asoka. We are told that Ashoka was a paternal ruler. In one of his edicts he class the people his children. Paternalism is a good virtue and is to be respected as such. Now, about his conquest of Orissa. Termendous bloodshed, we are told, was the price of this conquest. We are told also that Asoka shed bitter tears over this calamity. We can take it for granted that he shed tears at this bloodshed. For, after all, we are human beings. And it is human nature as a rule to sympathize with people in their miseries. In modern wars also kings and presidents of republics shed tears over the casualties occurring even among the enemies. It is, further, the custom to offer prayers and garlands at the tombs of *le soldat inconnu* (the unknown soldier) in all countries. Asoka's tender sentiments must have been touched on the occasion of the Orissan horrors. Here, however, as students of history we should be careful enough to note that in ancient times warfares were not very serious affairs in regard to bloodshed. Actual killings could hardly be numerous. Most of the casualties were in the nature of maimed bodies. The ankles, we may believe, might be sprained, the jaws half broken, the muscles swollen, the noses bleeding, and so on. Those wars were very akin to physical exercises and sports. All the same, Asoka's tears are not to be overlooked.

But did Asoka make Orissa free? Did he grant Orissa any "dominion status" or some sort of *swaraj* and self-rule? No. Instead of doing anything like this he swallowed Orissa and annexed it to the Maurya Empire. This gives another proof of the fact that Indians are as capable of political domination or militaristic imperialism as Europeans. There is hardly any difference as human beings between East and West.

Indians were not more moral and spiritual than Europeans, and Auropeans were not more militaristic, more materialistic, more power-loving and domination-loving than Indians. And therefore the philosophy that is today very popular in India, the metaphysics by discussing which we can get recognized overnight as brilliant philosophers, the ism which says that there is a fundamental difference between East and West in regard to outlook on life, life's viewpoints and world-conceptions are entirely fallacious.

WHAT IS AHIMSĀ ?

Now let us analyse the word *ahimsā*. That word has become very common nowadays. Unless we use the word in season and out of season we cannot digest our food. But what could this Sanskrit word have meant? We are taught by philosophers, historians and politicians also to believe that *ahimsā* is the special gift of mother India, the characteristic and exclusive contribution of India to world-culture. I should, therefore, like to know exactly in which period our mother India coined that word. Exactly what did mother India mean by this category, *ahimsā,* in the period? We should ask every-body to institute researches into the doctrine of *ahimsā*. We must ransack three orders of texts, the Buddhist Pali texts, the Jaina Prakrit texts, and finally, the Sanskrit Buddhist and Hindu texts. We shall have to ascertain, first, how many times that word has been used by our forefathers, and, secondly, how many times it was employed to mean the kind of *ahimsā* that is being propagated nowadays by our Indias scholars, leaders and philosophers as the special cult to India.

Researches reveal and without mock modesty it may be said that they are not very extensive—lead to the conclusion, a very simple proposition, that every child understands. In ancient and medieval India the word *ahimsā* signifies—"Do not be jealous, do not be envious, do not be malicious, etc." To a plain blunt man, *ahimsā* means simply absence of jealousy, envy, malice or hatred. This is not a very dangerous proposition after all. This is a copy-book maxim of morality discovered by every race and in every region. If this is to be paraded as the specific contribution of our mother India, we shall be challenged by the representatives of all races because this can be proven to be their contribution also. And if our mother India can not make any better show we should have to feel sorry for the poverty of her creativities. In any case, it is clear that by emphasizing this notion our leaders are serving to make India the laughing stock of all nations.

Another interpretation which can be discovered, not according to imagination but from the texts, is as follows: *Himsā*=killing. *Ahimsā*=non-killing, don't kill. Indians were taught not to kill. Yes. But not to kill what? This lamp post over here or the tree over there? The interpretation that is most common in Buddhistic literature and Jaina Prakrit literature is—"Do not kill animals." But orthodox Hindus know that many of us are used to animal sacrifices. Not every Bengali knows what Mother Kālī does in the non-Bengali parts of India. But our Bengali Kālī *Kalkattawali* eats goats. To a Bengali Hindu, therefore, animal sacrifice is perfectly legitimate. But we can take it that "do not kill an animal" was and continues to be a moral precept among Buddhists, Jainas and to a certain extent also among sections of Hindus, *e.g.,* Vaiṣṇavas. Animal sacrifice is likely to appear cruel in certain eyes. And, therefore, it is easy to believe that non-killing of animals is treated as an injunction of piety and mercy by some classes. All the same, we must not make too much of it as a doctrine or a philosophy. It is just a commonplace dictum of kindness. On this basis one can establish a Society for the prevention of cruelty to animals. Non-killing of animals is a very simple proposition, not an unreasonable proposition, and can be readily understood.

What did the benevolent and merciful Asoka do in this regard? Asoka issued a *firman* to forbid the killing of animals. So far so good. Whether that *firman* was an act of "positive" law we should like to ask our learned friends, the lawyers, to establish. We are not yet perfectly clear about that. To what extent were the edicts of Asoka regarded as the civil and criminal codes of India? We should like this topic to be taken up by students of historical jurisprudence. For the present, we believe that to a certain extent Asoka's *Hitopadeśa* was a sort of morality, perhaps positive morality, but whether it was positive law is not always beyond doubt, indeed, very often questionable.

Me this as it may, what did our Asoka say? He said something like the following: "Do not kill animals, and I am happy that in my regime during the last so many years as a result of my propaganda people have been observing *ahimsā*." But in the edicts he says likewise as follows: "If you my children do not follow my advice I have a sanction." And what is that sanction? Capital punishment. That is, men were to be killed by Asoka if they were to kill an animal. This is the interpretation of *ahimsā* in Indian history by the very champion and *avatar* of *ahimsā*.

These, then, are the two interpretations of *ahimsā*. Today *ahimsā* is being made to mean a third thing. It is being treated as equivalent to non-war, the abandonment of violence or killing in organized human groups. One group of human beings is not to kill another group of human beings, and there is to be no state of war. This is a new proposition altogether different from non-malice and non-killing of animals. The question is this: Does Asoka or does any Buddhist preacher or does even the Buddha himself ever banish war, *i.e.*, organized violence as an instrument for the decision of affairs between any two groups of human beings? Has war, *i.e.*, killing of human beings in organized groups been declared immoral and illegal in any of the Indian legal and moral codes? We ask if *ahimsā* in our Indian literature of the earliest times and of medieval times and later times has ever meant the renunciation or annihilation of war, *i.e.*, the abandonment of mutual killings between human groups. It would be necessary to know on how many occasions and by whom war was ever declared unjustifiable, immoral, and illegal in Indian history.

Indeed, it is very difficult to quote satisfying instances from Indian texts. In the present writer's judgment the concept of war as something illegal, immoral, unjustifiable is not an Indian doctrine. Ancient and medieval Indian thought, Hindu, or Moslim, can lay no claim to this concept. It is a contribution of the Western world to the problem of relations between groups. It is a doctrine of modern times and modern civilization. This doctrine is the creation of Europeans and Americans in the nineteenth century. Perhaps we can trace it back historically to the eighteenth century and even earlier. For the time being, we need not carry on antiquarian researches. So, for the present, *ahimsā*, meaning thereby pacifism in intergroup or international relations, is to be taken as an entirely modern category unknown in Indian political tradition, Indian philosophy, and Indian metaphysical literature.

The present writer is not a politician or a party man. We are masters of our conscience and have right to be pacifists in international morality if we care to. But while preaching or practising pacifism we have no right to believe or to propagate that we are observing *ahimsā* as known in ancient and medieval India. We may even give a new meaning to the old term *ahimsā* if we so desire. But we must not father our own view on old India. As pacifists we are following the modern Western thinkers, perhaps the Quakers, perhaps the socialists. May be, Jean Jaurès, the French socialist, is our *guru*. But we cannot pretend to follow the Jaina Tirthankaras or the Buddhist preachers who were utterby innocent of the limitation or abandonment of wars. Neither Mahāvīra nor Buddha nor Asoka understood *ahimsā* in the sense of international pacifism or socialist non-violence which we may be preaching today. We should have extensive researches carried on into this interesting problem. In case Mahāvīra, Buddha, or Asoka can be demonstrated to have forbidden warfare, *i.e.*, organized killing between groups as inhuman, unpolitical, illegal, and abominable, we should be very happy as Indians to claim for our fatherland some of the originators of the cult, albeit purely speculative and theoretical, with which the names of Abbé St. Pierre, Immannel Kant and others in the Western world are associated.

But situated as indology today is, we have to admit that in the matter of militarist domination Indians are as good or as bad as Europeans. If we take all the decades of Indian history and compare them with all the decades of European history, we shall have nothing to choose between the two on the score of *ahimsā*. The Chola Empire of Southern India was not based on *ahimsā*. It was the result of blood and iron. Neither Alauddin nor Akbar encountered *ahimsā* or practised it among the peoples of India, south, east or west. Let us take the Moghul Empire. What was it but a militarist-political domination? What was the Maratha Empire? Did it not embody the domination of one people over other peoples? The C.P., the U.P., and Gujarat need not be reminded of this fact. We cannot likewise ignore the fact that the Marathas as a people were the greatest world-conquerors of Indian history in the military-political fields. In the present writer's appraisal Shivaji was and continues to be the greatest Hindu of all ages. His exploits it was that rendered possible the establishment of a military-political empire that became the greatest world power on the Indian stage in the eighteenth century. In the interest of metaphysical neurosis or some pshychological aberrations the world cannot be compelled to ignore and forget this history of the last two hundred years.

No historian dealing with objective facts can deny or suppress the militaristic-political qualities of the dozens of Shivajis and hundreds of little *Sārvabhaumas* (worldrulers) that mother India produced from Vedic Sudās to Tipu, Baji, and Ranjit. The Hindus and Mussalmans of old India were not feeble-minded fools in any age of culture-history, whatever they may happen to be today.

IDEOLOGICAL IMPERIALISM

Up till now we have been talking of the militaristic-political domination. This is one kind of empire-building and imperialism. Now there is another kind of imperialism or domination. There one set of ideas is influenced, modified or conquered by another set, one system of morality is compelled to acknowledge the suzerainty or sovereignty of another system. The authority of another set of ideas, ideals and institutions replaces that of a traditional set. The arts and sciences, philosophies, religions, *mores,* manners and customs, and gods and goddesses of one people are replaced by those of another people. This domination or imperialism is ideological. It is impersonal, having hardly anything to do with any individual of flesh and blood.

Man is a brute by all means and tries to influence or conquer others physically and militarily. But it is also true that man is something of a non-brute, *i.e.,* man has tried to listen to reason, and to accept reason. It is very interesting to note that throughout the periods of militaristic-political domination, the domination of the other type, the ideological domination, ideological imperialism also has been going on, almost synchronous with the other imperialism. Very often the militaristic-political empire has had nothing to do with the ideological empire. Once in a while, the ideological empires have been established or influenced or promoted by military-political empires. But, as a rule, the two imperialisms have gone on independently of each other.

Let us take Islam, or Christianity which is older than Islam. As a system of ideas and ideals Christianity has conquered and dominated the world by influencing, modifying, moderating and subjugating the local rites, ceremonies, institutions, moral ideas, and gods and goddesses. Christianity as a system of conversions is one of the greatest ideological imperialisms the world has known. In social science it is the custom to use the term acculturation for this conversion. When one country or people is adopting the religion, customs, and manners of another, the first is being acculturated to the second, and the second likewise to the first. Christianization is an instance of world-domination by an adopted religion. It is imperialism on the ideological plane. The Christian empire is not confined to any particular continent. It has succeeded in encompassing the entire world with more or less doses of success. The Islamization of mankind has been relatively less extensive by the Christian standard.

We shall now mention another ideological imperialism. In the nineteenth and twentieth centuries, it is possible to say, democracy has established an empire among all mankind. The French Revolution, the ideas of 1789, started the world on this path. Today there is hardly anybody anywhere on earth that is not subject to the ideals of democracy, whatever that may mean. Thge undeniable fact is that democratic ideology is one of the most inspiring forces and vital urges among all races. The domination of the human spirit by democratic idealism is a remarkable imperialism of modern times.

Similarly one of the greatest world-empires is being enjoyed by science. Is there any human being today, in East or West, anywhere in the world, who is not subject to the rule of science, to the sovereignty or empire of science?

A fourth ideological empire is that of technocracy and industrialism and, along with them, capitalism. Since the beginning of the nineteenth century capitalism has been enjoing an empire among all peoples. This is an impersonal empire like Christianity or Islam, democracy and science.

Generally antithetic to capitalism is Marxism; the doctrine of Marx. Marxism or socialism in the nineteenth and twentieth centuries has been enjoying a world-empire. Its domination has reached even Asia including India. It is impossible for anybody to deny that socialism is directly or indirectly influencing the thoughts and activities of individuals here and there and everywhere. Socialism, therefore, is as great an ideological imperialism as Christianity or Islam, democracy, science, and capitalism.

So far we have mentioned the ideological imperialisms which are mainly non-Indian in origin. Does India afford illustrations of this second kind of imperialism? She does. India has given rise to ideas, ideals, *vidyās* and *kalās,* arts and sciences, manners and customs, philosophies, politics, moralities, religions, gods and goddesses, and sacred texts such as have conquered the world. Ideological imperialism is one of the greatest contributions of India to world-culture. India as a maker of chapters in world-history is thus to be placed in two different fields, first, as a contributor to militaristic-political domination, and secondly, as a contributor to ideological imperialism. Empire-building of two different kinds is to be credited to the culture or creativity of the Indian people.

Let us try to understand our Hinduism. In the first place, Hinduism is a cult or a religion. It has its gods and goddesses, rituals and ceremonies. In the second place, Hinduism is a system of culture, institutions, social philosophies. It is a system of arts and sciences, manners, beliefs and custome. Now, who established Hinduism? It was established by a small number of people, perhaps somewhere in Sindh or the Punjab, *i.e.,* on the banks of the Indus, the Kabul, the Ravi, or the Bias. The creative persons were perhaps a little colony of half a dozen or several dozen individuals. We call them *Riṣis*. What they called themselves we do not know. But they were creators, epoch-makers. These *Riṣis* established what later became Hinduism. In the beginning their creation or culture was nothing more than the burning of wood. It was fire applied to a few pieces of wood in which *ghee* was to be burnt. Considered objectively, *Yajna, Homa* and sacrifice is the pragmatic form of Hinduism as a religion.

The *Riṣis* who invented it were strong men, sturdy gymnasts, intellectual gymnasts and moral gymnasts, who along with the fire propagated a powerful cult of *Pancha Mahāyajna* (five great sacrifices or social duties). It was not some meanigless hocus-pocus that they started. They started a tremendous social dynamics embracing the multifarous interests of life in its entirety. And their motto was *charaiveti*, march on, march on, march on. That aggressiveness, that desire to proselytize, to influence, to convert, to go on conquering and to conquer is the kern of Hinduism as a religion. "We have lit this little fire," they said, "but it is not to remain confined to this little colony, to this our village. It has to be spread farther and farther. We are not to stay at home. There is that river, the cult has to spread to it, that river over there has to be crossed. And from village to village, from forest to forest, and from river to river, and on and on, it has to march, conquer, missionize until the whole world comes under its domination."

The *Riṣis* taught Young India to say, "*Ahamasmi sahamāna*, etc." "Mighty am I, superior by name upon the earth, conquering am I, all-conquering, completely conquering every region." This is the inspiration of Hinduism, the cult of *charaiveti* (march on), the culture of *digvijaya* (world-conquest), the philosophy of world-conversion.

This was not the mere enthusiasm of half a dozen nervous, rickety, malaria-stricken people, but the declaration of faith of those who actually marched on from one river to another and crossed one hill-top after another. The whole of India has come under their domination. Finally, an ideological empire has been established by what in our ignorance or absence of a better term, we describe as Hinduism. Hinduism is a world-conquering cult and culture, determined to organize missions in order to civilize or dominate the world. Hinduization is acculturation of diverse races, peoples and regions to Hindu norms and *mores*. We said that Christianity (or Islam), democracy, science, capitalism and socialism are ideological imperialisms or impersonal dominations and that these five isms or systems enjoy a world-position. Now as students, as mere intellectuals we cannot but objectively recognize Hinduism, understood whether as a system of cult or of culture, as another specimen of ideological world-imperialism of race-less, cosmopolitan and impersonal character.

The term 'world-empire' is being used in connection with Hinduism as a religion and as a culture. This is not a hyperbole. In the first place, the present writer's conception of the world is to be recalled as consisting in the very neighbourhood of the creative individual. Thus considered, the smallest territorial area conceivable can be aptly described as the conqueror's world. In the second place, India is a huge sub-continent, a world by itself. And last but not least, let us ask the question : "Is Hinduism confined to India?" And the answer is : "No."

The spirit of India has not rested content within the boundaries of the Indian sub-continent. Afghanistan and Central Asia were conquered by our Hindu religion and Hindu culture. Likewise was China conquered and it is in that conquest that we have to see the deeper significance of the Chinese Goodwill Missions of today. Burma and Siam were also similarly Hinduized. In Siam (or Thailand) we find that the names of rulers are derived from Rama, Vikrama, Varman, Jaya, Indra, Ananda, etc. Likewise in Indo-China do we encounter Hindu culture in daily life. In Sumatra, Java and the other Insulindian islands as well as in far-off Japan Hinduization is similarly manifest in temples, gods and goddesses, rituals and ceremonies. Korea, Manchuria, Mongolia, Siberia, Turkestan,—all these regions of Asia are to be recognized to a certain extent as the colonies of Hindu cult and Hindu culture. In one word, the whole of northern, southern and eastern Asia bears traces of Hindu ideological imperialism. This represents the domination of Hindu ideology over others, their acculturation to Hindu ideas and ideals.

Is Western Asia to be treated as outside the sphere of influence of Hindu imperialism? No. Hindu arts and sciences, algebra, arithmetic, *Ayurveda,* therapeutics, metallurgy, fables, stories, philosophies crossed the Himalaya mountains and the Khyber Pass. Hindu ideas were assimilated by the Iranian, Hellenic, Hellenistic and Romanized peoples. They were, later, accepted as the arts and sciences of the Muslims, the Saracens of Baghdad. From the latter they passed on to the Europeans who accepted them as some of the foundations of their mathematics, chemistry, medicine, etc. Thus our Hindu ideals, manners and sentiments which began at Mohenjodaro in Sindh and in the Punjab have spread everywhere in Asia and to a certain extent in Europe. Hinduism is then by all means a world-imperialism.

These Hindu sheres of influence were so many "Greater Indians" in Asia. The expansion of India consisted in the establishment of the ideological imperialism of Hindu cult and culture throughout the length and breadth of the Asian continent. These colonizing, missionizing or proselytizing enterprises of Indians outside the Indian frontiers may be said to have commenced in the third century B.C. The active period of *digvijaya* (world-conquest) or *charaiveti* (march on) of Hindu religion, arts and sciences continued until the thirteenth or fourteenth century. During these sixteen or seventeen hundred years India witnessed military-political vicissitudes of all sorts almost identical with those in contemporary Europe. The ideological dominations of the Hindus as established in the different regions of Asia were not necessarily of the functions of their military and political activities at home or abroad. This is an important item in connection with the ideological imperialism of the Hindus in ancient and medieval times which must never be lost sight of.

We have said before that the ideological empires of the world, viz., Christianity, socialism, etc., have no necessary connection with military-political imperialism. The two imperialisms are mainly independent of each other. If there is any contact between the two, that contact is often an accident. But scientifically speaking, it is impossible to demonstrate that political imperialism has been the cause and the only cause of ideological imperialism. The same is to be observed about Hindu ideological imperialism *vis-a-vis* Hindu political activities. The Hindu conquests in Asia from one end to the other were in the main non-political, non-military. Our ancient Indian culture went to Japan and was accepted by Japan but the Japanese knew hardly anything of Indian political and military achievements. If we take the case of Sumatra, Java, Bali, Borneo and other islands where Hindu culture still persists, we shall find that they were not, if at all, under the political domination of the South Indian Cholas for any long period. Political imperialism was hardly ever the basis of the ideological imperialism established by the Hindus. Indeed, militaristic-political domination may be removed almost entirely from the picture. No matter how many large, medium or small states were being established on Indian soil during this millennium and a half, no matter how many times we were fighting among ourselves, the conquests made by Hinduism as a religion and as a culture were going on from one country to another. The authors of the *Mahābhārata* and the *Rāmāyaṇa,* Manu, Buddha, Pāṇiṇi, Charaka, Patanjali, Nāgārjuna, and Kālidāsa were all the time conquering the world, very often supremely indifferent to the militaristic-political fortunes of their compatriots.

The story of all these ideological imperialisms or dominations, Indian as well as non-Indian, proves beyond question that almost invariably their progress is independent of political imperialisms or dominations. In order to be established as a dominant world-force an ideology does not have always to be backed up by a powerful political people or party. Indeed, the opposite picture is prominent on several occasions when "captive Greece captured Rome." Even a political slave can ideologically conquer the master.

INDIA'S ADDRESS IN THE MODERN WORLD

Attention may now be invited to the ideological empire of the twentieth century which we Indians—Hindus and Mussalmans—have commenced establishing,—although for the time being on rather modest basis,—in Asia, Europe, Africa, and, last but not least, America. This new empire is the second ideological contribution of India to world-culture. It is at present only in its rough, crude and humble beginnings. But one ought to be perfectly clear about the fact that even without, political domination, nay, political freedom, it is possible to influence, convert, capture and conquer the world in ideas, ideals, arts and sciences.

In the twentieth century we Indians are living under conditions of military-political subjection. Is it not ridiculous to think that a people that militarily and politically belongs to an alien empire should itself be credited with having established an ideological empire in the world? The answer to this and allied questions has already been furnished by the experiences of ideological world-imperalism discussed above. We have historical evidences to the effect that the ideological influence, conquest or domination is not necessarily a correlate of political activities.

We need not appeal always to the history of other epochs or other peoples in regard to human progress. Let us take the objective facts of India in the nineteenth and twentieth centuries. There is no doubt, be it repeated, that India is a subject country. And yet who, endowed with the objective sense, can doubt that the Indian people has been making progress in the same sense and along the same lines—always not perhaps to the same extent—as all the other peoples including the politically and militarily most dominant? The progress can be demonstrated by indices of all sorts. It should be necessary at the outset to bid adieu to sentimentalizings about the alleged golden age in old India's epochs of military-political freedom. In regard to the economic situation we have no answer questions like the following: Did the Marathas enjoy greater prosperity under Shivaji and Baji Rao than today? Did the Bengalis enjoy greater prosperity in the days of Ali Vardi Khan or Vijayasena? Did the Punjabis enjoy greater prosperity under the Khalsas or Anandapala? Did the people of Madras enjoy greater prosperity under Tipu Sultan or Rajendra Chola? Statistically, it is impossible to prove that India in the nineteenth and twentieth centuries has been becoming poorer and poorer. By all objective tests,—in the matter of transport, export and import, agricultural output, manufactures and semi-manufactures, housing, all sorts of articles for consumption, even in the matter of the *dhoti* which every Indian wears—by every economic index, it is possible to demonstrate that even in spite of foreign rule India has been progressing in the economic domain.

It does not belong to the present writer's science to furnish arguments in justification of political-military subjection. Nor is it necessary to wax eloquent over the blessings of sovereignty in external and internal affairs. The glories of political freedom are by all means to be accepted as first postulates. Politics is indeed a force in a human affairs and a powerful force. Freedom is a necessity for all mankind. But politics is not the only force. There are other forces not less powerful than freedom. A free country is not necessarily rich, nor is a subject country necessarily poor. However creative, inspiring and powerful political freedom may be as a spiritual and material force, it cannot, pragmatically considered, be taken to be the exclusive determinant in human civilization. A "political interpretation of history" in an *advaita* or monistic manner is as untenable as a "monistic economic interpretation" or a monistic Freudian (sexological) determinism.

We have today the beginnings of a new Indian Empire,—a new Indian nucleus of world-influences—which bids fair to be a worthy continuation of the ideological empire of the ancient and medieval Indians. True it is that in the nineteenth century there was a great break in Indian creativity and culture-making desire and power. After the overthrow of Tipu Sultan and Baji Rao and later of Ranjit Singh the entire Indian mentality became undoubtedly and almost entirely pessimistic. From one end of the country to the other, people lost all hopes. Was there anything to be done? European scholars, those "friends of India", came to us as teachers and we went to their country as pupils, as learners, and we were taught that our forefathers down to 1757, 1818 or 1857 were quite worthless people; and we were asked to believe that East was fundamentally different from West, and that there was nothing in common between the two. "You,Orientals," they said, "you do not understand life, human beings, the earth, this world of ours. You do not understand secular interests, forts and fortifications, health and sanitation, construction of roads, village organization, family life, law and polity. These are much too material things for your mentality. The spiritual genius of India has always considered them to be beneath notice." May be, why, almost certainly the Indians of that generation were flattered by such remarks coming from the Western "friends of India,"from men like Max Müller, for example.

What, according to these Westerners, were the Orientals fit for? They conferred on Asia and especially on India the glory of extra-mundane achievements, the credit of understanding in an extraordinary degree the affairs of the other-world, the spirit, the soul, communion with the divine, and what not. "Don't you see," said they in a seemingly appreciative manner, "how wonderful Indian intuition is? How exquisite and fine is the work of Indian imagination! Your *forte* lies in the life after death. You are past masters in that life. Your brain is used to the super-sensual, the esoteric, the refined and delicate concerns of the transcendental world. Stick to that as your splendid patrimony. Don't soil your hands by touching the materialistic and dirty things of the life below." That is the philosophy that Europe and America administered, not in homeopathic doses, but in big allopathic doses, to the intellectuals of India, those who later became the guardians of our morals and dominating personalities in our midst.

Naturally, as a consequence the East, India, was regarded as just a continent of molly-coddles and slaves to be dominated by Europeans and Americans. In foreign countries a man from the East meant a coolie, an Indian was equivalent to a slave. In Europe and America an Indian at best meant only a student, just a learner going there for an academic degree and coming back with a certificate written by a white hand, to be cashed in the cultural stock exchanges of India,—Government offices and such other establishments,—for a job of Rs. 250 to Rs. 1250 per month.

All the same, Indians—both Hindus and Mussalmans—were not unhappy to be thus entrusted by Eur-Americans with the glorious responsibility of managing the affairs of the Divine Communion. This was the position of India down to a particular time. But even India, often gullible as she is, could not be fooled all the time. The situation had to change. How could the transformation be accomplished? How did Eur-Americans as well as Indians get debamboozled into the realities of the world-situation? How did Eur-Americans as well as Indians themselves come to realize that Indians were human beings of flesh and blood and not some messengers of God?

The opportunity came when in 1893 a mammoth elearing-house of cultures was convoked on the shores of the lake of Michigan at Chicago in the U.S.A. It was the meeting-place of about 5,000 men and women. There were theologians and religious preachers, social scientists, anthropologists, philosophers, and natural scientists of the two hemispheres present. Most of them were white but a few were yellow and brown like ourselves. That cultural exchange also counted among its members millionaires and milliardaires, big businessmen, transportation experts, engineers, chemists and mill-owners. It was the assembly of 5,000 Americans, Europeans and Asians that received for the first time a rude shock of a peculiar character. The rude shock was due to a bombshell thrown in the midst of that huge pandemonium declaring the equality between East and West. For the first time in the history of modern civilization and after the overthrow of Baji Rao and Ranjit Singh was heard the voice of Young India in and through that bomb-shell. It was the voice of a human being, not an esoteric creature dealing in the spiritual goods of the other-world.

What he talked was perhaps not clear to many. But how he talked—the manner of his talk—was perceptible to all. It was challenging, it was a call to arms. The voice was that of modern India, an India bent upon a moral and intellectual tug of war with the world today. The audience had come to a Parliament fo Religions. The impact of that bomb-shell was religious, no doubt, but more than religious too. It covered the interests of entire human life, embracing as it did the whole problem of inter-racial contacts. The bomb-shell may be said to have announced to the world-pandemonium as follows:— "You, Eur-Americans, from now on be ready to consider yourselves to be the pupils of Asia and, of course, of India also as the creator of modern values,—just as we are not ashamed to declare ourselves as the pupils of Eur-America. Reciprocal discipleship or reciprocal mastership is to be the relation from now on. No onesided superiority or inferiority complex is to rule the international pattern tomorrow and day after tomorrow."That was, so to say, the Monroe Doctrine for Asia in the spiritual realm.

It went on, so to say, in the following strain: "You Europeans and Americans must not think that you are born to dominate Asia for all the centuries. Just note that you arenot going to have a greater domination on our Asian soil than Asians can have on Eur-American soil. We are going to dominate you ideologically to the same extent and in the same sense as you dominate us in the same field, although in military-political matters you happen to be our masters for the time being. If you want that our ideologies should be off Europe and America, from now on your ideologies should also have to be off Asia." This is the ideological Monroe Doctrine from the Asian side. The doctrine,—implying as it does "Hands off Asia" on the cultural plane,—was enumerated for the first time in the history of modern civilization by a young man born on the banks of the southern Ganges, and he was at once recognized as a re-creator of values, as a remaker of mankind, as a world conqueror. We refer to Swami Vivekananda.

THE RAMAKRISHNA EMPIRE

The desire and the power of the Indian people to create and to dominate in the world of modern values have been in evidence uninterruptedly since that event of 1893. The "ideas of 1905" constitute an important land-mark as embodying in a concrete form on the Indian soil the spirit of world-conquest manifested by Vivekananda in the U.S.A.

The Progress that we have been able to accomplish during the last fifty years, especially since the glorious revolution of 1905,—the *Swadeshi* movement, the *Swaraj* revolution of Young India,—the progress that has been achieved in industrialization, banking, insurance, commerce, etc., as well as in scientific researches, in activities on the international plane is something of which any people in the world can be proud. The political, economic and cultural activities of Indians—both Hindus and Muslims,—since 1905 are being watched by the entire world. What we are doing at Bombay, Calcutta, Lahore or Madras is attracting notice among all nations. It is being studies in New York, Tokyo, Berlin, Paris, Moscow, Rome and, last but not least, in London. It will not do to be blind to the reality that our thoughts, our aims and our movements are already world-commodities. This little trade union movement over here and that little political activity over there are all being commented upon in the newspapers of the world. India has succeeded in establishing world-contacts. Indians today are thus not tiny little bugs to be crushed out of existence according to the whims of a particular group of individuals living in a certain corner of the earth. India is a power,—of course, a junior power—among the powers of the world. She is influencing mankind in many directions although, no doubt, as yet not in a powerful manner. But men with eyes in East and West can see that Young India is already a creative force and has been establishing an address among the *Vishwa-shakti* (world-forces) in the realm of ideas, ideals and creativities of the ideological type.

Today there is hardly any journal of mathematics, physics, chemistry, geology, botany, zoology, medicine or the other natural sciences conducted by Europeans and Americans which is not publishing something by an Indian scholar or which does not review the work done by Indian scholars. Our Indian antiquarians and historians as well as researchers in the other human and social sciences have also come of age and have been recognized by European and American savants as their peers. This is a thing which was hardly known even down to 1905. In all these arts and sciences Indians today are not mere learners but have grown—although not in very large numbers yet—into teachers also. It is an aspect of world-domination in the sense of equality and constructive co-operation between

East and West which has to be visualized in connection with the new Indian Empire of the twentieth century. Vivekananda was the founder of this new Indian Empire because, in the present writer's opinion, previous to him hardly any Indian had ever been recognized in Europe and America as a world-conquering force.

This new Indian Empire is not identical and is not to be confounded with the influences of ancient Indian culture on the Eur-American culture of the last century and a half as noticeable in the romantic movement, "new thought" cults, theosophy, vegetarianism and so fourth. The modern West's interest in the old East, in the Asian literature, art, philosophy, etc., of bygone days, and in Orientalism as a branch of archaeological and antiquarian investigations is certainly an important feature in the contemporary contacts between India and Eur-America. But Vivekananda's pioneering goes much beyond this. It ushers in a new era of modern India's creations in the arts and sciences and co-operation with the modern West in the new problems and achievements of mankind.

Vivekananda is the first man to establish that empire, and it is lucky that with Vivekananda that empire did not cease to exist. He succeeded in leaving behind him a tradition of self-sacrifice, of the glorious vow of poverty, of spirituality combined with organizing power, and that tradition is embodied today in one of his creations, the Ramakrishna Mission. The activities of this Mission have reached in a somewhat stable albeit modest form several countries of Europe including England. The Mission is represented in South America also. In the United States of America it has centres in nearly a dozen cities. As is well known, the Mission has of course a network of institutions throughout India and Ceylon as well as Burma and the Federated Malaya States. Outside of Indian and Asian frontiers these institutions have served,—although not yet in very considerable proportions,—to bring Eur-American intellectuals, publicists, and culture-leaders into regular intercourse with the organizers of the Ramakrishna Order as well as other Indian scholars, businessmen and travellers. Contacts between East and West are thereby being maintained in Western centres of learning, commerce and politics on terms of equality and mutual goodwill. An international co-operation of this type had never been attempted in modern times previous to the establishment of this new Greater India. This is why the present writer has often described the Swamis of the Ramakrishna Mission as constituting the International Spiritual Service and the International Social Service of India. This body of cultural and ideological workers is not less profoundly constructive and significant for India and the world than the Indian Civil Service (I.C.S.), the Indian Medical Service (I.M.S.) the Indian Educational Service (I.E.S.), the Indian Police Service (I.P.S.) and so forth of the Government of India, or the several services that used to be maintained by the now defunct League of Nations.

The Ramkrishna Empire is not exclusively the work of the Ramkrishna Mission. It is the work of Industrialists, of scientists, of antiquarians, of poets, of painters, of religious missionaries, of business magnates, of trade unions, and of political leaders of all denominations. By political leaders,—although the present writer does not belong to any political party,—we mean not only people above forty but even young men and women between the ages of eighteen and twenty-five who are doing idealistic or constructive work. These young men and women are demostrating to the world, along with the adults in letters, science and industry, trade union organizers, businessmen and the Ramakrishna Mission that India is out conquering and to conquer. All those men and women, who are trying to crush to pieces the Himalayan obstacles that hamper the progress of India and to promote modern spirituality and society among the Indian people are establishing in their own personalities and in their daily activities that fundamental doctrine of equality between East and West and international cooperation on terms of mutuality.

The Ramakrishna Empire is still in its nonage. It has just commenced its career and is hardly yet adequately known. But among its architects is to be mentioned the legion of men and women who are working at home and abroad in the most diverse fields of thought and action and in the most heterogeneous ways. Whatever is being done by Indians in industry, commerce, science, education, literature, fine arts, politics, labour organization, religion and social service is a contribution to the strengthening of India's claims to recognition as a colleague of the other creative countries of the modern world. Not every builder of the Ramakrishna Empire is a religious preacher. Nor is every builder of this new Indian Empire a Hindu. The Mussalmans as well as the Christians of India have also been contributing to the Greater India as embodied in this Empire. It is not to be supposed that the Ramakrishna Empire is being constructed exclusively by the intellectuals and other high-brows. The industrial workingmen in the factories of India are no less valuable builders of this organization than the Tatas and other big industrialists. Nay, Indian emigrants in the different overseas lands of the two hemispheres are also powerfully helping forward the evolution of this new Indian Empire in so far as they are exhibiting their creativities in a manner which can be recognized by their non-Indian colleagues as of at least equal worth with their own work in the same lines. Every Indian man and every Indian woman, who embody in their daily thoughts and actions the desire and the power to influence, to convert and to dominate are to be listed in the ever-growing schedule of the pillars of the Ramakrishna Empire.

Why do we call this "Greater India" of today, this new Indian Empire of the twentieth century, the Ramakrishna Empire? Our logic is very elementary. Vivekananda used to describe all his own activities as the activities of his Master, Ramakrishna. The empire that was brought into being by his personality is therefore aptly to be described, in our estimation, as the Ramakrishna Empire. And this is what has been done as several occasions, at Rangoon, Karachi, Calcutta, Delhi, Patna, Bombay and elsewhere (1936-40).

For this logic we have some historical basis also. It is desirable once more to recall the first ideological empire of ancient and medieval India. That Greater India was the cumulative result of all sorts of Indian thoughts and enterprises carried on for over a millennium and a half. The workers were in many instances Brahminic Hindu in the narrow sectarian sense. Nor everybody among the Indian colonizers, missionaries and ideological empirebuilders of those days was thus strictly speaking a Buddhist. But it is very interesting that most of the Indian activities of that long period of history have come to be known in the world rightly or wrongly as Buddhist activities. The Greater Indias of those days have come to be described as so many bits of Buddhist India outside the Indian frontiers. That remarkable personality, Buddha, has furnished the name of the vast ideological empire of Indians throughout the Asian Continent.

Asia was conquered by the spirit of India as a whole, not by Buddhists as a sect or by Shaivas as a sect or by Vaishnavas as a sect. It is the stories of the *Rāmayana* and the *Mahābhārata* that conquered for India the painters, sculptures, poets and preachers of Asia. It is the laws of Manu by which social, economic and political norms of Asia were acculturated to Indian conditions. It is the Ayurvedic system of therapeutics that captured the medical experts of Asia. The *digvijaya* of decimal system of notation brought Asia within the Indian sphere of influence. Buddha was not the only Indian world-conqueror in Asia. And yet India is known in Asia as the land not so much of Rama, Shiva, Manu, Panini, Charaka and others as of Buddha. It is an accident of history perhaps. But it is a reality of international culture-contact.

Nothing is more curious than the fact that since the days of Yuan-Chwang, the Chinese scholar-organizer-educationist of the seventh century, even the *danton*, the twing that is used as tooth-stick, has been known in China as something Buddhist. And why? Because in the mule-loads of things Indian carried to China by Yuan-Chwang from the land of Buddha were to be found hundreds of articles not excluding the *danton*. It is as if we in Asia were to describe the steam-engine as Christian because in sooth it was imported into Asia along with many other things from Europe whose inhabitants happen to be Christian by faith.

The ideological empire of the Indian people that has been slowly but steadily evolving since 1893 is but an embodiment of the creative urges of all the self-conscious men and women of India in their entirety. But we are following the precedent furnished by history in order to describe it after Ramakrishna because he was the inspirer of Vivekananda, who, as the representative of Young India, succeeded in laying the first foundation-stone. The Ramakrishna Empire, then, as the successor of the Buddhist Empire, is growing into the second specimen of Indian ideological imperialism, constituting thereby another epoch of India in world-culture.

—DR. BINOY KUMAR SARKAR

15

INDIAN CULTURE AND EXTERNAL INFLUENCE

In considering Indian civilisation and its renascence, I suggested that a powerful new creation in all fields was our great need, the meaning of the renascence and the one way of preserving the civilisation. Confronted with the huge rush of modern life and thought, invaded by another dominant civilisation almost her opposite or inspired at least with a very different spirit to her own, India can only survive by confronting this raw, new, aggressive, powerful world with fresh diviner creations of her own spirit, cast in the mould of her own spiritual ideals. She must meet it by solving its greater problems,—which she cannot avoid, even if such avoidance could be thought desirable,—in her own way, through solutions arising out of her own being and from her own deepest and largest knowledge. In that connection I spoke of the acceptance and assimilation from the West of whatever in its knowledge, ideas, powers was assimilable, compatible with her spirit, reconcilable with her ideals, valuable for a new statement of life. This question of external influence and new creation from within is of very considerable importance; it calls for more than a passing mention. Especially it is necessary to form some more precise idea of what we mean by acceptance and of the actual effect of assimilation; for this is a problem of pressing incidence in which we have to get our ideas clear and fix firmly and seeingly on our line of solution.

But it is possible to hold that while new creation—and not a motionless sticking to old forms—is our one way of life and salvation, no acceptance of anything western is called for, we can find in ourselves all that we need; no considerable acceptance is possible without creating a breach which will bring pouring in the rest of the occidental deluge. That, if I have not misread it, is the sense of a comment on these articles in a Bengali literary periodical[1] which holds up the ideal of a new creation to arise from within entirely on national lines and in the national spirit. The writer takes his stand on a position which is common ground, that humanity is one, but different peoples are variant soul-forms of the common humanity. When we find the oneness, the principle of variation is not destroyed but finds rather its justification; it is not by abolishing ourselves, our own special temperament and power, that we can get at the living oneness, but by following it out and raising it to its highest possibilities of freedom and action. That is a truth which I have myself insisted on repeatedly, with regard to the modern idea and attempt at some kind of political unification of humanity, as a very important part of the psychological sense of social development, and again in this question of a particular people's life and culture in all its parts and manifestations. I have insisted that uniformity is not a real but a dead unity: uniformity kills life while real unity, if well founded, becomes vigorous and fruitful by a rich energy of variation. But the writer adds that the idea of taking over what is best in occidental civilisation is a false notion without a living meaning; to leave the bad and take the good sounds very well, but this bad and this good are not separable in that way: they are the inextricably mingled growth of one being, not separate blocks of a child's toy house set side by side and easily detachable,—and what is meant then by cutting out and taking one element and leaving the rest? If we take over a western ideal, we take it over from a living form which strikes us; we imitate that form, are subjugated by its spirit and natural tendencies, and the good and bad intertwined in the living growth come in upon us together and take united possession. In fact, we have been for a long time so imitating the West, trying to become like it or partly like it and have fortunately failed, for that would have meant creating a bastard or twy-natured culture; but twy-natured, as Tennyson makes his

Lucretius say, is no-natured and a bastard culture is no sound, truth-living culture. An entire return upon ourselves is our only way of salvation.

There is much to be said here, it seems to me, both in the way of confirmation and of modification. But let us be clear about the meaning of our terms. That the attempt in the last century which still in some directions continues,—to imitate European civilisation and to make ourselves a sort of brown Englishmen, to throw our ancient culture into the dust-bin and put on the livery or uniform of the West was a mistaken and illegitimate endeavour, I heartily agree. At the same time a certain amount of imitation, a great amount even, was, one might almost say, a biological necessity, at any rate a psychological necessity of the situation. Not only when a lesser meets a greater culture, but when a culture which has fallen into a state of comparative inactivity, sleep, contraction, is faced with, still more when it receives the direct shock of a waking, active, tremendously creative civilisation, finds thrown upon it novel and successful powers and functionings, sees an immense succession and development of new ideas and formations, it is impelled by the very instinct of like to take over these ideas and forms, to annex, to enrich itself, even to imitate and reproduce, and in one way or in another take large account and advantage of these new forces and opportunities. That is a phenomenon which has happened repeatedly in history, in a greater or lesser degree, in part or in totality. But if there is only a machanical imitation, if there is a subordination and servitude, the inactive or weaker culture perishes, it is swallowed up by the invading leviathan. And even short of that, in proportion as there is a leaning towards these undesirable things, it languishes, is unsuccessful in its attempt at annexation, loses besides the power of its own spirit. To recover its own centre, find its own base and do whatever it has to do in its own strength and genius is certainly the one way of salvation. But even then a certain amount of acceptance, of forms too,—some imitation, if all taking over of forms must be called imitation,—is inevitable. We have, for instance, taken over in literature the form of the novel, the short story, the critical essay among a number of other adoptions, in science not only the discoveries and inventions, but the method and instrumentation of inductive research, in politics the press, the platform, the forms and habits of agitation, the public association. I do not suppose that anyone seriously thinks of renouncing or exiling these modern additions to our life,—though they are not all of them by any means unmixed blessings,—on the ground that they are foreign importations. But the question is what we do with them and whether we can bring them to be instruments and by some characteristic modification moulds of our own spirit. If so, there has been an acceptance and an assimilation; if not, there has been merely a helpless imitation.

But the taking over of forms is not the heart of the question. When I speak of acceptance and assimilation, I am thinking of certain influences, ideas, energies brought forward with a great living force by Europe, which can awaken and enrich our own cultural activities and cultural being if we succeed in dealing with them a victorious power and originality, if we can bring them into our characteristic way of being and transform them by its shaping action. That was in fact what our own ancestors did, never losing their originality, never effacing their uniqueness, because always vigorously creating from within, with whatever knowledge or artistic suggestion from outside they thought worthy of acceptance or capable of an Indian treatment. But I would certainly repel the formula of taking the good and leaving the bad as a crudity, one of those facile formulas which catch the superficial mind but are unsound in conception. Obviously, if we "take over" anything, the good and the bad in it will come in together pell-mell. If we take over for instance that terrible, monstrous and compelling thing, that giant Asuric creation, European industrialism,—unfortunately we are being forced by circumstances to do it,—whether we take it in its form or its principle, we may under more favourable conditions develop by it our wealth and economic resources, but assuredly we shall get too its social discords and moral plagues and cruel problems, and I do not see how we shall avoid becoming the slaves of the economic aim in life and losing the spiritual principle of our culture.

But, besides, these terms good and bad in this connection mean nothing definite, give us no help. If I must use them, where they can have only a relative significance, in a matter not of ethics, but of an interchange between life and life, I must first give them this general significance that whatever helps me to find myself more intimately, nobly, with a greater and sounder possibility of self-expressive creation, is good; whatever carries me out of my orientation, whatever weakens and belittles my power, richness, breadth and height of self-being, is bad for me. If the distinction is so understood, it will be evident, I think, to any serious and critical mind which tries to fathom things, that the real point is not the taking over of this or that formal detail, which has only a sing value, for example, widow remarriage, but a dealing with great effective ideas, such as are the ideas, in the external field of life, of social and political liberty, equality, democracy. If I accept any of these ideas it is not because they are modern or European, which is in itself no recommendation, but because they are human, because they present fruitful viewpoints to the spirit, because they are things of the greatest importance in the future development of the life of man. What I mean by acceptance of the effective ideal of democracy,—the thing itself, never fully worked out, was present an an element in ancient Indian as in ancient European polity and society,—-is that I find its inclusion in our future way of living, in some shape, to be a necessity of our growth. What I mean by assimilation, is that we must not take it crudely in the European forms, but must go back to whatever corresponds to it, illumines its sense, justifies its highest purport in our own spiritual conception of life and existence, and in that light work out its extent, degree, form, relation to other ideas, application. To everything I would apply the same principle, to each in its own kind, after its proper Dharma, in its right measure of importance, its spiritual, intellectual, ethical, aesthetic, dynamic utility.

I take it as a self-evident law of individual being applicable to group-individuality, that it is neither desirable nor possible to exclude everything that comes in to us from outside. I take it as an equally self-evident law that a living organism, which grows not by accretion but by self-development and assimilation, must recast the things it takes in to suit the law and form and characteristic action of its biological or psychological body, reject what would be deleterious or poisonous to it,—and what is that but the non-assimilable?—take only what can be turned into useful stuff of self-expression. It is, to use an apt Sanskrit phrase employed in the Bengali tongue, *ātmasātkaraṇa,* an assimilative appropriation, a making the thing settle into oneself and turn into characteristic form of our self-being. The impossibility of entire rejection arises from the very fact of our being a term of diversity in a unity, not really separate from all other existence, but in relation with all that surrounds us, because in life this relation expresses itself very largely by a process of interchange. The undesirability of total rejection, even if it were entirely possible, arises from the fact that interchange with the environment is necessary to a healthy persistence and growth; the living organism which rejects all such interchange, would speedily languish and die of lathargy and inanition.

Mentally, vitally and physically I do not grow by a pure self-development from within in a virgin isolation; I am not a separate self-existent being proceeding from a past to a new becoming in a world of its own where no one is but itself, nothing works but its own inner powers and musings. There is in every individualised existence a double action, a self-development from within which is its greatest intimate power of being and by which it is itself, and a reception of impacts from outside which it has to accommodate to its own individuality and make into material of self-growth and self-power. The two operations are not mutually exclusive, nor is the second harmful to the first except when the inner genius is too weak to deal victoriously with its environmental world; on the contrary the reception of impacts stimulates in a vigorous and healthy being its force for self-development and is an aid to a greater and more pronouncedly characteristic self-determination. As we rise in the scale we find that the power of original development from within, of conscious self-determination increases more and more, while in those who live most powerfully in themselves it reaches striking, sometimes almost divine proportions. But at the same time we see that the allied power of seizing upon the impacts and suggestions of the outside world grows in proportion; those who live most powerfully in themselves, can also most largely use the world and all its material for the Self,—and, it must be added, most successfully help the world and enrich it out of their own being. The man who most finds and lives from the inner self, can most embrace the universal and become one with it; the *svarāṭ*, independent, self-possessed and self-ruler, can most be the *samrāṭ*, possessor and shaper of the world in which he lives, can most too grow one with all in the Atman. That is the truth this developing existence teaches us, and it is one of the greatest secrets of the old Indian spiritual knowledge.

Therefore to live in one's self, determining one's self-expression from one's own centre of being in accordance with one's own law of being, *svadharma*, is the first necessity. Not to be able to do that means disintegration of the life; not to do it sufficiently means languor, weakness, inefficiency, the danger of being oppressed by the environing forces and overborne; not to be able to do it wisely, intuitively, with a strong use of one's inner material and inner powers, means confusion, disorder and finally decline and loss of vitality. But also not to be able to use the material that the life around offers us, not to lay hold on it with an intuitive selection and a strong mastering assimilation is a serious deficiency and a danger to the existence. To a healthy individuality the external impact or entering energy, idea, influence may act as an irritant awakening the inner being to a sense of discord, incompatibility or peril, and then there is a struggle, an impulse and process of rejection; but even in this struggle, in this process of rejection there is some resultant of change and growth, some increment of the power and material of life; the energies of the being are stimulated and helped by the attack. It may act as a stimulus, awakening a new action of the self-consciousness and a sense of fresh possibility,—by comparison, by suggestion, by knowcking at locked doors and arousing slumbering energies. It may come in as a possible material which has then to be reshaped to a form of the inner energy, harmonised with the inner being, reinterpreted in the light of its own characteristic self-consciousness. In a great change of environment or a close meeting with a mass of invading influences all these processes work together and there is possibly much temporary perplexity and difficulty, many doubtful and perilous movements, but also the opportunity of a great self-developing transformation or an immense and vigorous renascence.

The group-soul differs from the individual only in being more self-sufficient by reason of its being as assemblage of many individual selves and capable within of many group variations. There is a constant inner interchange which may for a long time suffice to maintain the vitality, growth, power of developing activity, even when there is a restricted interchange with the rest of humanity. Greek civilisation,—after growing under the influence of Egyptian, Phoenician and other Oriental influences,—separated itself sharply from the non-Hellenic "barbarian" cultures and was able for some centuries to live within itself by a rich variation and internal interchange. There was the same phenomenon in ancient India of a culture living intensely from within in a profound differentiation from all surrounding cultures, its vitality rendered possible by an even greater richness of internal interchange and variation. Chinese civilisation offers a third instance. But at no time did Indian culture exclude altogether external influences; on the contrary a very great power of selective assimilation, subordination and transformation of external elements was a characteristic of its processes; it protected itself from any considerable or overwhelming invasion, but laid hands on and included whatever struck or impressed it and in the act of inclusion subjected it to a characteristic change which harmonised the new element with the spirit of its own culture. But nowadays any such strong separative aloofness as distinguished the ancient civilisations, is no longer possible; the races of mankind have come too close to each other, are being thrown together in a certain unavoidable life unity. We are confronted with the more difficult problem of living in the full stress of this greater interaction and imposing on its impacts the law of our being.

Any attempt to remain exactly what we were before the European invasion or to ignore in future the claims of a modern environment and necessity is foredoomed to an obvious failure. However much we may deplore some of the characteristics of that intervening period in which we were dominated by the western standpoint or move away from the standpoint back to our own characteristic way of seeing existence, we cannot get rid of a certain element of inevitable change it has produced upon us, any more than a man can go back in life to what he was some years ago and recover entire and unaffected a past mentality. Time and its influences have not only passed over him, but carried him forward in their stream. We cannot go backward to a past form of our being, but we can go forward to a large repossession of ourselves in which we shall make a better, more living, more real, more self-possessed use of the intervening experience. We can still thinkin the essential sense of the great spirit and ideals of our past, but the form of our thinking, our speaking, our development of them has changed by the very fact of new thought and experience; we see them not only in the old, but in new lights, we support them by the added strength of new viewpoints, even the old words we use acquire for us a modified, more extended and richer significance. Again, we cannot be "ourselves alone" in any narrow formal sense, because we must necessarily take account of the modern world around us and get full knowledge of it, otherwise we cannot life. But all such taking account of things, all added knowledge modifies our subjective being. My mind, with all that depends on it, is modified by what it observes and works upon, modified when it takes in from it fresh materials of thought, modified when it is wakened by its stimulus to new activities, modified even when it denies and rejects; for even an old thought or truth which I affirm against an opposing idea, becomes a new thought to me in the effort of affirmation and rejection, clothes itself with new aspects and issues. My life is modified in the same way by the life influences it has to encounter and confront. Finally, we cannot aovid dealing with the great governing ideas and problems of the modern world. The modern world is still mainly European, a world dominated by the European mind and western civilisation. We claim to set right this undue preponderance, to reassert the Asiatic and, for ourselves, the Indian mind and to preserve and develop the great values of Asiatic and of Indian civilisation. But the Asiatic or the Indian mind can only assert itself successfully by meeting these problems and by giving them a solution which will justify its own ideals and spirit.

The principle I have affirmed results both from the necessity of our nature and the necessity of things, of life,—fidelity to our own spirit, nature, ideals, the creation of our own characteristic forms in the new age and the new environment, but also a strong and masterful dealing with external influences which need not be and in the nature and of the situation cannot be a total rejection; therefore there must be an element of successful assimilation. There remains the very difficult question of the application of the principle,—the degree, the way, the guiding perceptions. To think that out we must look at each province of culture and, keeping always firm hold on a perception of what the Indian spirit is and the Indian ideal is, see how they can work upon the present situation and possibilities in each of these provinces and lead to a new victorious creation. In such thinking it will not do to be too dogmatic. Each capable Indian mind must think it out or, better, work it out in its own light and power,—as the Bengal artists are working it out in their own sphere,—and contribute some illumination or effectuation. The spirit of the Indian renascence will take care of the rest, that power of the universal Time-Spirit which has begun to move in our midst for the creation of a new and greater India.

—SRI AUROBINDO

REFERENCE :

1. *Narayan*, edited by Mr. C.R. Das.

16

INDIAN CULTURE IN THE WORLD PERSPECTIVE

A CASE STUDY OF ANNIE BESANT

In this paper an attempt will be made to examine and understand Annie Besant's ideas and concept about culture. What were her views about the world culture. How did she come in contact and appreciation of the Indian Culture. How she wanted India to meet the challenges of the western culture.

For Annie Besant Indian Culture was far superior to the Mushrom growth in the form of culture all over the world. India she felt was the mother of all religions and cradle of world civilization. She made an indepth study of the Indian Culture and wrote extensively on the subject. She wanted new India to evolve her own systems to the modern changed environment.

The answers to the above questions will be sought with the help of her writings, speeches, letters and through the study of her daily "New India" and the weekly.

I

When Annie Besant arrived in India she found the situation in the country was worse than she had imagined. Lord Macaulay who may be said to be the founder of the system of modern English education in India, maintained that 'the whole of Indian literature was not worth a single shelf of a good European Library'. No wonder that the system he designed produced a class of persons 'Indian in colour, but English in Tastes, in morals and intellect'. Sir George Birdwood has this to say of the results of that system :

> 'Gur (English) education has destroyed their love of their own literature.....and worst of all, their repose in their own traditional and national religion. It has disgusted them with their own homes, their parents, their sisters, their very wives. It has brought discontent into every family so far as its beneful influences have reached.'

'Its sinister shadow, 'He continues, involves' a slow poisoning of their spiritual life.'

Sir Ananda Coomaraswamy, who quotes the above passage in one of his lectures, goes on to say: 'I suppose there could be no better proof of all these things than is afforded by Pandit Jawaharlal Nehru's pathetic confession, 'I have become a queer mixture of East and West, out of place everywhere, at home nowhere'. These are not the words of free man, as Gandhi's always are, but the marks of a terrible soul-sickness, concludes Coomaraswamy.

This was the India to which destiny brought Annie Besant who counted no endeavour too difficult no sacrifice too high to restore India to her ancient glory. Many of her own patriotic sons and daughters had almost given up all hope when Annie Besant appeared on the scene with the reassurance, Your mother is not dead; she is only asleep and with the slogan 'Wake Up, India'.

II

With her tremendous energy and matchless eloquence she toured the length and breadth of the country, electrifying the Indian people with a new hope and a new spirit of dedicated service and sacrifice. She made sacred Kasi (Varanasi) the spiritual heart of India, her headquarters

She realized that the genius of India lay in religion and that any scheme for the regeneration of India must start with a religious revival. She learnt Sanskrit and made a translation of the Bhagavad Gita which is considered one of the most authentic translations of this great scripture of the Hindus.

The Christian missionaries were distributing free copies of the Bible to all students who passed the matriculation examination and Annie Besant insisted on all Hindu students being presented with copies of the Gita. She poured forth a wealth of knowledge which amazed her hearers and the learned Pandits of Benares hailed her as a persenification of Saraswati, the Goddess of Wisdom.

Her books like Hints on the Study of the Bhagavad Gita. The Wisdom of the Upanishads, Introduction of Yoga, The Self · nd its sheaths, Life after Death, 'Reincarnation', 'Karma' and 'Avataras' brought the essential teachings of Hinduism to the attention of educated Indians ignorant of Sanskrit, who marvelled at the treasures of their own religion which they had never known.

While Annie Besant paid the greatest attention to Hinduism she did not overlook the need for the revival of the other religions of the country. A series of lectures delivered at one of the International Conventions of the 'Theosophical Society' was published under the title 'Seven Great Religions' covering Hinduism, Jainism, Zoroastrianism, Buddhism, Christianity, Islam and Sikhism, bringing out the beauties of each faith and the essential identity of the basic teachings of all of them.

Annie Besant wrote, 'I may mention that while the first object of the Theosophical Society is to form a nucleus of the Universal Brotherhood of humanity without distinctions of race, creed, sex, caste or colour, its second object is to encourage a comparative study of religion, philosophy and science as a means of doing away with misunderstanding which separate man from man by demonstrating the validity of the basic truth on which Indian culture is founded, namely the declaration 'Ekam Sat, Viprah Bahudha Vadanti', Reality is only One; the learned ones speak of it in various ways.'

The message of the Gita,

Ye yatha mam prapadyanate
Tanstathaiva bhajamyaham

(By whichever path men approach me, by that path I welcome him) is fundamental to Hindu thought and culture. It is this spirit, not merely of widest tolerance, but positive appreciation of every religion as an expression of the one Divine Wisdom which made India welcome with open arms the various religions which came to her from abroad to add to the many religions and philosophies born on her own soil.

In spite of the exploitation of religion by political forces which resulted in the division of the country and the creation of the theoratic Muslim State of Pakistan, India is still the country which has the second largest Muslim population in the world-next only to Indonesia, India has thus successfully upheld her secular character. This is in keeping with her traditional culture based on the principle of 'Unit in Diversity' in which—while the uniqueness of every religion, every philosophy, every languages, every kind of customs and manners, every way of dress is given full scope of expression—the Indian genius creates out of all the diversity a unity which is characteristically Indian.

This is what Annie Besant has to say of the India of the future.

The Indian nation of the future is not to be a nation of one single religion only, but to embody the essence of all religions it will have in it the philosophy of Hinduism the valour and learning of Islam the purity of Zeroastrianism the love and tenderness of Buddhism the self sacrifice of Christianity. ......Every view of God is added to the views already held and so however infinity the perfection of God Himself, more and more knowledge of that perfect Being will come to India through the many religions horn on its soil and nourished by itself.

We are passing through times in which the fissiparous tendencies based on religiuous differences are once again exploited for political ends and we need now more than ever the Besant spirit of universal harmony.

III

Colonel Olcott had built up the famous Adyar Library for which he had collected rare manuscripts from all over the world. The Library now contains more than 18,000 manuscripts in Sanskrit, Pali, Prakrit, Persian, Arabic, Aramic, and other similar sacred and classical languages and the Pandits of the Library were bringing out in English and other modern languages translations of the original texts.

Annie Besant clearly forsaw the challanges to the Indian culture in the world perspective. Under her guidance thousands of copies of the daily practice (Sandhya), congregational temple worship (Nitya Puja Vidhanam), Vedic Upanayana and Marriage and other rituals in simple form with translations in English were printed and distributed by the Samaja to let the Hindus knew the meanings of the rituals they performed and rid the people of the dominance of the priests who exploited their credulity and ignorance.

The main objects of the Bharata Samaja were :

(a) To study the Sanatana Dharma and make its teachings available to all;

(b) To investigate the scheme of Hindu rituals and to adapt them to the needs and conditions of the time as well as to provide, as far as possible, for their being properly performed;

(c) To promote social welfare and eradicate social evils in the Hindu community;

(d) To promote tolerance good feeling and a spirit of cooperation between Hindus and the followers of other faiths.

The temples are open not only to Hindus but to followers of other faiths who wish to participate in this Hindu form of congregational worship. The social reorms included

(i) Breaking down of social disabilities and restrictions entailed by the mere reason of caste or sex (Women and non-Brahmins were entitled to conduct worship in the temples)

(ii) Eradication of reform of injurious customs such as early marriage and immature parentage, enforced widewheed, exaction of dowry from brides or bridegrooms.

Similar reform movements were started in other religions. There was the Liberal Catholic Church for reforms in the Christian religion the attempt of Colonel Olcott to bring all the scots of Buddhism to agree on Fourteen Fundamental Points as a common platform the simplification of the rituals and practices of the Zeroastrains the attempt to bring the Shia and Sunni sects of Islam together.

Annie Besant was responsible for the building of the various faiths at the headquarters of the Theosophical Society at Adyar where we have a Hindu Temple, a Christian Church, a Moslem Mosque, a Parsi (Zoroastrian) Agiary, a Buddhist Shrine and a Sikh Gurudwara. She also laid the foundation for a Hebrew Synagogue. Each of these places of worship is open to anyone who wishes to participate in its rituals thus giving practical shape to the idea of a fellowship of all faiths.

IV

I do not propose to say much about her political work except in so far as it touches on her impact on Indian culture. During India's freedom struggle much has happened to corrode and undetermine the foundations of Sanatana Dharma because of blind copying of Western values and Western methods.

Annie Besant points out, 'If we compare the fundamental idea of Sanatana Dharma with that of modern Western life, you will find that the ideal of the former is Dharma or duty whereas the Western idea is of rights.... Dharma means the obligations into which every man is born, to the parents, to te family, to the community, to the nation.... The elders guard and protect the child. The child in his manhood must repay the obligations in its turn.... Thus we come to the underlying idea of Manu, of Dharma-duties or obligations to the Devas for the gifts of nature, to ancestors whose heritage we have inherited; to fellow human beings who supply our various wants; to animals and plants to the Rishis of the past who have brought us to the stage of perfection we have so far attained. All these obligations are to be discharged if the cycle of life is to go on uninterrupted. Out of our recognition of these obligations or duties, the due performance of our Dharma grows the stability and the orderly progress of human life.'

In the West, however, another idea has grown up in recent times- in less than two centuries the idea that each is an individual, alone and apart, and that the very fact of birth invests him with certain rights. Society, according to this concept, rests not on mutual obligations but on individual rights which he may enforce by any means in his power. According to this view, law is only binding because people have accepted it and consented to it, yielding partially so that he may enjoy the reminder more fully. It is all a matter of contract. A marriage is no sacrament but a mutually accepted agreement. Each one asserts his rights without an equal emphasis on obligations. The result is continual struggle. The family no more represents all its members, as in the old Indian joint family system, but individuals each asserting his rights. The community similarly ceases to stress the obligations of each family constituting it. The legislature ceases to represent the nation as a whole but of parties or groups of conflicting interests. Nations cease to consider their mutual obligations for the common good of humanity as a whole and asserts each its right to unlimited sovereignty, which may extend to total destruction of another nation or nations.

One need hardly mention that if this trend continues unchecked and nations and individuals alike are not made to realize their mutual obligations there is the danger of the dissolution of the whole of modern civilization.

In spite of Annie Besants immense love for India, she was working on a larger framework than narrow nationalism. She worked with the forces of evolution and opposed revolution and anarchy. When Gandhiji started his Direct Action of Civil Disobedience and called on the ignorant masses and the immature students to break the laws of the land she wisely warned all concerned that they were undermining law and order and that once people learn to break one law they would go on to break all laws. She said, "You are sowing the wind you will reap the whirlwind."

We know only too well how true these words have been. So strongly did she feel on this subject that in her newspaper New India she declared, 'Brickbats must be met with Bullets', meaning that Law and Order must be maintained at all cost. This again is in keeping with Indian culture and tradition. In her book 'India-Bond or Free' she quotes examples of farmers in ancient Indian peacefully ploughing their fields while not far form the spot opposing armies were fighting a war.

She was working for larger and larger political federations—for a United States of Europe; for a Federation of South America and for a World Federation of Self-Governing Nations with a World Government which would do away with war. She was clear in her own mind that when such a World Federation comes it would be India's role to be the spiritual mother of all mankind.

In spite of the many setbacks which have occurred and the inhuman arms race in which the superpowers are indulging themselves, let us hope that Annie Besant's dream of a World Federation of Free Nations will materialise and that India will find her destined place as the spiritual mother of nations of the World.

—*DR. RAJ KUMAR*
ICHR, New Delhi

17

THE DEGENERATION OF INDIAN CULTURE

My intention is not to advocate basking in the luxury of this mother—Indian Culture. We have to come out of our groove, even if we are nourished by culture, to seek new horizons to fulfil our destiny. This cannot be done by ignoring culture or by looking only at the future or the present.

Culture has a magnetic power over our soul. Since it lives in the past, it drags us into the past. No race can progress by living in the past. Hence there is a paradox. But it is not so difficult to resolve it. Man is accustomed to facing sphinxes and solving riddles.

We have to find out the path of least wastage in this pull of the forces of the past and the present. Culture pulls us towards the past, whereas the problem of self-survival, in a fast moving world, asks us to remain in the present and dash towards the future. These two forces are constantly pulling at our soul and we often find all our energy wasted in this struggle. We have to change our approach if we wish to benefit from this. We must, first of all, cease to look upon it as a tragic situation. It is a great situation, full of hope, for the soul progresses only through opposites.

If our soul favouring either of these forces and takes up the role of Lord Vishnu at the churning of the ocean, the net gain will be the *nectar*. Lord Vishnu blessed both gods and demons. Let us welcome both these forces knowing that they are only engaged in a churning. A time will come when instead of these two opposites struggling, we shall find a third force developing in our soul which possesses the benefits of both.

Our culture has degenerated down the centuries owing to several reasons. The foremost among them was medieval, the unwillingness of our forefathers to face their problems as boldly as Nachiketa, Yudhisthira, Rama and Harishchandra had done. They lost the vigour to walk by their inner light. It appears that they were not prepared for the invasions and conquests of the foreigners. They never believed that they, being so greatly enlightened, could ever be subjugated. Besides, truth wins; they had a firm faith in this dictum. They thought truth and righteousness were on their side simply because they themselves never invaded foreign lands.

But ironically they were caught in the whirpool of defeat at a time when their spititual activities were at their finest bloom. They were stabbed when they were in a state of trance. They were deceived when they were dreaming of making the world a family. The shock was so complete that they completely seem to have lost the will to live and to assert themselves. They developed an attitude of avoiding issues and of playing hide and seek with them, and this attitude made them cowardly and disunited.

Indian Culture is a living thing, and does not merely mean only the finer things. All the bad points of our national character are also part of our culture. There have been attempts to show that Indian Culture is a stream of clear and transparent water. This is injurious and untrue. We cannot get rid of our bad habits if we do not trace out their source in our culture. We need not be afraid of defiling its sacred temple in doing so. Our philosophy, all our heritage, refutes the existence of evil. There is only good according to our racial genius. Evil is not the opposite of good. It is only a projection of ignorance. In our folly we plant evil as a parasite on good. Evil is a child of ignorance even as the sky flower is a child of imagination. Evil becomes a private reality for the soul whose ignorance produces or believes in it. The soul, being of the nature of the Real, has the inherent power to bestow the status of reality, at least for itself, to anything by believing.

We must therefore know that all these bad and shameful points of our national character are mere parasites, planted on our soul by our combined ignorance.

We have to trace their roots and unmask them in order to see the actual form in which they were originally planted on our soul. Very often we shall find that what we consider today to be a national evil has concealed beneath it a good point of our character. If only we could learn the art of neutralizing these parasites we shall regain our lost soul. We can never hope to conquer these evil forms by fighting them, for in this way we first make them existent. It was not for nothing that Christ asked his disciples not to resist evil.

The human soul has no enemy worse than sloth or inertia which lurks within it as if it were its very death wish. Something which can fulfil the wish of the Imperishable soul to die itself must be a very subtle killer. It is this enemy that produces ignorance, *i.e. moha* and anger as well as fear and hatred. They shroud the soul and isolate it form the world of facts. The stony ground against which it realizes its self-flowering is of facts. The soul gradually forgets this under the soporific of inertia.

It is this inertia which overtakes a stunned and deceived culture. It petrifies everything within it. All its good points cease to be active. It is a law of nature that if the good or the real does not act, it has to become a ground for the bad. Constant activity is a law of this world of actions. When good petrifies, inertia overtakes. It produces evil to begin its parasitic play.

Ancient Indians never believed in avoiding problems. They knew that to solve a problem is to stop its recurrence. It is also a law of nature that all our life a problem pursues us, assuming various forms, so long as we do not face and solve it. Once we have done this some other problem of a subtler type crops up. But we have crossed the ocean upto that level. This secret was perhaps known to all older people. Thus when Yudhisthira replies correctly to all the five questions of the Rakshasa, he not only lets him go but also helps him. Similarly the Russian hero who faces the ordeal of the witch Baba Yaga successfully, also receives her help in his mission. Thus evil is not real. It is only a means to our spiritual progress. Those who neither fear nor hate it, neither fall into its clever net nor become angry at it, discover the magic that melts it as mist and converts it into a slave of good like the Ginni of the lamp.

The forces of Indian Culture, which once led us to build a society on the rock foundations of love and sacrifice, have become magically transformed into their opposites. The sooner we accept this fact the better. Only those despair at this who identify facts with reality. Facts look stronger and larger than the truth and their doom lies in this. Nothing gains by growing larger than the Real. A lie is not only lesser than the truth. That which is larger than the truth is also a lie.

The petrification and mutilation of Indian culture is visible in our daily life. What we have today of our ancient culture is this. We have no alternative except to record these symptoms correctly and then try individually and socially to neutralize them. We shall thus discover this hidden culture.

A very important factor which ought not to be ignored is that Indian culture is no longer a self-integrated force. We have been dishonoured and humiliated a number of times. All those experiences have shattered its integrity. They have transformed into mutually contradictory forces like the mind of King Lear. Insulted and disgraced, she (our culture) has developed revengeful forces too. She was a goddess born of love. Our ancestors through acts of dharma and sacrifice had invoked her. This maiden's love and simplicity were repeatedly dishonoured by invaders. Insulted on account of love, she has developed a streak of petrification against love. It is expressed in our national character. We are intolerant of love-affairs. Our national genius works instinctively if it is put on the job of killing love between two persons.

The third streak is of exhibitionism. Instead of inner devotion we believe in show and display. Ritual developed later in Hinduism to such an extent that the reality has been hidden. We cannot approach the deity straight as our Vedic forefathers did. Somebody intervenes who knows the craft of worship, for love is not enough.

The fourth characteristic of our culture today is the tendency to understand only the language of fear and force. Even Tulsidas thought that fear begets love. People show a poor sense of responsibility towards the nation and towards society. They have an inhuman capacity to bear oppression and tyranny. Brutal, ruthless rulers and conquerors, upstarts have given this gift to our people.

Indian Culture has been hurt in her vitals. As we have seen, it has degenerated into the above four forces. It is this four-faced culture which our masses are living. A sweet reality has been transformed into bitter facts. But this process of unfolding can be reversed. These facts can neutralize each other and we can once again attain the original stream of sweetness and light. There is no reason for despair. This is an occasion for wakefulness and heightened spiritual activity. Life has something magical about it. Many of its forces disappear or get transformed into their opposites.

When a culture degenerates, it also develops a craving for things foreign. In fact it hopes to get revitalized by contact with them. Nirad C. Chaudhari's dilemma is nothing personal. There are many like him who feel lyrically about the English people. Such people are in fact doing a great service by exposing a strong trait of modern Indian Culture.

No culture can hope to regain its lost self in this way. This is in fact escapism. We run towards Western culture because the cultural force which we have inherited is tired of itself. It wants to run away from itself.

Gracelessness and lethargy are two more characteristics that have developed in our culture. All these seven qualities are embodied in our national character today. They are reflected in our politics, society and family. The graceful ways of living are being dropped because they now appear tiring and meaningless to us. The rhythm and lyrical aspect of our festivals and ceremonies is no longer known to our people. They are aware only of the superstitious element in them.

Caste, dowry, unhygienic ways of living, corruption, the harassing dirt, noise and shameless abuses that we find in public places like bus-stands, stations, trains, hospitals and courts are outer manifestations of these seven traits. We can not overcome them by fighting outwardly because they are a part of our character. Unless we overcome them internally we cannot hope to eradicate them. Despite all that the government has done to emancipate the lower castes and to eradicate the evils of caste, this has not resulted in the desired good. The impetus must come from within.

How to achieve this inner impetus? It is possible to achieve it if we act with patience and wisdom. These seven colours of our soul should not frighten us even though they are of alarming proportions. They are only cloud-elephants, gigantic but unreal.

Our soul has to take rebirth from this seven-headed mother of serpents. All the power that these seven heads possess once belonged to the soul and can again belong to it. It is only a play of folly that has transferred it. Folly is the dazed reply of intelligence to cleverness. Intelligence must not be shocked or angered by cleverness, nor has it to fight the latter. It has to manage a rebirth from it as Hanuman managed from Sirsa and Lanka, as Prahlad managed from Holika, as Savitri managed from Yama, as Krishna managed from Putana.

I am not telling anything new. I am only trying to remind the lulled racial genius of something which was taught by our great men. We are worshippers of Kali, the Goddess who destroys but only to give a rebirth, a new life. These vices in our national character and culture are to be taken as the terrible mother who is there to give us a rebirth. This terrible mother is flexible and can become a kind goddess like Mother Kali if only we realize her true function. God has not created these poisons to torture and blind us but ot make us stronger and wiser, a better image of Him. Illumination comes to us through such rational faith in God. We take into account all the cruel facts of experience. Only a deeper understanding of things makes us see the beneficial role that these facts can play in our evolution. It is a full use of science. Facts porperly handled create sweeter things than our best dreams.

The will to live by truth and to evolve racially has died in us. We have become seekers of individual destinies. All self-integrated forces are only good. When they disintegrate they breed confusion and a war of opposites. Our culture when integrated was a force serving love. All our rituals and details of daily life were expressions of love. When our culture got disintegrated its various elements became exaggerated and unruly. They became mutually contradictory.

Indian Culture is an outer manifestaion of love. This love was an integration of four elements, *i.e.* complete faithfulness like that of a dog, godly virtues, interest in the life of others, and the desire to unite in depth removing all veils from the soul. When love disintegrated it broke into these forces, this time exaggerated and mutilated. It is a law of nature that when something disintegrates its constituents become more powerful and uncontrollable than the whole. The disintegration of an atom is an ample. The neutrons, the protons and the electrons were happily checking each other's energy, but when disintegration sets in, they all become unruly.

When these four constituents break up they also become exaggerated and negative in character. Faithfulness becomes blind faith. The self-bestowing godly virtues become godly pride and isolation to the total exclusion of others. Both these traits are only too visible in Hinduism to need any discussion. Faith in God degenerated into faith in the verdict of the priest and his craft. At the same time Hinduism became too proud of its purity, closing its doors so firmly that even the Hindus could not return to it once they had forsaken it.

Interest in the life of others got transformed into a callous interference in their life. Nirad C.Chaudhary has caricatured this trait sufficiently.

The fourth characteristic of love, *i.e.* to unite without keeping any veil, is the fire which leads it to a complete union of souls. After disintegration, it gets changed into a craving for the nude. We believe in exposing others publicly till they have no shred with which to hide themselves. Instead of helping a good man publicly, to become better, we start picking holes. We like to prove that he is a hypocrite. It is a popular saying in India that the happiest are the naked for they have nothing to hide. Those who try to hide their shame are always harassed and insulted.

Our culture has been deformed and petrified. This was not originally intended to be so by our forefathers. Nor is the seed of our culture diseased. Unless we trace our way back to the sources again; unless by an act of will we neutralize the perversions and insist upon the flowering of the essence, we cannot fulfil our destiny.

We lost the original track of our culture because except during the earliest days we ceased exercising our will. To drop the will is the same as to adopt regression. The ancient Indians knew this. But later on they started believing that to negate the will was a pious way of living. Experience has taught us that to negate the will is the same as to submit it to the will of others. If the other happens to be a foreign invader, his will is bound to be the opposite of our will. To submit to his will is the same as to adopt a will to die. It is in this way that a deathwish has overtaken our culture.

The Bhagavad Gita expects us to exercise our will freely—'Yatha ichchasi tatha kuru.' Our ancestors had realized that to destroy the will was to fight nature. A better way was known to control its vagaries. This was a training which subjected the will to intellect and the intellect to love. This discipline takes away the sting from the will. It becomes an instrument of love, *i.e.* God.

We must exercise our will if we want to come out of the coils of the death-wish. It is better to err by will than to negate it. Will is our *Karma-Sanskara.* To negate it is not the same as to free the soul of this bondage. Therefore we avail nothing by killing the will. The suitable particles of *karma* continue to cling to the soul. Will only expresses our soul in the outer world. A true seeker sees his real face in his actions. In order to get rid of a wrong will one has to go deeper. One gains nothing by destroying the will. It is only a symptom of some archetypal force or *karmic* matter clinging to our soul. We have to neutralize that parasite.

Our race took to the wrong path of destroying will. It has only taken us away from ourselves. We have developed a complex character. We have to correct this error. We have to learn again to live by will like our great ancestors and to subject will to a true intellect. This will transform all the vices, discussed above, into strong good forces in our character, for that is their original form.

THE DANGER TO INDIAN CULTURE

I have said already that it is unreasonable to think of the indestructibility of Indian Culture. This stream was formed by a mass of aspirations, thoughts, longings and attempts at self-realization. Nothing can hold this except a passion to live by the true aspirations and ends of life. The fact that our culture has withstood all ravages in the past does not mean that it will do so in the future as well. If it stood its ground, it was due to the untiring and unbroken faith of our people in the lofty and the true, which never lost its vigour. Today faith has paled, and all of a sudden, under the clouds of new slogans a confused and unrealistic approach to life has cropped up. So much sacrificed! The butchering of the whole of life for mere material gains! One who desires to witness this may go to the people among whom life is sapping fast and where an artificial haste seems to have darkened and thrown away the inherent urges of life, which were once so clear and understandable even to the common man.

Indian Culture did not stand only because of the deep seed of spirituality. It was the profound urge to know, not to negate, that provided its daily strength. All through the ages woman was held in high esteem for her natural virtues and man could understand her. This appreciation encouraged them to grow as they are and helped men to supplement their virtues. Social life thus never came to mask-plays and arid flights. Even with so many severe forms of asceticism, society kept on giving woman her due regard. It did not criticize her for what nature did not give her. As the principle of creation, as the Ganga herself, the source of our corn and life; as the power of destruction, as Durga and Kali; as Prakrti herself as the constant playmate of Purusha, the source of his fulfilment and delusion, the element of the feminine permeated the daily details of our life. Even ascetic systems like Jainism developed the concept of goddesses and the feminine. Buddhism developed the theme of the feminine within the divine folds of Buddha, in the form of *tathagata-garbha* or *prajnaparimita, i.e.* Nature, Prakrti, the principle of the feminine, mother of the Buddhas and also in the form of goddesses like Tara and Manjusri. Even sex, the feared factor between the two, was boldly understood in its true significance so that nothing remained to check the free and uninhibited mixing of the two for mutual fulfilment. This was the process of giving growth to a culture on the stem of life. It was this active and free response of the sexes to each other, without mutual fear and hatred, that helped the culture of India to face all iconoclasts and shocks.

Today in the isolated pursuit of material progress, power and strength, the feminine has no place. Little do they know that this new society has not considered them at all in founding itself. In fulfilling its requirements women are not doing the job of the physical slaves alone, but of slaves in the soul. Strange that such total slavery should be acceptable to woman in an age so full of the clamour of the freedom and emancipation of woman. What an irony it is that the freedom and emancipation of woman should be judged by her becoming imperfect man, a mocking copy of man, and not in expressing herself!

The profound respect for woman that existed only a decade back has already disappeared. Humiliated and admired only for their physique and sexual prospects, girls can already be seen as moving pictures of frustration. Shorn of the glory that circles them only in the mind of a people, nourished on a comprehensive and enlightened culture, they have no way left for self-expression except through pursuing the ways of man. Young persons in our country, considering themselves very advanced, look upon woman only as a source of light entertainment. With this loss of intimate union between the two sexes, India has chosen her road to doom even on the primrose path of freedom. Where women wail, where women are cheated and crushed, life decays.

"He who denies anything to a woman is a coward," cried Varahamihira long ago. Today she is being denied her very nature. With the decay of the profound concept of the feminine, Indian culture has already come to a fast decline. There will be nothing to wonder at if in the near future it is replaced by hollowness and a loud but empty freedom. It is this particular way of life and understanding of freedom against which India will have to take a stand if the future of democracy and the free life is to be saved from oblivion. This will be India's particular service to herself, to humanity, and to all tortured people. It is true that even freedom can corrupt. It is true that the noblest of our ideas may corrupt, since corruption lies not in the idea but in our understanding of it. When it is only for an immediate and narrow purpose of ours that we employ a noble idea, the result cannot be anything but corruption. If freedom prepares us to disregard nature and the truth of life and only becomes an instrument of negation and arrogant theorization and self-impositions, it becomes hardly distinguishable from oblivion. It is not the goal of culture to put an end to experimentation. If that were to happen, culture would be putting an end to itself, since without dynamism, without zest for the future and advancement and for regions of light, it would be a dead thing, confined to the archives. The sole demand that culture makes of a man is to display utter sincerity towards himself and, as such, search for the widening regions of light and perfection—a search with many sighs, 'chercher en genmiscent!' as Pascal cried.

No altruistic principle, no creed or noble aspiration unites men better than sincerity to their inner self. Living by creeds and principles we are always liable to excesses, inflexibility and falsehoods. But when we observe truth towards ourselves, and sincerity, and make an honest search for light and fulfilment, we do so, not only for ourselves, but for others too.

INDIA TODAY

Everybody says India is passing through a building phase. A leaning towards machines and fastness are the strongest developing traits in the Indian character. With this relaxation has set in various vital parts of our life. Is it our coming out of an age-old darkness? Or is it a step towards another kind of darkness? Or is it simply the imbalanced expression of a long supressed urge to have our own way and destiny. There is no doubt that whatever is being done, has its source in an urge for advancement.

The main and troubling question is whether this is really an advancement or a mere drift in the contemporary current. There will be many to whom even this is not sufficiently alarming. They would retort that moving with the times is a wise and practical way for a people to live.

For the first time in history, India has started giving priority to the physical conditions of life. It has been thought that material advancement is not only essential but the only way to survive in the present-day world. Implicitly, a queer, though common, feeling persists that we have a sufficient reservoir of spirituality and that material advancement will take us to the very acme of civilization. We are feeling the burden that freedom has brought, the burden to look after the multi-faced life of a country. We can no more blame nor depend on the foreigners. The urge for betterment has no natural outlet in negation and mere criticism. We have to act and build our future. Living under such stress we are likely to be come hectic and over-swayed, more obsessed by the urge for progress than working thoughtfully and properly. But giving due weight to all these considerations, one has yet to find a satisfactory and encouraging note for whatever is being done on the individual, social, economic and political plane. It is not that the element of reason is missing. It is not as if our steps are always thoughtless and that we lack a proper understanding of the material and conditions towards which we are moving. But perhaps it is not reason alone which works out a human situation. Reason itself presupposes a moving will behind it. And much depends on this moving will, for reason is a double-edged weapon. One might say that the moving will aims at progress; and that reason has been chosen to fulfil it. Now the question arises whether this will is well-informed; whether it is balanced and imbued with a sincere understanding of advancement.

Advancement could simply be movement, even a damagingly one-sided one, and at times even a move towards oblivion. When a tremendous release of energy floods the life of a nation with intensified activity, such questions are better thought out at all levels. It is not merely that all action does not lead to betterment. Again, every urge is not necessaritly sincere and does not work to realize it self. At times it is feeble, one-sided, hectic and uninformed, resulting in a mockery of the life of a people. Life-energy in itself is uniformed. It does not know the direction it is taking, and merely for the reason that it is energy spent itself on the nearest cause. When an aim is not defined clearly, and when roads are not built by those who can think more clearly and far into things, such purposeless energy in the masses is bound to result in confusion, thoughtless wastage, frustration and disturbance. It is always dangerous to rouse the sleeping sources of energy. It is dangerous that they should be aroused with slogans and left to a people.

Lovers of the free life and of individual thinking will perhaps object saying that nobody, howsoever elevated, has the right to think for others. It is true. But such idealism works only in ideal conditions. And whatever the human scene has been throughout history it has never been ideal. The masses always expect to be given a clear lead. Not only this, most of them are greatly averse to thinking before acting. They have an inborn inclination to lean on someone. If they are told about the intrinsic freedom of each individual and the fundamental right of each person to think for himself, they are not likely to take this seriously. They are more likely to become arrogant and stubborn. The masses belonging to certain advanced countries are an illustration of this. Freedom of all kinds that became their slogan has brought them no real emancipation. Instead, it has blurred the possibility of true advancement and happiness in countries where material resources and comforts are highly developed. The mere possession of the notion of uncompromising freedom without it being exercised with true knowledge depraves a people.

And no poison is more potent than the one which though not originally poison, turns out to be such under the peculiar conditions of a particular situation. It is possible for the very idea of freedom to ruin a people. What is freedom but a consciousness of right and a sincere urge for it? When it is not so, it is only an awareness of rights and crude self-assertion or cynical indifference.

Human life can never be happy with such pedantic and vulgar self-assertion or complacency. The mass frustration, the rush for life, the waywardness, the lack of a healthy alternative to hectic rushing all these unhappy conditions of modern life are the doings of the vice of freedom more than of anything else. Regrettably, in the human condition it is possible for any Noble Idea to corrupt and ruin.

Such is the hallucination of progress too. The common run of men are more fascinated by its lustre. A nation never progresses by entrusting slogans to its people. The slogan has to be supplied with proper food, so that its growth in life and mind may be sound and clear. It these attributes are lacking, every noble passion or urge is more likely to land us in confusion. What one feels about India is that by and large people have been left with the notion that progress implies hunting out everything that has a smell of the old and this is largely a negative process. On the positive side the country is working only in thoughtless imitation of exotic ideologies and transplanting them onto indigenous soil by cleansing them of their native suggestions.

Anyone can perceive the seeds of decay and total ruin in such a process. Already much that was serene and happy in our life has died out. The apostles of progress argue that this is but a natural stage in the course of advancement.

It is easy to wash away the gains of ages. Nothing works better than the force of a noble idea. Nobody puts barriers before a noble idea, and it has full freedom to do all it can in its devastating sweep. After all, nothing in a society is in itself indestructible. If certain things refuse to die this is not because of their value and force alone, but much because the people pay attention to them. During centuries of slavery and political imposition the perennial waters of culture did not die in this country. The greater the oppression the greater the inner resistance that sprang up to match it. The result of this was a singular spiritual courage and love of values among a people even in conditions of political degradation. If this culture did not die it is not because it had something in it which prevented its death. The finest flowering of human endeavours and aspiration wither away if the human soil does not react to them. The strongest ideas and the truest thoughts fail to survive on their own. It is only the living heart of a people where they live to be immortal. It is always in the passionate adherence of a people that a set of values refuses to perish. It is not so surprising as ironical that a culture which could not be effaced by mighty empires and the clash of swords, by temptations and threats of annihilation, should have run so thin within thirty years of independence. The benuding of India has occurred when her own sons are endowed with the might to protect her! Anything can create a paradox in the human situation. It will be painful for coming generations to learn that so much was accomplished in negating the spirit of India by her free, democratic and freedom-loving sons—the heralders of a new heaven over her old decayed maidenhood!

Certain elements of our life that were alive only a few years ago, have gone into chronicles and museums. And it is well for the sons of India to feel proud of their preservation! Everything that formed the grand link between a depraved generation with the most massive and living period of our past, whether known to history or not, is going back, receding into the cold of the past and becoming the treasured item of an old culture. The fabric of Indian life has been pierced and the weavers are no longer in a position to set the piece into its old oneness. A growth beyond the past is nowhere in sight. We are perhaps tired of being Indians. The base on which this entire manifestation was raised is slipping, and how long will it take, one wonders, for the great culture of India to join the dead procession of the cultures of the Nile and Babylon!

There is nothing inevitable about a culture or a way of life. All real worth that a culture possesses is to be found in its richness, maturity, comprehensiveness and in a wider response to the demands of life. There is no point in lamenting that something of ours is fading away in face of the brilliance of something against which it cannot stand. It would indeed be an achievement to find something richer to add to the past. The agony of our present decay springs from the fact that it is not with open and descriminating eyes that we are emerging into the present from the past. It is a lustre-obsession, a lead given by the thoughtless and the ill-bred. It is the sophisters and the decadents, who have brought us to this confusion. To discover the insufficiency of our culture and to enrich life with a richer outlook, would be a homage to the source springs of life. But to remove our culture simply for the desire to be something other than ourselves is to invite annihilation. It is not easy to restore links in the flow of a culture when a gap intervenes and dissociates the future from the past.

THE LOSS OF COMMON VALUES

Until independence one could say that India has pursued the spiritual road. This is not to suggest that Indians have always been spiritualists in any active sense. Nonetheless it would not be wrong to suggest that spiritualism has been the core of Indian life. This means that all our actions and ways had some common spiritual values and base and people were unanimous in accepting them. Those who pursued worldly way knew that their's was an inferior search and were not so arrogant as to look upon it merely as a different way of life. This Indian social scene never presented the kind of chaos as exists at present. This common acceptance of values opened up vistas for those who sought to pursue a higher life, and such persons were honoured and understood. The racial consciousness was common, and people understood and discriminated instinctively between the higher and the inferior ways of life. Perhaps it was this ability of the Indian people, this unanimity, this common love of the higher and a sound sense of discrimination, that sustained the people through all social and political degradation. It was this innate and unmutilated sense which kept the spiritually united amidst a variety of pursuits and social conditions.

It is painful to observe that this perennial sense of truth and values, this love of the higher and the nobler, which could not be destroyed by invasions and foreign rule, has been destroyed most easily within these thirty years of independence, though with the best of intentions owing to narrow self-pursuits.

It is inevitable that there should be some incongruity between thoughts and deeds. Deeds are but reflections of thoughts under various conditions. As such our deeds can never be euqal to our thoughts. Yet so long as thoughts are noble and fine the hope for betterment is not lost for then we know what betterment consists of. People know that it is an improvement in conditions which is to be brought about so that deeds may properly mirror thoughts. Life under such conditions has a known and clear objective. Progress is the improvement in conditions and in the environment to suit the best of our thoughts. If the unanimity of spirit and its lofty yearnings are given up, the other unanimity of actions being absent, people will never know what is meant by improvement in conditions. The improved social and material conditions soon drop relating themselves inevitably to some higher end and become an end in themselves. Thus people enter into a race which never ends and brings no happiness to life. It reduces them to constant activity and activity aimed at no comprehensive and life-enriching end. This has already happened in the case of many people in the West.

Culture in itself has no meaning or value. It is of value because it renders fulfilment of life. It is a force which makes life realize all that is best in the course of existence. It links earth with heaven at every step. Man is an impossible child of both time and eternity. Born in circumstances when everything is definite and limited, he yet has urges and infinite dreams. Something surges within him and impels him towards a higher and freer flight. To call this vague, foolish and adolescent is to give it names. It is this vague, childish and dreamy side which has realized the highest aspirations of man and has given his dusty life the unknown wings of hope, the call of beauty and joy and the will to live. With all its material fullness the world would be nothing to man without these elements.

Culture aims at accepting the whole of man without cutting off of any part of his self. It is the discovery of a way whereby he may fulfil all his parts. A child is born in a society which has through hundreds of years of experience realized certain positive values, the alternatives to which are chaos. As a normal person the child grows up with those values and accepts them and regulates his life according to them without much effort. In case of a bolder individual the values are not only accepted but further refined and added to. Sometimes he discovers things that are futile and dead and yet are cherished by people out of an ignorant attachment to them. But one endowed with real understanding and goodwill never revolts against such things in the popular fashion. Never has human consciousness improved by wild jerks. A people shocked by the revolt of a brilliant man only gets shattered and disintegrated. All improvement is brought through intimacy and mutual understanding. Persons who really intend to improve upon the racial consciousness of their people—like the Buddha—travel a path of additions and improvements, never of subtraction and negation.

The culture of a people is expressed in the various elements of their racial consciousness—their common experience on grounds of certain fundamental values, their common sufferings, their strivings in the quest of happiness, their common sense of Beauty, Truth and the Good, their myths and faith. These elements and others come to form a common stream of consciousness. New experiences come up. All the while old faiths and ideals keep on revitalizing themselves under new conditions. When something grows dead and meaningless, it disappears and newer elements come to replace it. Sometimes stagnant waters are stirred by finer persons so that they do not turn into dogmas and make people rigid and lifeless. The reason why India could continue such a long, unbroken record of history and culture is due to the fact that the common values were never imposed. They were passionately adhered to by people since it was their inner call, denying which life would be meaningless. It is thus that they reacted strongly to everything shaky, merely brilliant or born of personal prejudices and frustrations. This strong reaction was a self-growth in each individual soul. Empires rose and fell, and mighty arms came and subdued the valleys of the Ganges and the Krishna, but the base of Indian life never disintegrated. Indians continued to be one people, endowed with one faith and, as such, all these vicissitudes made little impact on their inner life. Even as the holy Ganges roars every year fresh from the lap of the Himalayas, so did these people, crushed, always humiliated and played upon, arose smiling, suffering and yet intact. The sort of man has rarely shown such innate resistance to the powers of evil and negation.

Today we have come to question those values. We are entitled to do so since there is no reason why people should abide by a scale of values which have realised no good or has ceased to be good. However, the question remains: is it true that the old values have realised no good for us? Perhaps the strong verdict of 'no' will come forth from all quarters in India. Yet it may be argued that these values were not sufficient to face the calls of life, and that they debarred us from a big, practical side of it. We did not look upon practical life with seriousness. This cannot be denied. The very history of the Indian people shows a certain insufficency of interest on the practical side. We cannot live in isolation, and in a world so narrowed by science, it would not only be imprudent to do so, but also suicidal. New ways must come up. But to negate irrationally everything from the past because of some obsession will merely deprive us of confidence and proper growth. The old values form the root in us plucking which thoughtlessly we remain nothing but merely tossing on the waves of time and conditions, a spiritless people with blinded energy.

These values are the very substance of our life and to remove something of them must be the task of construction and self-enrichment alone, and not of negation and a search for ease and comfort. Unfortunately modern India did not start with a nobler yearning. The yearning is confined to a pursuit of wealth and technical equality with the West. Since this did not really come as a call of the new India but only of a few excited and brilliant Indians, it could find no echo in the heart of the people. The result is the loss of happiness from national life, the spiritual degradation of people, their demoralization, and a hectic rush all around. This always results when an idea, howsoever good and well-meaning, is imposed before it has matured into a common urge. Unless the individual accepts it, an idea, whether good or bad, is an imposition on him. It can never realize his freedom. A welfare state's function is to inform the individual, to convince him of the good envisaged and to let the process of development become an expression of the urges of common life. The process is tedious but it is for this that distinction is made between totalitarian, autocratic and democratic forms of government.

It may be objected that to suggest that the people should first be prepared for changes is to indulge in a lengthy waste of time. This could be avoided by changing first and then acclimatizing the people to it. Perhaps the objection is a natural one from persons in position of power. But the counter question world be: could be ever acclimatize people to changes that have not their sanction behind them? At best we may get them used to such changes. But as long as the inside remains denied and unnurtured, a people will gain only unhappiness, confusion, oblivion and slavery. This disharmony between their actions and inner cravings will lay the seeds of the utter ruin and break up of their society. Already signs have appeared. With nothing to abide by, the age-old lyricism of life is starving. Fed with insincere, thoughtless and vague speeches, and standing amidst amazing and incomprehensible changes, the common man, crushed with homely worries, and lacking in exceptional energy to question and understand, has followed the course of surrender. Once surrender sets in, the very talk of culture, national emancipation and individual realization becomes vulger. The love of freedom of a government is not judged by how much opposition it can tolerate but by the higher and positive effort that it makes to understand silent opposition. The call of life, tortured and denied, does not pierce the isolated cells of leadership and personal ambitions. The millions that suffer and who will never voice their protest, since they have no courage, sense, leisure or urge for it, will never be heard. The country will keep along the high path of progress. A longer and even increasing estrangement between people and policies may set in thus creating incongruity between the ills of life and their cures. The result of this can be envisaged—total destruction of the people and their life and the flourishing of big plants, big machines, big show-pieces like cultural academies and big self-consolatory prizes to artists and litterateurs, in fact everything big. And when one thinks that all this has been done with good intentions! Life has lost its link with everything being done for it.

It is a half-theory of life which is being pursued. Schemes are being evolved for it, and the earthly, earth-laden life remains buried somewhere under heaps of frozen minds and hearts. Will someone suggest that this is a fact which is not known? Truth has not to be brought back to man. It is another matter that infatuated with the power of leadership and self-glory, or blinded by theories and schemes, we may prefer to ignore this. We may become hardened and denaturalized, living in conditions away from life and reacting to it. It is difficult for man to revise candidly. Under modern democratic conditions of party politics where the opposition is ever ready to spot mistakes and exploit them not in the interests of truth but for propaganda and other vulgar gains, such frankness is presumably the work of great moral courage.

THE MODERN MYTH OF PROGRESS

India has opened a new chapter of sufferings for herself since, for the first time, our middle classes have also come under the slogan of progress. Progress? It is merely to become like the upper classes in fashion, behaviour and living. And progress for the upper classes? To become like the most progressive people in the world in material possessions and modes of living. And progress for those most progressive people in the world? To have new adventures with matter and appetites; to find new ways of revolt and to throw away everything inherent and old. For them ideals are but a brutal denial of all ideals. What is disastrous is the spirit in which this course of progress has been laid. The spirit is the spirit of negation, of denial, of frustration. It presumes life to be absurd. It declares that the few excitements and pleasures that are possible ought to be snatched without waiting. It is a constant drift from life, *i.e.* from its base, its depth, into the isolation of the pleasure-hunt.

The whole generation has, therefore, taken a tired look, and it appears that questions of deep interest to life interest none. Only brooding, time-killing, and vain philosophic queries we indulge in. The result is that the cheapest and the charlatans who simply pose; those who in utter cowardice never dare for life and resign themselves to a joyless career of excitement and waywardness have become leaders. Man seems to have embraced living death. The course followed is modern cowardice in which everything, youth, joy, splendour, seems to be running fast, afraid of itself. The two profound causes are lack of courage and the fear-complex. Man has lost his spiritual stature in his uncommon and hysterical love of matter. Having neglected the essence of his life so long, he is not prepared to face the question of revitalizing it. Life has become inactive, almost dead, and only dead winds and darkness seem to come from it whenever one tries to look at it. It is thus that man has achieved his estrangement from life. Never in history have people in such large number become devoid of the very feelings of love and passion. Much as they try to excite these feelings artificially they fail, and the family life of a couple in the most advanced countries breaks down on obscure grounds. Often the couple fail to find a definite, explicit reason. Sometimes it is 'mental cruelty' and 'perversity'. Sometimes two persons show their irrational hatred for each other within a short time. The trouble today is that they no longer find hatred only a feeling in them which may be controlled or cured. It seems to have changed places with the life impulse itself.

On all such occasions the first call is from the home, from their own denied self and life. Since there is no outlet in such nostalgia they take to brooding so that nothing outer holds real interest for them. It only men and women worked sincerely they would realise that progress in a human sense is not just imitation of what is different, nor of those who are more prosperous or advanced, nor merely an excited pursuit after intellectual fashions or wealth. Progress for man is to turn everything dark in himself towards light. This is done by showing sincerity to oneself.

It is impossible to enjoy life and its true emotions without facing the accumulated mass of darkness in our crushed and denied souls. The course of life is an arduous, rather pleasant, search for light. Everything in life when seriously and honestly turned towards light results in joy. It is on this road that we discover life and its elementary feelings and build a culture. For what is culture but a restoration of life to itself, to its natural state and true flowering. It is only a deathless desire for the whole of truth and the courage to face it.

IS INDUSTRIALIZATION PROGRESS?

Indian Culture is not someting pertaining to history and the ancient world, but a way of life evolved earlier for all times to come. Undoubtedly Indian Culture includes the ancient world since it was then that this flow of consciousness formed itself. But to call it only ancient is to locate it in an period dead and past. Culture is co-extensive with life. It it merely aims at dragging life back, it is not true to itself and becomes something which is only of historical and scholarly interest. Nothing of this can be ignored. Yet, the question must be asked since in our times efforts are being made to replace culture wholesale. Who is making these efforts? Perhaps nobody, since neither individuals nor the government have so far expressed any revolt against it. There is an urge for advancement and newer things and it is commonly thought that the old values do not help in these changing times. It is in fact this thought that nurtures a sense of nagation. The old values are insufficient. What are the new values? When one poses this question one faces only blankness everwhere. There is no serious attempt to look at the changed position and find out a better way. Dissatisfaction with the present state of affairs can lead towards progress only if there is some serious and genuine urge for it. The tendency of the common man is to go for mere negations. To unburden oneself of the holy and exacting values is an easy process towards which the masses will always be eager to run. India faces danger because this dissatisfaction with the past has not been matched by an equal urge for construction. In the absence of such an urge the normal and inevitable course has already been taken—the run towards a denial of values and imitation of others.

The hectic call of industrialization can hardly be expected to provide a sound urge for progress. It has only aroused a lust for steel and power and for better living conditions. People do not realize that without the cherishing of values this so-called progress is bound to result in chaos and dissipation. An increase in material prosperity in itself means nothing. There is no serious harm in this so long as a people does not resign its primary citizenship of a finer world. It would appear today from the heat and rush of life, from the colour of material pursuits, and from a total closing of the eye to the finer and the spiritually valuable that industrialization has replaced everything else for India. A people notorious for their religious feelings becomes dangerous under such conditions. Their instinct makes them develop anything they take a liking to into a religion. Already a cynical appreciation of material civilizations has come to the surface. This industrialization has also resulted in the most dangerous type of democratization, leading to the homogeneity of all, the degeneration of all, the levelling of all. It is obvious that in a society pursuing industrial emancipation so religiously, and where values of a different kind are considered to be an old-fashioned obsession, culture will be left only to the out-of-the ordinary to cherish in an extraordinary way. They will be more prone to develop cynical attitudes. Such results we have already noticed in the West, where the love of finer things has isolated individuals so completely that their isolation has unfortunately nurtured in them a peculiar self-pride, imbalance and cynicism. They have been reduced to an item of curiosity for the masses, something both admirable and laughable. Away from the current of life, in their superior isolation, they fail to effect any improvement on the life surrounding them, and live in a state of unhappy tensions. Nothing could be more tragic than a living condition in which natural love for finer and subtler things, for the everyday simple music of life, ceases to be part of normal life.

I believe it is such a fashioning of life towards which our entire education and way of life is moving. The few individuals who manage to struggle clear of this are very few. It is not just a few individuals endowed with finer qualities that change the tide of life. The tide of life keeps itself attuned to the urge of the common man. The common man ought to be fed on the material which we want him to cherish in life. It is useless for a few leaders to lament the loss of values and illumined response to life among the people when they have not provided the conditions where such things can flourish. The whoie nation thinks today in a crude, narrow and material manner. It is perhaps considered unmodern to think in any other way. It is this blind enthusiasm for technology and industrialization that threatens to hurl India into an abyss where not only the grand heritage of thousands of years will be no more, but where also nothing will be left to rebuild a society for ages to come. Little do we realize the total ruin that this heralding of a new age has devised for this country.

To look far into the wildest dreams of the enthusiasts of industrialization, India projects the picture of an industrial paradise. To change India into this may be a happy fulfilment for persons whom depravity and spiritual and mental slavery have closed to the real and genuine joys of life. To those who have thought of life as a richer possibility, in its many contents and diverse parts, such estrangement will proclaim sheer emptiness. The life of a people does not become richer by virtue of self-alienation and an abrupt surrender of their heritage. To isolate only one activity, that of industry, and advance it at the peril of all else may result in the progress of industry, but not of man. What is more, it is bound to usher in decay in the very value of life and of man, reducing him into a sub-machine or a tool of a society where the real individuals will be big plants and machines. Man retains his superiority only because he claims himself to be richer product of nature endowed with elements and urges that are owned by no other species. Once these elements and urges are starved, his superiority will be demolished. He will no more own those virtues which make him self-confident and place him above others. Bereft of them, conscious only of one greatness, *i.e.* the mechanic and material, his small frail body will be no match for the machines and will reveal no sign of superiority. It is this which will make him feel like a misplaced master whose inferiors are immensely his superiors. It is this feeling of emptiness that he will have before big machines, and thus a silent, untold, unspeakable frustration will set in, poisoning the whole of life and making a leap towards further enslavement under industry, inevitable.

These conclusions are not merely imaginary. The living conditions in industrially-advanced countries, even in those that were somewhat vigilant about the preservation of their values, exhibit this unbearable torture and frustration, where man though owning everything, yet does not derive even the pleasure of possession. Here are people estranged from themselves breathing in the void of the present. For such people what else remains but to search hard after pleasure, excitement and againt industry—industry even when they do not need it and even if they have to destroy the surplus output; for there is no other way known to life to live and express itself.

Where industry reigns, where industry and matter are the religion of the day, only those will be considered exalted who are its closest allies. And who are they? Often the depraved, often those whose brains and psychological conditions find no affinity with the higher and finer objects and forms of life and who therefore find it inevitable to mould and to be moulded by matter.

THE MODERNIZED INDIAN WOMAN

It is painful to look at the modernized women in India moving under a state of self hypnotism, hollow, bereft of any personality and almost shattered. The ideal of Indian womanhood seems to have broken down largely among the upper and, to a certain extent, the middle classes. Woman here too has learnt the ways of self-befooling and of hard exteriors. Stiff and straight looks have become the mark of yough ladies of education and advancement. It is difficult to come across women, except in 'unprogressive' circles, who emit a glow of feminine grace.

Beauty and grace are not poses and they are not composed of mere mannerisms, or of constant concentration on the outer self. They are natural expressions of a whole integrated personality which has not chosen the course of selfestrangement. For ages such drillings in mannerisms were resented in India even among the higher classes. Suddenly, however, the Indian woman has also taken note of this easy way of appearing virtuous and graceful without undergoing suffering and striving for these qualities. These are signs of utter decay. Evil does not rest in half nude bodies or in a growing frankness and freedom among ladies, but in self-delusion, self-hypnotism and sophistry. This reduces the difference between truth and falsehood among a people. It appears that the sense and love for truth of the Indian people has come to a sudden wane. The lower classes, of course, even today and even in their ignorance and poverty hold in some way to the inner road. But for how long will this negative resistance of ignorance and poverty stand up against the penetration of this falsehood? True, their protest derives its strength from something stronger too. This is their racial consciousness. The myths and tales, the cultural elements of a common heritage, have taught them of another kind of life. But without a proper conditioning of this protest through enlightened and sincere education, they will not be able to withstand the lure of immediate, though temporal, conquests. With an increase in wealth, India will make such transformation even among the lowest possible. And there it will be, when it will be, in its vulgarest form.

Often one hears champions of women's cause rejoicing at this tremendous change. For the first time Indian woman is said to be tasting freedom; that she has for the first time come out of her age-old slavery. The rejoicing is as much hollow as baffling. What was this salvery from which Indian woman has managed so sudden as escape? Was it her dependence on man or tending the house and children? Was it her world of being confined to the home?

It would be a misunderstanding of the sense of freedom to insist that freedom for woman consists in coming out of the home. As freedom for the farmer does not consist in coming out of his field, so freedom for woman does not consist in coming out of her home. Home forms the little isolated world which woman beautifies and enriches with the unique endowments of sweetness, simplicity and the intrinsic sense of beauty and good that nature has given her. She has not formed physically or temperamentally to face the subtle clash of material desires and political orgies of the outer world. She is not a rival of man. If so she has a lasting reason for frustration since nature has handicapped her. It would be unreasonable and wilful to think that nature cherishes some purposeful enmity towards woman. Having handicapped her in some way nature has compensated her in other ways. All of us can hope for fulfilment within our nature. If we feel frustrated because of the fact that we are not like our opposites, it may create a revolt within us. Such attempts can never bring fulfilment and happines. If woman aims at competing with man in the industrial and political world, she may develop hard muscles and even a masculine form and habits. But this will cause mortification to her because her little woman's heart will get denied under this false crust. She will be denied a woman's body too, a fundamental denial, with the inner yearning remaining as feminine as ever.

Masculine habits and manners of life will not procure for her the prized end. The more she drifts towards the masculine, the further she goes away from herself, finally becoming a totally torn and broken maid, ready to give herself up to anyone who can make her feel a woman. This drift towards the masculine, long celebrated by Western women, has brought them to frustration. It is thoughtless and foolish to seek an end which does not bring our inner self to flower and which only takes us away, away from ourselves. It should not be the aim of the Indian woman to develop the muscles of men and their hardness, or even their fatness of ankles and peculiar deformities, which only lead to the worries of a self-destructive and complicated life.

For women to go to the factory and work there, or to the office and to a job, and then join their husbands for "a sweet homely evening" may be a totalitarian ideal aiming at the absurd but not an ideal aimed at natural life. A house in which the two, husband and wife, meet in the evenings and in the mornings or on holidays, each occupied with the false burdens of an alienated life will soon be reduced to a hostel, and both of them will become strangers to each other. In keeping man human and loving, it is the woman's hand which plays the larger part. With a mind occupied with the house and the thoughts of a happy family, it is woman herself who constitutes the home for man. It is she who imbues the home with her thoughts and love and finer feelings. By making her busy elsewhere and overstraining her gentler nerves with the worries of an external life to which she does not belong, we shall take away every possibility of the display of those riches which nature has bestowed on her. Without these riches the association of man and woman cannot sustain its charm. Nothing makes one sadder than to see women occupied in masculine jobs. To look at most wage-earning girls, employed in offices and the professions, is to behold pathetic self-denying persons who have somehow fallen into a wrong current.

Woman seeks fulfilment by giving expression to those virtues which are inherent in her nature. They are different than those of man. It is in the safe undisturbed surroundings of a home and in complete mastery over it that she expresses her finest urges. All her education, culture and refinement come into play here.

It may be said that this presupposes an incurable duality between man and woman and thus strikes at the very root of the oneness of all life. But the realization of the oneness of all life does not imply the blurring of distinctions. Rather it is the fullest manifestation of distinctions which, at their highest stage, realize oneness. Any artificial attempt to drop distinctions will only result in an unnatural state of affairs and in confusion.

It is obvious that Indian women have not progressed after independence although they may have come closer in imitation to their western prototypes. Education has come to them, no doubt, more widely. They have gone to work in factories and offices. They have succeeded in gaining the self-deceiving slumber of the so-called advanced women who have over the years directed their genius towards fields that have brought them neither hope nor fulfilment. In the old days of the Roman and Arab markets where women were sold and auctioned, they knew their weakness and exploitation. Never in history, at least in India, has woman allowed herself to be the toy of man. The old annals and those of the medieval Rajputs show what woman thought of herself. Though weak and confined to the home, could she be exploited as the pleasure hunt of man? Even if this happened, the whole of her interior boiled in opposition to this. The frail light of inner truth and the faint hope of refuge in it, and a vow to abide by this inner light, sustained women in their darkest days. When conquerors came our women proudly burnt themselves and considered death loftier than a disgraced life. When they were prevented from doing so, even when they were raped, in their rape and dishonour the conquerors could not break the integrity of their soul, which was so closely woven round the fire of dharma. It was this love of dharma, of truth, which saved women from being engulfed by the various enslaving practices. In the deepest degradation of this country, the flame of dharma was kept high by our ordinary and illiterate women.

It is this sense of dharma as the inner meaning and significance of life that has decayed suddenly. Dharma has unfortunately come to stand for its objective meaning, *i.e.* religion. Westernized thinking has done its biggest harm in identifying for the common Indian dharma with religion. But in the remote villages where the impact of western education has not penetrated even through secondary sources, this identification is yet unknown. Dharma to them is still the way of life which they have been adhering to, and it is inner.

The idea that despite its social aspect, dharma for us has been something purely individual—svadharma—has suddenly been blurred. Dharma was not something imposed, no common scale of values chosen by all, but the very inner call of one's own life. As such it was the untaught inner call, the guide and the principle of life. Without it there was no light, no free step. No matter in how faint a way the common man understood it, he held to it as fast as he could. It is this inner meaning, self-born, infusing our body and soul with one light, which has been lost in a confusion of terminologies.

It is true that women have lost their fascination. The aura of love and respect which used to be the approach of young men towards women has gone. Women today stand before them only as differing partners in the carnal play, weak competitors in the race for power. This has reduced the prestige of woman. Rather frantically they have taken to poses and tasteless exposition to keep up their attraction. But the respectfuly approach to women was a spontaneous reaction to a natural, fuller and spiritual way of life. It is the fineness of heart and a will to adhere to inner truth which have vanished.

Already in advanced circles women have realized a loss of communication with men. They no more occupy the world of his highest thoughts and fancies. An isolation has appeared between their two worlds. Inspite of an increase in free mingling, love and respect are rarely to be found among young men today towards women. Once values are found to be superfluous, or something cheap and artificial replaces them, the fine threads of human bondage get broken. Women lose everything with this loss. By adopting a pose, without caring for inner enrichment and light, they lose the very magnetism they have for man. They lose not only the love and respect of man but also inner clam and happiness, inner strength and fulfilment. With the light withdrawn, hollow, dispirited, enlivened by nothing inborn, nothing remains for women.

Industrialization under such self-disgrace brings them the biggest share of hardships. In their inner lives both men and women face a void. They were created to enrich each other by love and mutual acceptance, but this is not possible unless they abide by their inner light. In an industrial society there will be many influences affecting the self-estrangement of man. It is essential that women keep themselves away from such influences, so that in their proximity to nature and truth they may manage a return for man to find himself. In a society homogeneously industrial, it is inevitable that through a continuous process of negation both sides of the human species should be destroyed. Denuded of their inner richness, self-estranged, they will have nothing in common.

THE MODERN FRUSTRATION

The biggest enemies of life are disillusionment and frustration. All noble urges and aspirations are struggles agtainst hard facts. They are our refusal to bow down before greed, narrowness and selfishness. Whenever we lose faith in them disillusionment sets. It is something like being disgraced. Everything in us is keen on revolting against it and yet no alternative seems at hand. Man comes to a void where old values appear lustreless and the foundation for the future is lost.

It is not so much the shortcomings of our ideals as a certain working of the death-instinct in us which realizes this. Every ideal that we know is short of the whole. It is only in our heart and unflinching adherence that it raises itself to the whole. Sometimes new facts emerge, and we start distrusting our ideals. It is futile to hope that a surrender of the old ideal will bring us the desired strength. It will only lead to breakage and a total loss. It is not petty gains which should command the allegiance of our soul. The soul is wedded to something different and no change of custom brings it any happiness. Disillusionment has its cause in a desertion of the true road, not in an awareness of the wicked nature of the world. This is a plain fact about the world and no new revelation. Those who would not be satisfied with anything less, walk on the grand path inspite of everything. Life is not for the calculator, the man who always weighs all. Disillusionment and frustration are the lot of the weak and of the small seekers. Those who have realized the great truth that gains do not consist in possessions or in returns from others but in the ability to maintain lofty feelings and a head raised high, what care they for what the world thinks of their loftiness? They do not allow themselves to be regulated by the cynicism of the world. To struggle against cynicism and to fight it on the same level of give and take is to develop another kind of cynicism. It is not given to the human soul to maintain purity and richness and lofty feelings and also cynicism.

To walk on the higher road certainly involves a certain element of resignedness and also a little divine foolery. If we look around too much and assess the returns and the attitudes of others, we are in danger of falling a prey to a greater cynicism. Those who choose the nobler heights have no other end in view.

Our life-long struggle against disillusionment and frustration is the struggle of life against living death. It is the inner significance of a culture. A culture which fails to feed this struggle spontaneously passes into history. Everything in life has the possibility of disillusioning and frustrating us. Frustration or disillusionment are the reactions of the weak who cannot dare into truth. We getout of life what we dare of it. Life lives for those who see it and dare to share it. Culture is the constant effort to retain and advance all that is fine and noble. It is with their culture, the rich and true way of life that has evolved, that people fight the powers of darkness. When these weapons reach the common people through the efforts of their great men a people becomes strong and true.

Today the danger that India faces in many-sided. Suddenly, the emancipated race of great and dedicated persons seems to have vanished. People are engrossed in petty struggles, and the growing tendency to idealize such meaningless and base ways of life has taken away the element of fire from life. It is tragic seeing underlings make their way to the top and those at the top toppling down, lost, bereft of faith. When a country becomes so fully engaged with matter, life becomes a version of cynicism. To cynicism are given the most placid ways of destroying everything.

One of the most important reasons for modern frustration and emptiness is mutual exclusion of the two sexes. It would appear that never before was their world so completely divided, and so fully self-alienated. A man's life today is empty of woman and so is the reverse. The mutual sharing of life in depth is something totally lost. *Kama* is no more a *purushartha* of life. It is not the strong force which is said to have its roots in the very sources of life. Now it has become only a function and an appetite. It is physical, and people take special pride in mentioning that they have brought it to the level of the skin. It is no longer the mysterious troubling darkness of their being.

Little do we realize that the loss of the yearning for the opposite in its wholeness has brought a profound emptiness which is irreparable through any other means. Those who have negated the opposite from their life by making it only physical and superficial have become prey to many kinds of bifurcation and torture. The sight of the self-hypnotised person is no rarity today. Young men running after artificial ideals of frankness, boldness and masculinity have made themselves pathetically hypocritical, cruel and self-obsessed. The negation of the opposite is bound to create such psychological complications.

Everywhere in nature the inevitability of sharing of life between the masculine and the feminine is apparent. It is this sharing which is the cause of all evolution and fullness. The more this association goes down to the depth, the richer and fuller life becomes. To all feeling and sensitive individuals it is obvious that nature did not image her ideal in man or woman single and alone. Nature has conceived her highest type in a being of one sex who has realized the opposite too within. Merely to be locked in each others's arms, out of physical necessity or the necessity for accommodating each other, whilst in our hearts we are nothing but strangers to each other, is cowardice of the highest type.

Indian myths and legends of powerful men, mighty warriors and great men nowhere idealize the merely 'masculine' man. Veda Vyasa, the highest embodiment of our racial genius, has given us in his heroes—Krishna, Karna, Arjuna, Bhima—men who though masculine in the highest degree had not reached great heights through a negation of the feminine in their nature. Manliness was never confused with cruelty and ruthlessness as it was in the epic wisdom of Europe. The Hindus took special pleasure in giving an almost feminine lustre to the face of the heroes, the boldest, bravest and the most heroic by all standards. The concept of the *ardhanarisvara*—He who is half-feminine—is not a profound myth but the base on which Hindu life has formed itself. To negate the opposite entirely is the same as not to be. To be purely masculine or purely feminine is the same as being neither.

It was left to Goethe in the West to realize the profound significance of the opposite. The 'eaternal feminine' was to him, when he had gone through the agonized journey of Faust, 'the constant emancipator of man.' This certainly is not the same thing as turning towards the opposite sex with a sexual craze. It is the flow of our nature towards the opposite. It is seeking fulfilment in the opposite. Unless the feminine becomes the eternal urge for man, the very yearning of his soul, self-fulfilment and joy can never be had. Woman to him otherwise shall be only a toy, a thing of amusement. This is all negative and based on ignorance, and not only mean but humiliating. The place of woman is different and deeper for men. She is the very half of nature. Unless she is given this natural seat, surrendering all sophistry and falsehood, life cannot bloom. So it is with woman. As long as man remains only the opposite and the exploiter to her, she will always be dominated by him and become bifurcated within. When he becomes the very half without whom Nature does not sing her melodies, she becomes free of tensions and comes on a road to self-fulfilment. It is a yearning for the opposite which brings freedom from our egg-shell isolation, rigidity and the still waters of life. When the interplay with the opposite becomes free in the depths of our nature, emptiness ends and all that we do has a tendency to become worship. Culture would not have become something so superfluous and objective for us, a study for scholars, had this tragic mutual exclusion of the two sexes not come about. Culture, arts, the joys of life, all the finest aspirations and achievements of life can mean nothing to a half nature. These full products of life remain attractive and inspiring only when we are not isolated as masculine or feminine but have realized an inner profusion where each is both.

It is thus that we reach a state where in self-abundance we become naturally free of all craving and struggle. Those who choose the path of negation achieve another kind of end which in its purity and suffering is awesome but fruitless, empty and tortuous. It is unhappy, unproductive and hopelessly mortifying. Without fulfilment through the opposite every kind of nobility, idealism and moral perfection reduces itself to a useless exercies and never becomes spontaneous. This yearning for the opposite is only a phase of our yearning for the whole.

MODERN DEMOCRACIES TOO EXPLOITING THE INDIVIDUAL

Our civilization has brought disintegration of the individual since it has trusted the process of refinement to suppression and its eye never cares to probe beneath. All our social institutions, including law and the State, insist only upon proper behaviour. This suffices for the social ends of law and order, therefore nothing more is sought. Little do we care to assess the price that we have to pay for this. Our civilization has come to a certain impasse where it has made the very word social organization bereft of any intrinsic value. The value of a society is in developing mutual sympathy and understanding among individuals. A true social organization provides us freedom from anxiety and insecurity.

Society in our days has come to assume an independent life. It no more lives for the individual and in the individual. It has developed its own life and it claims rights for its existence and support from the individual.

This inevitability has given the social organization a brutal type of relaxation and insensitivity to the problems of the individual. True, the days of tyrants are gone. Today, however, those very institutions that have risen to replace them have assumed their role. It is a big problem and one on which a great deal of the future of mankind rests. By adopting these suppressing tactics the democratic institutions have been acting almost in the totalitarian fashion. True, it is parliaments that function here and not closed in castles from which orders are issued. But this makes little difference if the parliament finds complete fulfilment in staging mutual showdowns by different parties.

It is a dangerous game that modern democracy is playing. Instead of working for its true ends—to let each individual find expression and self-realization—it has adopted the clever ways of imposing itself. This spirit is the same old spirit of tyrants and self-seekers. This has already resulted in loss of faith among people in democracy itself. If they cling to it, it is because its deal still holds out some hope, whereas its opposite has blighted all. The day is not far off when democracy will be buried in the very grave dug by its clever adherents.

The first and foremost task before all well-meaning individuals the world over is to work for the integration of each human soul. We can gain nothing by destroying human material. This may be in the interests of a few uncommonly mean persons in power, but can never be in the interests of society, of mankind or of the individual. A society which seeks harmony through suppression has no solution to offer and deserves to be liquidated since it carries within itself the seed of despair and ruin to millions.

It is here that we have to pose the question again and again—"whither, whither?"

THE SEED OF DESPAIR IN OUR TIMES

It is not a taste for problems that has driven me to this analysis and criticism. It avails one little to criticize and it is only a concern for human sufferings that gives criticism the little meaning that it has. All criticism is worthwhile only as a cleansing approach to light and truth. In itself it is futile, and, if indulged for sheer pleasure, merely cynical and absurd.

Life today is profoundly tragic since there is no one that does not suffer on account of negations and the oblivion of values. When the finest in us is crushed by ignorance, false allurements or a falling in the whirlpool of self-deception, we ourselves are the chief sufferers. Today the whole human race is paying this bitter price. It seems as if the dark ages have revisited us like a big bird with all-embracing black wings. The sixth century before Christ might perhaps have witnessed a similar confusion of values which called for the mighty spirits of men like the Buddha and Mahavira to teach man to stand against this total danger of annihilation There is no value that has not been questioned and laughed at today, nothing noble and sacred that has not been mocked at.

There would be no justification for man perhaps to submit to anything noble or fine if it were not to sustain his own true inner being, the being that has become clouded. Instead of clarifying the mist and making it clear so that its voice and urges could come to us, we have preferred to be cynics, to be martyrs of our own frustration. It is hopeless when the urge to the fine is dropped as mere illusion and facts are taken to be all that truth means. We seem to have fallen prey to this fallacy. True, the human ego has been found to be the home of many vile passions and meaner longings. But should we derive horrid conclusions from this? Should we say that all talk of perfect beauty and purity, of higher joys and spiritual freedom are false mental creations, purely ideal, lacking in truth? It is only a dispirited and broken generation that would so completely lose sight of the lofty. True, our generation has sufficient reason to be such a one since the sufferings and fears of war and annihilation have hardened us. But should the human race stop at that? A future has to be built, a future which life may take pride in recognising as its own. Can such a disheartened state bring us anywhere close to a future? The future, as it appears today, is the same sad extension of the present. It is gloomy, lifeless, with only a few sparks of excitement and then tiredness.

The sins of the ages sit heavily on us. The very nature of man has been mutilated and changed. That which we recognise to be the hard and base truth about him is in fact no truth. His incurable seeming meanness and selfishness are no essential part of him. They are only results of a wrong direction taken and inhuman experiences. It is this which has become our psychological truth. It is not what truth is in its essence but what it has become; what it should never have become.

The psychological state of man is a creation of his experience, desires and views. It is fear, obsession and disillusionment caused by unhappy experiences that take him to despondency. It would be a mistake to call it the truth of life. This mistake, on a wider level, is current as the foremost superstition of our age. In art, literature and common life it is this which has been accepted with the solemnity of truth. A weak but sensitive soul comes, faces a few odds of life and gets broken. This soul appears with a brush and paints all the squares and horrors and scars within it unmindful of the utter chaos of its language. This is taken as something great merely because it is sincere. But art is not only sincerity to oneself. Art symbolises above all the human struggle against darkness, against all that tends to cover life with layers of ugliness. The artist is not worth his profession if through art his only aim is to express the wreckage of his soul. His positive contribution to life is in struggling through art for a superior light where this wreckage may be repaired.

Whenever literature, art, music or philosophy become confined only to a form of self-expression, decay sets in. Above all, they are to be our passages, our attempts for not getting broken, to enkindle faith in something noble and lofty that keeps the self in its proper course and helps against its crushing by the merest details of daily life.

Art is the product of a spontaneous urge for expression—expression above all of joy within. Till an artist reaches this stage, by a constant strengthening of his spirit and raising it to a higher level, it is impossible for his soul to seek artistic expression. If he insists upon expressing himself before such maturity he is a pedant and does not know what art is. With the mosaic pattern of a soul that the artist has within, the true form of expression for him must be an attempt at understanding his own chaos and bringing it to the surface. If he is satisfied merely in depicting those brilliant and dark patches in queer drawings and poems, he is deceiving himself and befooling others. A broken soul first cries out for self-integration. It is only after conquering those patches and breakages and rising above them, that the real urge to express through art comes. Art is essentially the product of inner music.

THE CORRUPTING INFLUENCE OF EXPERIENCES

It is a misfortune that the process of resurrecting India did not mature with an appreciation of the whole of life and its various demands. In going in for industrialization its likely imbalancing effects on the life of millions was never considered. Over-won by the driving passion for the fulfilment of our industrial destiny, no thought was ever given to the fact that if this imbalance and disturbance in the life of millions was essential, it was also essential that the lost balance be restored. Progress is dubious if its requirements are a hopeless surrender of the equilibrium. All change has to justify itself by aiming at a higher equilibrium. When an evolving society is lacking in such a goal, the best changes have a tendency to misguide. A highly industrialized society can be a gain only if the people recognise the road to uncompromising light. Otherwise the mechanical rigours, the exacting demands and hopeless rush of materialistic ends deny the human fountains. When, therefore, the moment of prosperity and material advancement arrives, the inner conditions of a happy life may be lost altogether. Falsehood, surface living, sophistry and other instant measures of adaptation to a mechanical society replace the very milk of human life. It is simply horrible to envisage a society which has lost its native system of values. This is not a mere picture representing an idea in the abstract. Nothing seems to be inevitable with man. Constant depravity and mean conditions of living can cause such injuries to human nature.

Culture is a continuous process of awakening life to the calls of beauty, light and love. It is man's struggle against disillusionment and vulgarization. The experiences of life are often hard and disenchanting. They not only make us aware of human nature and its various deformities but also mould us accordingly. It is this aspect of experience which is highly injurious and destructive. We lose all our higher urges and the desire for self-perfection. As practical persons we cannot afford to ignore the nature of persons living around us.

The danger comes from a cowardly element in man which makes him equate the world of his experience with the whole world, and that part of a man's personality that he has known with the whole of him. The strong desire to be practical and successful makes a man take such hasty steps. The hope for something different and the charm of the new are rather irritating to practicality. The biggest loss that man derives from this is in the very roots of life, in its verve, enthusiasm and joy. Life becomes stale for him.

Culture is the brave call of light, in a disillusioning and deceitful world. It is a reminder to man that the truth of human nature is different. He has only seen what man has made of himself; what he would never have become had ignorance and self-clouding desires not been so strong. Culture gives him faith in himself and is a vow not to break his heart amidst gloom and deception. It gives him love enough for light to stand alone. Where then is the cause for disillusionment? Someone whispers. All have changed. All have betrayed. This does not mean however that light has changed or truth has betrayed.

It is not enough to see things as they are for it is not given to us to see things as they are. We only see facets and that too through the colour of our personality. What we know in life about things is certainly not the whole truth about them. Science has revealed how the most insignificant dust particle is full of tremendous energy. Culture makes it possible for us to live gracefully with this partial truth. Today man has lost faith in man in his savage narrow realism.

When we start recognising this implicit profundity in everything, our experience does not blind us. The realisation of something nobler and greater permeating all corrects the error. We do not become prisoners of the modern savages—the disillusioned realists. It makes us assess people properly both in their explicit and implicit virtues.

Not that under soe spiritual intoxication we cease seeing the distortions in human nature. Only these distortions do not paralyse our nobler urges.

THE EMANCIPATION OF WOMAN

The very essence of the vitality of Indian Culture rests in the position that it gave to woman. The cultures of Greece, Rome and Egypt decayed because in their pursuit of the higher life they became more and more manly, stiff one-sided and inflexible. Ultimately they arrived at a stage where the female got utterly excluded. The world became the property of man, and woman found herself in it hardly different from various other objects to be enjoyed by man. Excluded from the flow of life in a society where the higher engagements of man—not only war and the struggle for power, or even art and literature—gave her no place inseparable from man, woman became isolated and weak. She realised the world of difference that had come between her and man. She also found that in the lonely, hard and proud interior of man—the soldier—she was a stranger. Only as an object of psysical attraction, a satiator of appetite and a relief in softness did she attract man. She was an object to relax with from the tension and heat of ambitious life and war.

Not much is known of the early protests of woman against such alienation. It is true that any protest from her could not have lasted long without support from man. Man had drifted away and in his total manliness could not have taken into account the aspirations of woman, whom religion also found feeble and tempting. The work left for women amongst all classes was to please the warriors, the senators and the rich ones. A corrective from Dante or a few others could not have meant much when the whole stream of consciousness was running towards its opposite. The more ambitious kind of women sought manly pursuits, reducing themselves to the state of lisping man, violating their nature, to be lost further in the gloom of negation and frustration. We have, therefore, heard stories of cruel self-torturing and unwomanly women.

In ancient India, on the other hand, woman continued to be a part of life in all its aspects. The relations between men and women are bound to be artificial and short-lived when a whole stream of racial consciousness has bifurcated the two. The very aim of modern culture is towards the goals of men—power, strength, self-assertion. But the soul that lives in us is not composed entirely of man. Without the realisation of the opposite, which is already within, which is only to be recognised, we can never attain fulfilment. To insist on the purely manly virtues is merely to insist on one half in us and to cancel the other half. To cancel any part of our being is to suffocate the whole and go away from truth, enslaved by certain fashionable thoughts. Already the humiliation and dangers arising from the exclusion of women have appeared. She cannot compete with man in the race for power and strength. Such are not the ends of her nature. As a protest, she has cultivated the art of displaying more and more of her self, fearing neglect from man. She has become more affected—all signs which are by mistake taken for advancement whereas they are nothing but signs of fear, frustration and decay. Many of them have chosen man's ideals and found ways to be further violated and emptied within. With the increase in material resources, India has discovered new dimensions of family and social unhappiness—haughtiness, disrespect for woman, snobbery and hypocrisy. It is futile to marvel at the strength and deathlessness of our culture which has endured for thousands of years against thousands of shocks. The signs of the liquidation of this culture are already apparent. Abandoning the lyrical, rich and profuse life, men are choosing an empty, falsely active and psychologically diseased life as their ideal. To cope with them, women are chasing the same ideals as their disgraced counterparts. It is vain and thoughtlessly complacent to think of the immortality and inner strength of Indian Culture or of any other culture. The Chinese have wiped out a culture, matching our own in richness and vitality, within a few years of narrow materialistic thinking and living.

Denuded, broken in our essence, split and emptied in our personality within a few years, we stand dazed and ruined, with no way out but to advance on the same road. This is the subtle way in which the powers of darkness and death choose to ruin man. They come through the very sacred sources that we never suspect. Conditions are the same the world over with the apparent results of waywardness and wastage. The fight of the two power blocks is not likely to be of light against darkness, but rather of darkness smothering darkness, people fighting out of an inner vacuum, finding no invitation from life, no rhythm in it. Never were values and truth so obliterated, confused and unconvincing as today. Anything true can appeal to us only if we remain close to nature. Devoid of one half of our nature—the feminine—we stare at truth only with masculine eyes, which draw only half a deceptive figure of it. Truth and values do not bloom in egoistic and narrow hearts. This growth cannot occur on a soil which is untouched by the principle of the opposite. Never was man confined to only one half in him so religiously, with such strong prejudices and with a feeling or alienation for the other half within him.

The life of a people gains its strength from the total recognition of everything within. In order to be strong, we have not to negate that which is delicate and opposite in us. To impose upon woman masculine patterns is cowardice and suicidal. The ideals we are imposing upon woman are not only foolish, selfish and thoughtless, but artificial and ridiculous. Ultimately society here too will become exclusively 'manly'. Both ends and means will become manly and everything will have to suit their purpose. The vigour of the feminine, the tender and human corrective that it can provide, will be missing. Above all this will be the realisation of man as he sees himself and not of man as nature made him, endowing him with various elements of the opposite sex. All such elements will be excluded. The realisation or fulfilment of so chemically 'pure' a man, will bring happiness neither to him nor to society.

The proper ends for us grow from within. A code which comes from without ought to possess the sanctity of that which originally grows from within. The ends for woman could not be remote from her nature. Whatever she can do for self-fulfilment, she can never do by alienating herself or by choosing manly ideals. Man is her counterpart, the constant opposite and by yearning for him she realises the manifestation of her inner riches. It is by remaining true to herself, and by insisting on her acceptance by society as such, that she can save her honour and happiness. It is a shame and a delusion to consider the copying of the manly virtues to be a sign of progress. That will in fact be the total exploitation of woman by man, injurious to both. By demanding from man an understanding of her nature and ends and by including them in the fabric of a common society, she can best serve the ends of life, time and eternity. It is through this assimilation of opposites that society can aim at such goals which will not destroy women and children. It would be a pity for woman and a two-fold deception both to the nation and to woman not to question the purely manly ends that our society has chosen, after giving them rights on paper at par with man. The voice of man has always been mistaken for the voice of woman too, for her timidness and lack of faith in herself, for her shame at the strange difference of her demands from those of man. Those who become advanced become somewhat of a sub-man. The scales of feminine advancement too are measured by manly virtues. Such advanced woman speak with the borrowed voices of men, vulgarizing and denying themselves. What India needs today at this critical period is true women leaders, representing their sex, unashamed of its lack of manly virtues and glorifying those virtues that nature has given them. Thus they can check the self-complacency, intemperance and self-approval of man and can save society from total ruin after the purely manly ideal. Leaning only towards either man or woman, human society will soon find itself in ruins. Democracy does not consist merely in listening to the voice of all stratas of society. It consists above all in managing expression to the two distinct voices of the two natural divisions of mankind, man and woman, a fact which always gets ignored in the cry of the materialistic division. When this distinction is properly realised and the day society takes this into account, cruelty, artificiality, emptiness and excesses will vanish and a road leading to the true ends of life will be laid.

It is not only an economic or political destiny that a people has to fulfil; it is the destiny of all life. Under all creeds today it is human beings that are suffering. Truthfully did the Hindus say: "Where woman is worshipped, there the gods dwell." This worshipping was not a form of mental slavery. Heeding to this counsel, Indians gave to woman that regard which the West can never understand. According to their ways of thinking, the Indian woman has perhaps enjoyed only a slavish career. They must be taught that freedom is not a mere matter of space, of remaining indoors or outdoors. Woman could fulfil herself in this society under all conditions, even when confined to the home, owing to the systematic encouragement given to her inner nature. The freedom of woman is possible only if we create conditions in which she can fulfil her nature. If woman is an equal citizen and a living person whose ends are to be kept in mind in building a society, the present self-acquisitive and neglectful attitude towards woman will have to be given up by man. The equality of woman does not consist in granting her opportunities to take the jobs of man. It consists in recognising her differing nature and creating such jobs as will suit her and help in the flowering of her nature. Man has dominated woman not by any other process but by indoctrinating her with so-called manly ideals, crushing her nature within and making her feel humiliated and insignificant. Man has thus forced her in this subtle way to adopt his ends and thus accept him as her superior. Whatever the outward changes, the inner consciousness runs to be so. Woman's humiliations are endless and various in form. Even as a feminine creature she has preferred to be judged merely by the lusty standards of man.

Woman need not fear violation or a denial of her duty to cooperate with man whilst claiming the need for true expression of her nature. Cooperation is not subjugation. It is not total surrender or a denial of inner truth. On the contrary, by insisting on their inner turth, by feeling proud in displaying their natural virtues, they can cooperate with man in the highest sense and give of their best towards the formation of a well-founded and strong society.

THE TRUE UNION OF THE SEXES

The mutual fulfilment of the two sexes has come to an end. They are now only objects of desire and a necessity to each other. They are concessions to each other. The grand concept of each completing the other, evolved long ago in the image of *ardha-nariswara,* has died out. With this, the possibility of a positive, life-long union has come to an end. As objects merely of desires and concessions to each other's weaknesses the very association of man and woman bases itself on negations, on weak foundations. They will soon become objects of hatred towards, each other, and each will struggle to oust the other from his or her life. It is in a situation like this that the modern deluded mind sees freedom. But how hopeless this can be is apparent from the vast number of men and women haters that exist in the advanced societies. The two sexes cannot achieve any happiness or fulfilment by hateful mutual exclusion. The possibility of a complete mutual acceptance can be envisaged only when it is not through weakness that the strength of our being. If it is only hunger that prompts an urge for the other sex, this will only lead to fetters, hatred and decadence. Love is a gift, a continuous giving by a soul that knows the upward road. It is not possible to achieve this in a hectic life whose aim is to run away from inner questions. It is when desire for union springs as the very call of life that a true foundation for union of the two sexes in laid. Such an urge is no fiction or philosophic speculation. The very desire on the surface presupposes it. The relationship between man and woman unfortunately suffers from several old inhibitions and prejudices. It is supposed to be something basically evil. Those who do not consider it so, do so often without any deeper realisation of the correct situation. The very genesis of evil is traced to this association with the result that in most cases people do not dare to think of the relationship in depth. They do not wish to consider in depth something which has already darkened them on the surface with excitement, shameful sexuality and desire.

In India, from the earliest times the importance of sex was realised in its deepest sense. Of the four *purusharthas* the ancient Indians put sex as one. Lest certain prudish elders should try to conceal this dark and supposedly shameful part of life from the young, sex was depicted boldly in temples and in the sacred books. The erotic was not denied, but openly accepted as a symptom of a deeper craving, the craving of opposites to be one. Sex was raised to a spiritual level. The complete flowering of the erotic was the same as the flowering of the soul. It was not an appetite, carnal and mean, but the throbbing of the soul to attain its highest destiny. When understood in depth and brought to true flowering without any obsessions sex had no ends other than the highest, in fact the same ends as the longing for freedom and beauty.

It is not by denial but by correct appreciation that we can get rid of what we call the dark in life. While giving due recognition to sex right from the days of the *Brihadaranyaka,* our sages emphasized that, if sex is pursued in isolation, for the sake of physical pleasure alone and without a proper understanding of its significance and depth, it will not fulfil its real purpose. It will then contradict the other *purusharthas* such as dharma and total freedom or *moksha*. This will cause a split in the human personality. That life alone is meaningful in which all the *purusharthas* converage towards one end.

Culture would be a meaningless exercise if it did not take all the urges and appetites of life into account. It would merely negate itself if in its efforts to absorb all such urges it failed to regulate them into a unified dynamism where each promoted the ends of the other. Cultures have perished, mainly because of a growing inflexibility and their insistence upon retaining certain good, though stilled, characteristics which, in their decay, they claimed to be signs of purity. Such rigours found no place in the foundations of Indian Culture. The folds of this culture were expected to grow ever as life grows. This growth in fact represented nothing but willingness to face the whole of life.

There is no reason for introducing the sexual revolt of the West into this country. The western revolt was directed against a consciousness which until the 19th Century—except among a small and enlightened circle— considered woman as immensely inferior to man and the unquestioned representative of hell on earth. To those who reposed faith in religion, sex was the very symbol of sin and thus never acceptable to them. It was this rigid religious consciousness which caused the many-sided revolt in the West on the theme of sex in art, in literature and in philosophy. As is but natural in all such revolts the result was perversion. Revolt rarely maintains a sense of proportion. It prefers to expand, and in the very act of expansion ruins the very cause it stands for. In revolting against a false and narrow consciousness, western men ended up by revolting against the true spirit of the relationship between the two sexes. A bold denial of all restraint and grace in the satisfaction of physical thirst was the price demanded by a long tortured consciousness. This denial of everything else gave rise to many kinds of revolutionaries, whose needs led to the preparations of yet another cage for man. This cage was the isolated pursuit of sex, of accepting sex, but accepting it only at a surface level. Sex could hardly have any higher purpose before an eye obsessed by lust. All talk of a higher purpose is merely laughable to such men. It is this laughter which proves that sex has still not been accepted in full. For the inner soul it is still only carnal and base, with no resemblance to itself. Modern man, even in his shameless and frank sexuality, has not accepted sex fully. He is still inhibited, and his soul is closed to it. When the soul realises this appetite to be the symptom of a deeper appetite, sex will rise to its true significance and become a *purushartha,* a value of life. The division within us will be broken and in its acceptance by the inner self, sex will become purged of all mean lust.

The history of Western Culture has opened a new and tragic chapter. Hatred has appeared against sex and frigidity, and this is the direct result of the opposition within us between the flesh and the spirit. It was thought by the ancient Indians that it was wrong to think that the appetites of the body were all degrading and different from those of the spirit. These appetites were not different, and the appetites of the body in their depth sprang from the soul itself. If traced to their sources with composure and a deathless urge for light, all divisions will be gone. Sex will lose all notions of lust and sin. It is thus that desires are conquered, and not by suppression, cancellation or confinement to the physical level. In the fire of the spirit everything gets purified. If the spirit of man is the seed of the Lord, there is no reason why we should fear in taking desires to it. It is not desires that corrupt but our obsession; our lack of understanding of the true significance of desires. The are symptoms of a nobler spiritual craving of total union and freedom.

■■■■